Super Easy

MEDITERRANEAN

DIET COOKBOOK for Beginners

2000 Days of Quick, Tasty & Nutritious Recipes Book for Everyday Meals to Live a Healthier Life | No-Stress 30-Day Meal Plan

Wendeline Daalmeijer

TABLE OF CONTENTS

INTRODUCTION

Welcome to the vibrant world of the Mediterranean Diet, a lifestyle that transcends mere eating habits and invites you to embark on a journey towards better health, joy, and longevity. This introduction serves as your gateway to understanding the essence of this celebrated diet, which is not just a regimen but a rich tapestry woven from centuries of tradition, culture, and culinary excellence.

A Journey Through History

The Mediterranean Diet is rooted in the dietary patterns of the countries bordering the Mediterranean Sea, including Greece, Italy, Spain, and parts of North Africa. It harks back to the ancient civilizations that thrived in these regions, where food was not just sustenance but a way of life. The diet was shaped by a unique confluence of geography, climate, and cultural exchanges, resulting in a diverse and flavorful cuisine.

Historical records and archaeological findings suggest that the diet of the ancient Greeks and Romans was rich in fruits, vegetables, whole grains, and legumes, complemented by moderate amounts of fish, dairy, and wine. Olive oil, a staple of the Mediterranean Diet, has been produced in the region for over 6,000 years. This historical context underscores the diet's deep-rooted connection to the land and its people, offering a timeless model for healthy living.

The Science Behind the Diet

The Mediterranean Diet gained international recognition in the mid-20th century through the pioneering research of Dr. Ancel Keys and his colleagues, who identified the diet's remarkable health benefits. Subsequent studies have consistently shown that this dietary pattern is associated with a reduced risk of chronic diseases such as heart disease, stroke, diabetes, and certain cancers. The diet is also linked to improved cognitive function and longevity.

The secret to the Mediterranean Diet's health benefits lies in its emphasis on whole, minimally processed foods rich in nutrients, antioxidants, and healthy fats. Olive oil, the cornerstone of the diet, is high in monounsaturated fats and polyphenols, which have been shown to reduce inflammation and improve cardiovascular health. The diet also includes an abundance of fiber from fruits, vegetables, and whole grains, which promotes digestive health and helps maintain a healthy weight.

Beyond Nutrition: A Way of Life

The Mediterranean Diet is more than just a collection of foods; it embodies a holistic approach to living well. It emphasizes the importance of enjoying meals with family and friends, savoring the flavors of fresh, seasonal ingredients, and practicing mindful eating. This communal aspect of dining fosters strong social bonds and enhances overall well-being.

Physical activity is another integral component of the Mediterranean lifestyle. Historically, the people of the Mediterranean region engaged in regular physical activity through farming, fishing, and daily tasks. Today, this translates to incorporating moderate exercise, such as walking, into one's daily routine, further contributing to the diet's health benefits.

The Culinary Experience

At its heart, the Mediterranean Diet is a celebration of food. It invites you to explore a diverse array of dishes that are as delightful to the palate as they are nourishing to the body. Imagine the vibrant colors and bold flavors of a Greek salad with ripe tomatoes, crisp cucumbers, tangy feta cheese, and olives drizzled with extra virgin olive oil. Picture a Spanish paella brimming with succulent seafood, aromatic saffron, and hearty vegetables.

The recipes in this book are designed to capture the essence of Mediterranean cooking, highlighting simple yet flavorful ingredients. From classic dishes like Italian bruschetta and Moroccan tagine to innovative twists on traditional favorites, each recipe is a testament to the culinary richness of the Mediterranean region.

Embracing the Mediterranean Diet

Adopting the Mediterranean Diet is not about restrictive eating or following rigid rules. Instead, it encourages a flexible and enjoyable approach to food that can be adapted to individual tastes and lifestyles. Whether you are a seasoned cook or a kitchen novice, the recipes and tips in this book will inspire you to embrace the Mediterranean way of eating and living.

Begin by incorporating more fruits, vegetables, whole grains, and healthy fats into your meals. Experiment with new recipes and ingredients, and take the time to savor the process of cooking and eating. Remember that the Mediterranean Diet is not a quick-fix solution but a lifelong commitment to better health and well-being.

As you turn the pages of this book, you will discover that the Mediterranean Diet is much more than a diet; it is a celebration of life. It is an invitation to slow down, enjoy the simple pleasures of good food, and connect with loved ones. It is a path to health that is sustainable, enjoyable, and deeply rooted in tradition. Welcome to the Mediterranean Diet – a timeless journey to a healthier, happier you.

Chapter 1

Mediterranean Diet Meal Plan

Chapter 1: Mediterranean Diet Meal Plan

Meal planning is often perceived as a mundane chore, but within the Mediterranean Diet, it transforms into an exciting adventure. Imagine embarking on a culinary journey that not only tantalizes your taste buds but also nourishes your body and soul. This chapter is designed to guide you through the art of meal planning in the context of the Mediterranean Diet, with a special focus on the Mediterranean Diet Pyramid. Together, these tools will empower you to create balanced, delicious, and health-promoting meals effortlessly.

The Mediterranean Diet Pyramid: A Blueprint for Healthy Eating

The Mediterranean Diet Pyramid is more than a simple guideline; it is a visual representation of a lifestyle steeped in tradition, culture, and nutritional wisdom. Developed by Oldways, Harvard School of Public Health, and the World Health Organization, this pyramid emphasizes foods that have been the cornerstone of Mediterranean eating for centuries. Let's explore the different levels of the pyramid and uncover how each contributes to a well-rounded, nutritious diet.

The Base: Physical Activity and Social Connections

At the foundation of the Mediterranean Diet Pyramid lies an often-overlooked element: lifestyle. Regular physical activity, such as walking, cycling, or gardening, is essential. Equally important is the emphasis on communal meals. Sharing food with family and friends enhances emotional well-being and fosters a sense of community, making eating a joyful and meaningful experience.

Daily Consumption: Fruits, Vegetables, Grains, and Healthy Fats

The next level of the pyramid highlights the foods that should form the basis of your daily meals.

Fruits and Vegetables: Abundant in vitamins, minerals, antioxidants, and fiber, fruits and vegetables are the cornerstone of the Mediterranean Diet. Aim to fill half your plate with these colorful, nutrient-dense foods at every meal.

Whole Grains: Replace refined grains with whole grains such as quinoa, bulgur, and farro. These grains are rich in fiber, which aids in digestion and helps maintain steady blood sugar levels.

Healthy Fats: Extra virgin olive oil, nuts, and seeds provide essential fatty acids and have anti-inflammatory properties. These fats are not only heart-healthy but also enhance the flavors of Mediterranean dishes.

Legumes: Beans, lentils, and chickpeas are excellent sources of plant-based protein and fiber. They are versatile and can be incorporated into soups, salads, and main dishes.

Weekly Consumption: Fish, Poultry, Eggs, and Dairy

The middle tier of the pyramid includes foods that should be eaten a few times per week.

Fish and Seafood: Rich in omega-3 fatty acids, fish such as salmon, sardines, and mackerel support cardiovascular health. Aim to include fish in your meals at least twice a week.

Poultry and Eggs: While red meat is limited, lean poultry and eggs provide high-quality protein and essential nutrients. Include these in moderation, focusing on variety and balance.

Dairy: Cheese and yogurt are traditional components of the Mediterranean Diet, providing calcium and probiotics. Opt for fermented dairy products like Greek yogurt, which supports gut health.

Occasional Consumption: Red Meat and Sweets

At the top of the pyramid, you'll find foods that should be consumed sparingly.

Red Meat: Enjoy red meat occasionally, selecting lean cuts and practicing portion control. Use it more as a flavoring rather than the centerpiece of your meals.

Sweets: Sweets, particularly those with added sugars, are reserved for special occasions. Instead, satisfy your sweet tooth with fresh fruit or a small piece of dark chocolate.

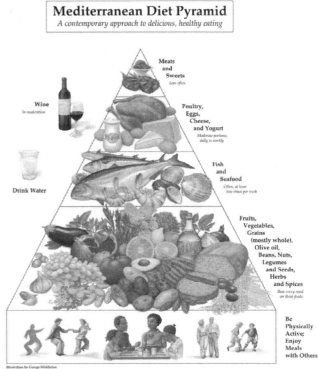

Mediterranean Diet Pyramid
A contemporary approach to delicious, healthy eating

© 2009 Oldways Preservation and Exchange Trust • www.oldwayspt.org

Practical Tips for Mediterranean Meal Planning

Embrace Seasonal and Local Produce
One of the joys of the Mediterranean Diet is its reliance on fresh, seasonal, and local produce. Plan your meals around what's available at your local farmers' market or what's in season. This not only ensures peak flavor and nutrition but also supports sustainable farming practices.

Batch Cooking and Meal Prep
To make meal planning more manageable, consider batch cooking and meal prepping. Spend a few hours each week preparing large batches of grains, roasting vegetables, and cooking proteins. Store these components in the refrigerator or freezer, allowing you to mix and match ingredients for quick and easy meals throughout the week.

Variety and Balance:
Variety is the spice of life, and it's also a key principle of the Mediterranean Diet. Ensure your meal plans include a wide range of fruits, vegetables, grains, and proteins to provide a comprehensive array of nutrients. Balance your meals by including a source of protein, healthy fat, and fiber to keep you satisfied and energized.

Mindful Eating
Mindful eating is a practice that aligns perfectly with the Mediterranean lifestyle. Take the time to savor your meals, pay attention to the flavors and textures, and listen to your body's hunger and fullness cues. This practice enhances your dining experience and promotes better digestion and satisfaction.

Conclusion

The Mediterranean Diet Pyramid serves as a comprehensive guide to meal planning, emphasizing balance, variety, and enjoyment. By incorporating the principles of this time-honored diet, you can create meals that are not only delicious and satisfying but also profoundly nourishing. As you delve deeper into the Mediterranean way of eating, you'll discover that meal planning is not just a task, but an opportunity to celebrate food, culture, and health in every bite.

30-Day Meal Plan

DAYS	BREAKFAST	LUNCH	DINNER	SNACK/DESSERT
1	Creamy Cinnamon Porridge 9	Barley Risotto 17	Chicken with Lemon Asparagus 23	Salted Almonds 52
2	Marinara Eggs with Parsley 9	Moroccan Vegetables and Chickpeas 18	Sicilian Kale and Tuna Bowl 42	Dried Fruit Compote 74
3	Mediterranean-Inspired White Smoothie 9	Domatorizo (Greek Tomato Rice) 21	Pomegranate-Glazed Chicken 25	Garlic-Lemon Hummus 52
4	Greek Yogurt and Berries 9	Herbed Barley 20	Red Curry Flank Steak 34	Blueberry Pomegranate Granita 74
5	Portobello Eggs Benedict 12	Greek-Style Pea Casserole 20	Salmon with Garlicky Broccoli Rabe and White Beans 45	Whole Wheat Pitas 56
6	C+C Overnight Oats 13	Amaranth Salad 20	Hoisin Turkey Burgers 24	Honey-Rosemary Almonds 55
7	Enjoy-Your-Veggies Breakfast 14	Sea Salt Soybeans 20	Moroccan Lamb Roast 40	No-Mayo Tuna Salad Cucumber Bites 54
8	Spinach and Feta Egg Bake 15	Sun-Dried Tomato Rice 17	Mediterranean Cod Stew 46	Black-Eyed Pea "Caviar" 54
9	Smoked Salmon Egg Scramble with Dill and Chives 10	Lebanese Rice and Broken Noodles with Cabbage 21	Lemon-Oregano Grilled Shrimp 48	Tirokafteri (Spicy Feta and Yogurt Dip) 54
10	Strawberry Basil Honey Ricotta Toast 10	Apple Couscous with Curry 20	Brazilian Tempero Baiano Chicken Drumsticks 26	Garlic-Parmesan Croutons 54
11	Greek Yogurt Parfait 10	Black-Eyed Peas with Olive Oil and Herbs 19	Braised Short Ribs with Fennel and Pickled Grapes 35	Stuffed Cucumber Cups 52
12	Savory Feta, Spinach, and Red Pepper Muffins 10	Spanish Rice 17	Poached Octopus 42	Baked Eggplant Baba Ganoush 54
13	Berry Warming Smoothie 10	Mediterranean Lentil Casserole 21	Rosemary Salmon 45	Crispy Spiced Chickpeas 53
14	Morning Buzz Iced Coffee 11	Bulgur with Red Pepper and Goat Cheese 19	Personal Cauliflower Pizzas 29	Flatbread with Ricotta and Orange-Raisin Relish 53
15	Mashed Chickpea, Feta, and Avocado Toast 11	Garlicky Split Chickpea Curry 19	Beef Bourguignon with Egg Noodles 35	Goat's Cheese & Hazelnut Dip 53

DAYS	BREAKFAST	LUNCH	DINNER	SNACK/DESSERT
16	Jalapeño Popper Egg Cups 11	Brown Rice Vegetable Bowl with Roasted Red Pepper Dressing 18	Niçoise Chicken 27	Manchego Crackers 53
17	Spinach, Sun-Dried Tomato, and Feta Egg Wraps 11	White Bean Soup with Kale and Lemon 18	Shrimp Foil Packets 48	Garlic Edamame 55
18	Broccoli-Mushroom Frittata 11	Three-Grain Pilaf 17	Greek Lamb Burgers 39	Black Bean Corn Dip 55
19	Egg Salad with Red Pepper and Dill 12	Herbed Polenta 18	Seafood Paella 44	Sweet-and-Spicy Nuts 55
20	Gluten-Free Granola Cereal 12	Vegetarian Dinner Loaf 19	Spiced Lamb Stew with Fennel and Dates 39	Classic Hummus with Tahini 56
21	Greek Eggs and Potatoes 15	Couscous with Crab and Lemon 91	Roast Pork Tenderloin with Cherry-Balsamic Sauce 33	Black Olive and Lentil Pesto 56
22	Cauliflower Avocado Toast 12	Toasted Couscous with Feta, Cucumber, and Tomato 90	Fish Tagine 47	Pesto Cucumber Boats 56
23	Nuts and Fruit Oatmeal 14	Mediterranean Spice-Crusted Salmon over White Beans 43	Braised Striped Bass with Zucchini and Tomatoes 49	Grilled Stone Fruit 76
24	Spiced Potatoes with Chickpeas 14	Mixed Vegetable Couscous 91	Moroccan Crusted Sea Bass 44	Cinnamon-Apple Chips 55
25	Berry Breakfast Smoothie 13	Fettuccine with Tomatoes and Pesto 91	Almond-Encrusted Salmon 49	Mascarpone and Fig Crostini 76
26	Berry Baked Oatmeal 13	Penne with Roasted Vegetables 90	Roast Chicken 24	Shrimp and Chickpea Fritters 52
27	Golden Egg Skillet 13	Walnut Spaghetti 92	Chicken Breasts Stuffed with Feta and Spinach 28	S'mores 76
28	Blueberry-Lemon Tea Cakes 13	Couscous with Tomatoes and Olives 91	Braised Pork with Broccoli Rabe and Sage 40	Tortilla Fried Pies 77
29	Mexican Breakfast Pepper Rings 15	Israeli Salad with Nuts and Seeds 81	Grilled Kefta 37	Date and Honey Almond Milk Ice Cream 77
30	Egg in a "Pepper Hole" with Avocado 14	Asparagus Salad 81	Pesto-Glazed Chicken Breasts 29	Cinnamon-Stewed Dried Plums with Greek Yogurt 78

Chapter 2

Breakfasts

Chapter 2 Breakfasts

Creamy Cinnamon Porridge

Prep time: 10 minutes | Cook time: 10 minutes | Serves 2

- ¼ cup coconut milk
- ¾ cup unsweetened almond milk or water
- ¼ cup almond butter or hazelnut butter
- 1 tablespoon virgin coconut oil
- 2 tablespoons chia seeds
- 1 tablespoon flax meal
- 1 teaspoon cinnamon
- ¼ cup macadamia nuts
- ¼ cup hazelnuts
- 4 Brazil nuts
- Optional: low-carb sweetener, to taste
- ¼ cup unsweetened large coconut flakes
- 1 tablespoon cacao nibs

1. In a small saucepan, mix the coconut milk and almond milk and heat over medium heat. Once hot (not boiling), take off the heat. Add the almond butter and coconut oil. Stir until well combined. If needed, use an immersion blender and process until smooth. 2. Add the chia seeds, flax meal, and cinnamon, and leave to rest for 5 to 10 minutes. Roughly chop the macadamias, hazelnuts, and Brazil nuts and stir in. Add sweetener, if using, and stir. Transfer to serving bowls. In a small skillet, dry-roast the coconut flakes over medium-high heat for 1 to 2 minutes, until lightly toasted and fragrant. Top the porridge with the toasted coconut flakes and cacao nibs (or you can use chopped 100% chocolate). Serve immediately or store in the fridge for up to 3 days.

Per Serving:
calories: 646 | fat: 61g | protein: 13g | carbs: 23g | fiber: 10g | sodium: 40mg

Marinara Eggs with Parsley

Prep time: 5 minutes |Cook time: 15 minutes| Serves: 6

- 1 tablespoon extra-virgin olive oil
- 1 cup chopped onion (about ½ medium onion)
- 2 garlic cloves, minced (about 1 teaspoon)
- 2 (14½-ounce / 411-g) cans Italian diced tomatoes,
- undrained, no salt added
- 6 large eggs
- ½ cup chopped fresh flat-leaf (Italian) parsley
- Crusty Italian bread and grated Parmesan or Romano cheese, for serving (optional)

1. In a large skillet over medium-high heat, heat the oil. Add the onion and cook for 5 minutes, stirring occasionally. Add the garlic and cook for 1 minute. 2. Pour the tomatoes with their juices over the onion mixture and cook until bubbling, 2 to 3 minutes. While waiting for the tomato mixture to bubble, crack one egg into a small custard cup or coffee mug. 3. When the tomato mixture bubbles, lower the heat to medium. Then use a large spoon to make six indentations in the tomato mixture. Gently pour the first cracked egg into one indentation and repeat, cracking the remaining eggs, one at a time, into the custard cup and pouring one into each indentation. Cover the skillet and cook for 6 to 7 minutes, or until the eggs are done to your liking (about 6 minutes for soft-cooked, 7 minutes for harder cooked). 4. Top with the parsley, and serve with the bread and grated cheese, if desired.

Per Serving:
calories: 127 | fat: 7g | protein: 8g | carbs: 8g | fiber: 2g | sodium: 82mg

Mediterranean-Inspired White Smoothie

Prep time: 5 minutes | Cook time: 0 minutes | Serves

- ½ medium apple (any variety), peeled, halved, and seeded
- 5 roasted almonds
- ½ medium frozen banana, sliced (be sure to peel the
- banana before freezing)
- ¼ cup full-fat Greek yogurt
- ½ cup low-fat 1% milk
- ¼ teaspoon ground cinnamon
- ½ teaspoon honey

1. Combine all the ingredients in a blender. Process until smooth. 2. Pour into a glass and serve promptly. (This recipe is best consumed fresh.)

Per Serving:
calories: 236 | fat: 7g | protein: 8g | carbs: 40g | fiber: 5g | sodium: 84mg

Greek Yogurt and Berries

Prep time: 5 minutes | Cook time: 30 minutes | Serves 4

- 4 cups plain full-fat Greek yogurt
- 1 cup granola
- ½ cup blackberries
- 2 bananas, sliced and frozen
- 1 teaspoon chia seeds, for
- topping
- 1 teaspoon chopped fresh mint leaves, for topping
- 4 teaspoons honey, for topping (optional)

1. Evenly divide the yogurt among four bowls. Top with the granola, blackberries, bananas, chia seeds, mint, and honey (if desired), dividing evenly among the bowls. Serve.

Per Serving:
calories: 283 | fat: 9g | protein: 12g | carbs: 42g | fiber: 5g | sodium: 115mg

Smoked Salmon Egg Scramble with Dill and Chives

Prep time: 5 minutes | Cook time: 5 minutes | Serves 2

- 4 large eggs
- 1 tablespoon milk
- 1 tablespoon fresh chives, minced
- 1 tablespoon fresh dill, minced
- ¼ teaspoon kosher salt
- ⅛ teaspoon freshly ground black pepper
- 2 teaspoons extra-virgin olive oil
- 2 ounces (57 g) smoked salmon, thinly sliced

1. In a large bowl, whisk together the eggs, milk, chives, dill, salt, and pepper. 2. Heat the olive oil in a medium skillet or sauté pan over medium heat. Add the egg mixture and cook for about 3 minutes, stirring occasionally. 3. Add the salmon and cook until the eggs are set but moist, about 1 minute.

Per Serving:
calories: 325 | fat: 26g | protein: 23g | carbs: 1g | fiber: 0g | sodium: 455mg

Strawberry Basil Honey Ricotta Toast

Prep time: 10 minutes | Cook time: 0 minutes | Serves 2

- 4 slices of whole-grain bread
- ½ cup ricotta cheese (whole milk or low-fat)
- 1 tablespoon honey
- Sea salt
- 1 cup fresh strawberries, sliced
- 4 large fresh basil leaves, sliced into thin shreds

1. Toast the bread. 2. In a small bowl, combine the ricotta, honey, and a pinch or two of sea salt. Taste and add additional honey or salt if desired. 3. Spread the mixture evenly over each slice of bread (about 2 tablespoons per slice). 4. Top each piece with sliced strawberries and a few pieces of shredded basil.

Per Serving:
calories: 275 | fat: 8g | protein: 15g | carbs: 41g | fiber: 5g | sodium: 323mg

Greek Yogurt Parfait

Prep time: 5 minutes | Cook time: 0 minutes | Serves 1

- ½ cup plain whole-milk Greek yogurt
- 2 tablespoons heavy whipping cream
- ¼ cup frozen berries, thawed with juices
- ½ teaspoon vanilla or
- almond extract (optional)
- ¼ teaspoon ground cinnamon (optional)
- 1 tablespoon ground flaxseed
- 2 tablespoons chopped nuts (walnuts or pecans)

1. In a small bowl or glass, combine the yogurt, heavy whipping cream, thawed berries in their juice, vanilla or almond extract (if using), cinnamon (if using), and flaxseed and stir well until smooth. Top with chopped nuts and enjoy.

Per Serving:
calories: 333 | fat: 27g | protein: 10g | carbs: 15g | fiber: 4g | sodium: 71mg

Savory Feta, Spinach, and Red Pepper Muffins

Prep time: 10 minutes | Cook time: 22 minutes | Serves 12

- 2 cups all-purpose flour
- ¾ cup whole-wheat flour
- ¼ cup granulated sugar
- 2 teaspoons baking powder
- 1 teaspoon paprika
- ¾ teaspoonp salt
- ½ cup extra virgin olive oil
- 2 eggs
- ¾ cup low-fat 2% milk
- ¾ cup crumbled feta
- 1¼ cups fresh baby leaf spinach, thinly sliced
- ⅓ cup jarred red peppers, drained, patted dry, and chopped

1. Preheat the oven to 375°F (190°C) and line a large muffin pan with 12 muffin liners. 2. In a large bowl, combine the all-purpose flour, whole-wheat flour, sugar, baking powder, paprika, and salt. Mix well.3.In a medium bowl, whisk the olive oil, eggs, and milk. 4. Add the wet ingredients to the dry ingredients, and use a wooden spoon to stir until the ingredients are just blended and form a thick dough. 5. Add the feta, spinach, and peppers, and mix gently until all the ingredients are incorporated. Evenly divide the mixture among the muffin liners. 6. Transfer to the oven, and bake for 25 minutes or until a toothpick inserted into the middle of a muffin comes out clean. 7. Set the muffins aside to cool for 10 minutes, and remove them from the pan. Store in an airtight container in the refrigerator for up to 3 days. (Remove from the refrigerator 10 minutes before consuming.)

Per Serving:
calories: 243 | fat: 12g | protein: 6g | carbs: 27g | fiber: 2g | sodium: 306mg

Berry Warming Smoothie

Prep time: 5 minutes | Cook time: 0 minutes | Serves 1

- ⅔ cup plain kefir or plain yogurt
- ½ cup frozen mixed berries
- ½ cup baby spinach
- ½ cup cucumber, chopped
- 2 tablespoons unsweetened shredded coconut
- ¼ teaspoon grated ginger
- ¼ teaspoon ground cinnamon
- ¼ teaspoon ground nutmeg
- ⅛ teaspoon ground cardamom
- ¼ teaspoon vanilla extract (optional)

1. In a blender or Vitamix, add all the ingredients. Blend to combine.

Per Serving:
calories: 165 | fat: 7g | protein: 7g | carbs: 20g | fiber: 4g | sodium: 100mg

Spinach, Sun-Dried Tomato, and Feta Egg Wraps

Prep time: 10 minutes | Cook time: 7 minutes | Serves 2

- 1 tablespoon olive oil
- ¼ cup minced onion
- 3 to 4 tablespoons minced sun-dried tomatoes in olive oil and herbs
- 3 large eggs, beaten
- 1½ cups packed baby spinach
- 1 ounce (28 g) crumbled feta cheese
- Salt
- 2 (8-inch) whole-wheat tortillas

1. In a large skillet, heat the olive oil over medium-high heat. Add the onion and tomatoes and sauté for about 3 minutes. 2. Turn the heat down to medium. Add the beaten eggs and stir to scramble them. 3. Add the spinach and stir to combine. Sprinkle the feta cheese over the eggs. Add salt to taste. 4. Warm the tortillas in the microwave for about 20 seconds each. 5. Fill each tortilla with half of the egg mixture. Fold in half or roll them up and serve.

Per Serving:
calories: 435 | fat: 28g | protein: 17g | carbs: 31g | fiber: 6g | sodium: 552mg

Jalapeño Popper Egg Cups

Prep time: 10 minutes | Cook time: 10 minutes | Serves 2

- 4 large eggs
- ¼ cup chopped pickled jalapeños
- 2 ounces (57 g) full-fat
- cream cheese
- ½ cup shredded sharp Cheddar cheese

1. In a medium bowl, beat the eggs, then pour into four silicone muffin cups. 2. In a large microwave-safe bowl, place jalapeños, cream cheese, and Cheddar. Microwave for 30 seconds and stir. Take a spoonful, approximately ¼ of the mixture, and place it in the center of one of the egg cups. Repeat with remaining mixture. 3. Place egg cups into the air fryer basket. 4. Adjust the temperature to 320ºF (160ºC) and bake for 10 minutes. 5. Serve warm.

Per Serving:
calories: 375 | fat: 30g | protein: 23g | carbs: 3g | fiber: 0g | sodium: 445mg

Broccoli-Mushroom Frittata

Prep time: 10 minutes | Cook time: 20 minutes | Serves 2

- 1 tablespoon olive oil
- 1½ cups broccoli florets, finely chopped
- ½ cup sliced brown mushrooms
- ¼ cup finely chopped onion
- ½ teaspoon salt
- ¼ teaspoon freshly ground black pepper
- 6 eggs
- ¼ cup Parmesan cheese

1. In a nonstick cake pan, combine the olive oil, broccoli, mushrooms, onion, salt, and pepper. Stir until the vegetables are thoroughly coated with oil. Place the cake pan in the air fryer basket and set the air fryer to 400ºF (204ºC). Air fry for 5 minutes until the vegetables soften. 2. Meanwhile, in a medium bowl, whisk the eggs and Parmesan until thoroughly combined. Pour the egg mixture into the pan and shake gently to distribute the vegetables. Air fry for another 15 minutes until the eggs are set. 3. Remove from the air fryer and let sit for 5 minutes to cool slightly. Use a silicone spatula to gently lift the frittata onto a plate before serving.

Per Serving:
calories: 329 | fat: 23g | protein: 24g | carbs: 6g | fiber: 0g | sodium: 793mg

Morning Buzz Iced Coffee

Prep time: 10 minutes | Cook time: 0 minutes | Serves 1

- 1 cup freshly brewed strong black coffee, cooled slightly
- 1 tablespoon extra-virgin olive oil
- 1 tablespoon half-and-half or heavy cream (optional)
- 1 teaspoon MCT oil (optional)
- ⅛ teaspoon almond extract
- ⅛ teaspoon ground cinnamon

1. Pour the slightly cooled coffee into a blender or large glass (if using an immersion blender). 2. Add the olive oil, half-and-half (if using), MCT oil (if using), almond extract, and cinnamon. 3. Blend well until smooth and creamy. Drink warm and enjoy.

Per Serving:
calories: 124 | fat: 14g | protein: 0g | carbs: 0g | fiber: 0g | sodium: 5mg

Mashed Chickpea, Feta, and Avocado Toast

Prep time: 10 minutes |Cook time: 0 minutes| Serves: 4

- 1 (15-ounce / 425-g) can chickpeas, drained and rinsed
- 1 avocado, pitted
- ½ cup diced feta cheese (about 2 ounces / 57 g)
- 2 teaspoons freshly
- squeezed lemon juice or 1 tablespoon orange juice
- ½ teaspoon freshly ground black pepper
- 4 pieces multigrain toast
- 2 teaspoons honey

1. Put the chickpeas in a large bowl. Scoop the avocado flesh into the bowl. 2. With a potato masher or large fork, mash the ingredients together until the mix has a spreadable consistency. It doesn't need to be totally smooth. 3. Add the feta, lemon juice, and pepper, and mix well. 4. Evenly divide the mash onto the four pieces of toast and spread with a knife. Drizzle with honey and serve.

Per Serving:
calories: 301 | fat: 14g | protein: 12g | carbs: 35g | fiber: 11g | sodium: 450mg

Egg Salad with Red Pepper and Dill

Prep time: 5 minutes | Cook time: 10 minutes | Serves 6

- 6 large eggs
- 1 cup water
- 1 tablespoon olive oil
- 1 medium red bell pepper, seeded and chopped
- ¼ teaspoon salt
- ¼ teaspoon ground black pepper
- ½ cup low-fat plain Greek yogurt
- 2 tablespoons chopped fresh dill

1. Have ready a large bowl of ice water. Place rack or egg holder into bottom of the Instant Pot®. 2. Arrange eggs on rack or holder and add water to the Instant Pot®. Close lid, set steam release to Sealing, press the Manual button, and set time to 5 minutes. 3. When the timer beeps, let pressure release naturally for 5 minutes, then quick-release the remaining pressure until the float valve drops. Press the Cancel button and open lid. Carefully transfer eggs to the bowl of ice water. Let stand in ice water for 10 minutes, then peel, chop, and add eggs to a medium bowl. 4. Clean out pot, dry well, and return to machine. Press the Sauté button and heat oil. Add bell pepper, salt, and black pepper. Cook, stirring often, until bell pepper is tender, about 5 minutes. Transfer to bowl with eggs. 5. Add yogurt and dill to bowl, and fold to combine. Cover and chill for 1 hour before serving.

Per Serving:
calories: 111 | fat: 8g | protein: 8g | carbs: 3g | fiber: 0g | sodium: 178mg

Gluten-Free Granola Cereal

Prep time: 7 minutes | Cook time: 30 minutes | Makes 3½ cups

- Oil, for spraying
- 1½ cups gluten-free rolled oats
- ½ cup chopped walnuts
- ½ cup chopped almonds
- ½ cup pumpkin seeds
- ¼ cup maple syrup or honey
- 1 tablespoon toasted sesame oil or vegetable oil
- 1 teaspoon ground cinnamon
- ½ teaspoon salt
- ½ cup dried cranberries

1. Preheat the air fryer to 250°F (121°C). Line the air fryer basket with parchment and spray lightly with oil. (Do not skip the step of lining the basket; the parchment will keep the granola from falling through the holes.) 2. In a large bowl, mix together the oats, walnuts, almonds, pumpkin seeds, maple syrup, sesame oil, cinnamon, and salt. 3. Spread the mixture in an even layer in the prepared basket. 4. Cook for 30 minutes, stirring every 10 minutes. 5. Transfer the granola to a bowl, add the dried cranberries, and toss to combine. 6. Let cool to room temperature before storing in an airtight container.

Per Serving:
calories: 322 | fat: 17g | protein: 11g | carbs: 35g | fiber: 6g | sodium: 170mg

Cauliflower Avocado Toast

Prep time: 15 minutes | Cook time: 8 minutes | Serves 2

- 1 (12 ounces / 340 g) steamer bag cauliflower
- 1 large egg
- ½ cup shredded Mozzarella cheese
- 1 ripe medium avocado
- ½ teaspoon garlic powder
- ¼ teaspoon ground black pepper

1. Cook cauliflower according to package instructions. Remove from bag and place into cheesecloth or clean towel to remove excess moisture. 2. Place cauliflower into a large bowl and mix in egg and Mozzarella. Cut a piece of parchment to fit your air fryer basket. Separate the cauliflower mixture into two, and place it on the parchment in two mounds. Press out the cauliflower mounds into a ¼-inch-thick rectangle. Place the parchment into the air fryer basket. 3. Adjust the temperature to 400°F (204°C) and set the timer for 8 minutes. 4. Flip the cauliflower halfway through the cooking time. 5. When the timer beeps, remove the parchment and allow the cauliflower to cool 5 minutes. 6. Cut open the avocado and remove the pit. Scoop out the inside, place it in a medium bowl, and mash it with garlic powder and pepper. Spread onto the cauliflower. Serve immediately.

Per Serving:
calories: 321 | fat: 22g | protein: 16g | carbs: 19g | fiber: 10g | sodium: 99mg

Portobello Eggs Benedict

Prep time: 10 minutes | Cook time: 10 to 14 minutes | Serves 2

- 1 tablespoon olive oil
- 2 cloves garlic, minced
- ¼ teaspoon dried thyme
- 2 portobello mushrooms, stems removed and gills scraped out
- 2 Roma tomatoes, halved lengthwise
- Salt and freshly ground
- black pepper, to taste
- 2 large eggs
- 2 tablespoons grated Pecorino Romano cheese
- 1 tablespoon chopped fresh parsley, for garnish
- 1 teaspoon truffle oil (optional)

1. Preheat the air fryer to 400°F (204°C). 2. In a small bowl, combine the olive oil, garlic, and thyme. Brush the mixture over the mushrooms and tomatoes until thoroughly coated. Season to taste with salt and freshly ground black pepper. 3. Arrange the vegetables, cut side up, in the air fryer basket. Crack an egg into the center of each mushroom and sprinkle with cheese. Air fry for 10 to 14 minutes until the vegetables are tender and the whites are firm. When cool enough to handle, coarsely chop the tomatoes and place on top of the eggs. Scatter parsley on top and drizzle with truffle oil, if desired, just before serving.

Per Serving:
calories: 189 | fat: 13g | protein: 11g | carbs: 7g | fiber: 2g | sodium: 87mg

Berry Breakfast Smoothie

Prep time: 5 minutes | Cook time: 0 minutes | Serves 1

- ½ cup vanilla low-fat Greek yogurt
- ¼ cup low-fat milk
- ½ cup fresh or frozen
- blueberries or strawberries (or a combination)
- 6 to 8 ice cubes

1. Place the Greek yogurt, milk, and berries in a blender and blend until the berries are liquefied. Add the ice cubes and blend on high until thick and smooth. Serve immediately.

Per Serving:
calories: 158 | fat: 3g | protein: 9g | carbs: 25g | fiber: 1g | sodium: 110mg

Berry Baked Oatmeal

Prep time: 10 minutes | Cook time: 45 to 50 minutes | Serves 8

- 2 cups gluten-free rolled oats
- 2 cups (10-ounce / 283-g bag) frozen mixed berries (blueberries and raspberries work best)
- 2 cups plain, unsweetened almond milk
- 1 cup plain Greek yogurt
- ¼ cup maple syrup
- 2 tablespoons extra-virgin olive oil
- 2 teaspoons ground cinnamon
- 1 teaspoon baking powder
- 1 teaspoon vanilla extract
- ½ teaspoon kosher salt
- ¼ teaspoon ground nutmeg
- ⅛ teaspoon ground cloves

1. Preheat the oven to 375ºF (190ºC). 2. Mix all the ingredients together in a large bowl. Pour into a 9-by-13-inch baking dish. Bake for 45 to 50 minutes, or until golden brown.

Per Serving:
calories: 180 | fat: 6g | protein: 6g | carbs: 28g | fiber: 4g | sodium: 180mg

Golden Egg Skillet

Prep time: 15 minutes | Cook time: 20 minutes | Serves 2

- 2 tablespoons extra-virgin avocado oil or ghee
- 2 medium spring onions, white and green parts separated, sliced
- 1 clove garlic, minced
- 3½ ounces (99 g) Swiss chard or collard greens, stalks and leaves separated, chopped
- 1 medium zucchini, sliced into coins
- 2 tablespoons water
- 1 teaspoon Dijon or yellow mustard
- ½ teaspoon ground turmeric
- ¼ teaspoon black pepper
- Salt, to taste
- 4 large eggs
- ¾ cup grated Manchego or Pecorino Romano cheese
- 2 tablespoons (30 ml) extra-virgin olive oil

1. Preheat the oven to 360°F (182ºC) fan assisted or 400°F (205ºC) conventional. 2. Grease a large, ovenproof skillet (with a lid) with the avocado oil. Cook the white parts of the spring onions and the garlic for about 1 minute, until just fragrant. Add the chard stalks, zucchini, and water. Stir, then cover with a lid. Cook over medium-low heat for about 10 minutes or until the zucchini is tender. Add the mustard, turmeric, pepper, and salt. Add the chard leaves and cook until just wilted. 3. Use a spatula to make 4 wells in the mixture. Crack an egg into each well and cook until the egg whites start to set while the yolks are still runny. Top with the cheese, transfer to the oven, and bake for 5 to 7 minutes. Remove from the oven and sprinkle with the reserved spring onions. Drizzle with the olive oil and serve warm.

Per Serving:
calories: 600 | fat: 49g | protein: 31g | carbs: 10g | fiber: 4g | sodium: 213mg

C+C Overnight Oats

Prep time: 5 minutes | Cook time: 0 minutes | Serves 2

- ½ cup vanilla, unsweetened almond milk (not Silk brand)
- ½ cup rolled oats
- 2 tablespoons sliced almonds
- 2 tablespoons simple sugar
- liquid sweetener
- 1 teaspoon chia seeds
- ¼ teaspoon ground cardamom
- ¼ teaspoon ground cinnamon

1. In a mason jar, combine the almond milk, oats, almonds, liquid sweetener, chia seeds, cardamom, and cinnamon and shake well. Store in the refrigerator for 8 to 24 hours, then serve cold or heated.

Per Serving:
calories: 131 | fat: 6g | protein: 5g | carbs: 17g | fiber: 4g | sodium: 45mg

Blueberry-Lemon Tea Cakes

Prep time: 10 minutes | Cook time: 25 minutes | Serves 12

- 4 eggs
- ½ cup granulated sugar
- Grated peel of 1 lemon
- 1½ cups all-purpose flour
- ¾ cup fine cornmeal
- 2 teaspoons baking powder
- 1 teaspoon kosher salt
- 1 cup extra-virgin olive oil
- 1½ cups fresh or frozen blueberries

1. Preheat the oven to 350°F(180ºC). Grease a 12-cup muffin pan or line with paper liners. 2. With an electric mixer set to medium speed, beat the eggs and sugar together until they are pale and fluffy. Stir in the lemon peel. 3. In a medium bowl, stir together the flour, cornmeal, baking powder, and salt. With the mixer on low speed, alternate adding the flour mixture and oil to the egg mixture. Fold in the blueberries. 4. Dollop the batter into the muffin pan. Bake until the tops are golden and a toothpick inserted in the middle comes out clean, 20 to 25 minutes.

Per Serving:
calories: 317 | fat: 20g | protein: 4g | carbs: 31g | fiber: 2g | sodium: 217mg

Spiced Potatoes with Chickpeas

Prep time: 10 minutes | Cook time: 10 minutes | Serves 4

- ¼ cup olive oil
- 3 medium potatoes, peeled and shredded
- 2 cups finely chopped baby spinach
- 1 medium onion, finely diced
- 1 tablespoon minced fresh ginger
- 1 teaspoon ground cumin
- 1 teaspoon ground coriander
- ½ teaspoon ground turmeric
- ½ teaspoon salt
- 1 (15-ounce / 425-g) can chickpeas, drained and rinsed
- 1 medium zucchini, diced
- ¼ cup chopped cilantro
- 1 cup plain yogurt

1. Heat the olive oil in a large skillet over medium heat. Add the potatoes, spinach, onions, ginger, cumin, coriander, turmeric, and salt and stir to mix well. Spread the mixture out into an even layer and let cook, without stirring, for about 5 minutes until the potatoes are crisp and browned on the bottom. 2. Add the chickpeas and zucchini and mix to combine, breaking up the layer of potatoes. Spread the mixture out again into an even layer and continue to cook, without stirring, for another 5 minutes or so, until the potatoes are crisp on the bottom. 3. To serve, garnish with cilantro and yogurt.

Per Serving:
calories: 679 | fat: 20g | protein: 28g | carbs: 100g | fiber: 24g | sodium: 388mg

Enjoy-Your-Veggies Breakfast

Prep time: 20 minutes | Cook time: 10 minutes | Serves 4

- 1 tablespoon olive oil
- 1 small sweet onion, peeled and diced
- 2 large carrots, peeled and diced
- 2 medium potatoes, peeled and diced
- 1 stalk celery, diced
- 1 large red bell pepper, seeded and diced
- 1 tablespoon low-sodium soy sauce
- ¼ cup water
- 1 cup diced peeled zucchini or summer squash
- 2 medium tomatoes, peeled and diced
- 2 cups cooked brown rice
- ½ teaspoon ground black pepper

1. Press the Sauté button on the Instant Pot® and heat oil. Add onion and cook until just tender, about 2 minutes. 2. Stir in carrots, potatoes, celery, and bell pepper and cook until just tender, about 2 minutes. Add soy sauce and water. Press the Cancel button. 3. Close lid, set steam release to Sealing, press the Manual button, and set time to 2 minutes. When the timer beeps, quick-release the pressure until the float valve drops. Press the Cancel button. 4. Open lid and add squash and tomatoes, and stir. Close lid, set steam release to Sealing, press the Manual button, and set time to 1 minute. When the timer beeps, quick-release the pressure until the float valve drops. Press the Cancel button and open lid. 5. Serve over rice and sprinkle with black pepper.

Per Serving:
calories: 224 | fat: 5g | protein: 6g | carbs: 41g | fiber: 5g | sodium: 159mg

Nuts and Fruit Oatmeal

Prep time: 10 minutes | Cook time: 7 minutes | Serves 2

- 1 cup rolled oats
- 1¼ cups water
- ¼ cup orange juice
- 1 medium pear, peeled, cored, and cubed
- ¼ cup dried cherries
- ¼ cup chopped walnuts
- 1 tablespoon honey
- ¼ teaspoon ground ginger
- ¼ teaspoon ground cinnamon
- ⅛ teaspoon salt

1. Place oats, water, orange juice, pear, cherries, walnuts, honey, ginger, cinnamon, and salt in the Instant Pot®. Stir to combine. 2. Close lid, set steam release to Sealing, press the Manual button, and set time to 7 minutes. When the timer beeps, let pressure release naturally, about 20 minutes. Press the Cancel button, open lid, and stir well. Serve warm.

Per Serving:
calories: 362 | fat: 8g | protein: 7g | carbs: 69g | fiber: 8g | sodium: 164mg

Egg in a "Pepper Hole" with Avocado

Prep time: 15 minutes | Cook time: 5 minutes | Serves 4

- 4 bell peppers, any color
- 1 tablespoon extra-virgin olive oil
- 8 large eggs
- ¾ teaspoon kosher salt, divided
- ¼ teaspoon freshly ground
- black pepper, divided
- 1 avocado, peeled, pitted, and diced
- ¼ cup red onion, diced
- ¼ cup fresh basil, chopped
- Juice of ½ lime

1. Stem and seed the bell peppers. Cut 2 (2-inch-thick) rings from each pepper. Chop the remaining bell pepper into small dice, and set aside. 2. Heat the olive oil in a large skillet over medium heat. Add 4 bell pepper rings, then crack 1 egg in the middle of each ring. Season with ¼ teaspoon of the salt and ⅛ teaspoon of the black pepper. Cook until the egg whites are mostly set but the yolks are still runny, 2 to 3 minutes. Gently flip and cook 1 additional minute for over easy. Move the egg-bell pepper rings to a platter or onto plates, and repeat with the remaining 4 bell pepper rings. 3. In a medium bowl, combine the avocado, onion, basil, lime juice, reserved diced bell pepper, the remaining ¼ teaspoon kosher salt, and the remaining ⅛ teaspoon black pepper. Divide among the 4 plates.

Per Serving:
2 egg-pepper rings: calories: 270 | fat: 19g | protein: 15g | carbs: 12g | fiber: 5g | sodium: 360mg

Spinach and Feta Egg Bake

Prep time: 7 minutes | Cook time: 23 to 25 minutes | Serves 2

- Avocado oil spray
- ⅓ cup diced red onion
- 1 cup frozen chopped spinach, thawed and drained
- 4 large eggs
- ¼ cup heavy (whipping) cream

- Sea salt and freshly ground black pepper, to taste
- ¼ teaspoon cayenne pepper
- ½ cup crumbled feta cheese
- ¼ cup shredded Parmesan cheese

1. Spray a deep pan with oil. Put the onion in the pan, and place the pan in the air fryer basket. Set the air fryer to 350°F (177°C) and bake for 7 minutes. 2. Sprinkle the spinach over the onion. 3. In a medium bowl, beat the eggs, heavy cream, salt, black pepper, and cayenne. Pour this mixture over the vegetables. 4. Top with the feta and Parmesan cheese. Bake for 16 to 18 minutes, until the eggs are set and lightly brown.

Per Serving:
calories: 366 | fat: 26g | protein: 25g | carbs: 8g | fiber: 3g | sodium: 520mg

Mexican Breakfast Pepper Rings

Prep time: 5 minutes | Cook time: 10 minutes | Serves 4

- Olive oil
- 1 large red, yellow, or orange bell pepper, cut into four ¾-inch rings

- 4 eggs
- Salt and freshly ground black pepper, to taste
- 2 teaspoons salsa

1. Preheat the air fryer to 350°F (177°C). Lightly spray a baking pan with olive oil. 2. Place 2 bell pepper rings on the pan. Crack one egg into each bell pepper ring. Season with salt and black pepper. 3. Spoon ½ teaspoon of salsa on top of each egg. 4. Place the pan in the air fryer basket. Air fry until the yolk is slightly runny, 5 to 6 minutes or until the yolk is fully cooked, 8 to 10 minutes. 5. Repeat with the remaining 2 pepper rings. Serve hot.

Per Serving:
calories: 76 | fat: 4g | protein: 6g | carbs: 3g | fiber: 1g | sodium: 83mg

Greek Eggs and Potatoes

Prep time: 5 minutes | Cook time: 30 minutes | Serves 4

- 3 medium tomatoes, seeded and coarsely chopped
- 2 tablespoons fresh chopped basil
- 1 garlic clove, minced
- 2 tablespoons plus ½ cup olive oil, divided

- Sea salt and freshly ground pepper, to taste
- 3 large russet potatoes
- 4 large eggs
- 1 teaspoon fresh oregano, chopped

1. Put tomatoes in a food processor and purée them, skins and all. 2. Add the basil, garlic, 2 tablespoons olive oil, sea salt, and freshly ground pepper, and pulse to combine. 3. Put the mixture in a large skillet over low heat and cook, covered, for 20–25 minutes, or until the sauce has thickened and is bubbly. 4. Meanwhile, dice the potatoes into small cubes. Put ½ cup olive oil in a nonstick skillet over medium-low heat. 5. Fry the potatoes for 5 minutes until crisp and browned on the outside, then cover and reduce heat to low. Steam potatoes until done. 6. Carefully crack the eggs into the tomato sauce. Cook over low heat until the eggs are set in the sauce, about 6 minutes. 7. Remove the potatoes from the pan and drain them on paper towels, then place them in a bowl. 8. Sprinkle with sea salt and freshly ground pepper to taste and top with the oregano. 9. Carefully remove the eggs with a slotted spoon and place them on a plate with the potatoes. Spoon sauce over the top and serve.

Per Serving:
calories: 548 | fat: 32g | protein: 13g | carbs: 54g | fiber: 5g | sodium: 90mg

Beans and Grains

Chapter 3 Beans and Grains

Barley Risotto

Prep time: 10 minutes | Cook time: 30 minutes | Serves 6

- 2 tablespoons olive oil
- 1 large onion, peeled and diced
- 1 clove garlic, peeled and minced
- 1 stalk celery, finely minced
- 1½ cups pearl barley, rinsed and drained
- ⅓ cup dried mushrooms
- 4 cups low-sodium chicken broth
- 2¼ cups water
- 1 cup grated Parmesan cheese
- 2 tablespoons minced fresh parsley
- ¼ teaspoon salt

1. Press the Sauté button on the Instant Pot® and heat oil. Add onion and sauté 5 minutes. Add garlic and cook 30 seconds. Stir in celery, barley, mushrooms, broth, and water. Press the Cancel button. 2. Close lid, set steam release to Sealing, press the Manual button, and set time to 18 minutes. When the timer beeps, quick-release the pressure until the float valve drops and open the lid. 3. Drain off excess liquid, leaving enough to leave the risotto slightly soupy. Press the Cancel button, then press the Sauté button and cook until thickened, about 5 minutes. Stir in cheese, parsley, and salt. Serve immediately.

Per Serving:
calories: 175 | fat: 9g | protein: 10g | carbs: 13g | fiber: 2g | sodium: 447mg

Sun-Dried Tomato Rice

Prep time: 10 minutes | Cook time: 30 minutes | Serves 8

- 2 tablespoons extra-virgin olive oil
- ½ medium yellow onion, peeled and chopped
- 2 cloves garlic, peeled and minced
- 1 cup chopped sun-dried tomatoes in oil, drained
- 1 tablespoon tomato paste
- 2 cups brown rice
- 2¼ cups water
- ½ cup chopped fresh basil
- ¼ teaspoon salt
- ½ teaspoon ground black pepper

1. Press the Sauté button on the Instant Pot® and heat oil. Add onion and cook until soft, about 6 minutes. Add garlic and sun-dried tomatoes and cook until fragrant, about 30 seconds. Add tomato paste, rice, and water, and stir well. Press the Cancel button. 2. Close lid, set steam release to Sealing, press the Manual button, and set time to 22 minutes. When the timer beeps, let pressure release naturally for 10 minutes, then quick-release the remaining pressure. Open lid and fold in basil. Season with salt and pepper.

Serve warm.

Per Serving:
calories: 114 | fat: 4g | protein: 2g | carbs: 18g | fiber: 2g | sodium: 112mg

Spanish Rice

Prep time: 10 minutes | Cook time: 20 minutes | Serves 4

- 2 tablespoons extra-virgin olive oil
- 1 medium onion, finely chopped
- 1 large tomato, finely diced
- 2 tablespoons tomato paste
- 1 teaspoon smoked paprika
- 1 teaspoon salt
- 1½ cups basmati rice
- 3 cups water

1. In a medium pot over medium heat, cook the olive oil, onion, and tomato for 3 minutes. 2. Stir in the tomato paste, paprika, salt, and rice. Cook for 1 minute. 3. Add the water, cover the pot, and turn the heat to low. Cook for 12 minutes. 4. Gently toss the rice, cover, and cook for another 3 minutes.

Per Serving:
calories: 328 | fat: 7g | protein: 6g | carbs: 60g | fiber: 2g | sodium: 651mg

Three-Grain Pilaf

Prep time: 10 minutes | Cook time: 10 minutes | Serves 6

- 2 tablespoons extra-virgin olive oil
- ½ cup sliced scallions
- 1 cup jasmine rice
- ½ cup millet
- ½ cup quinoa, rinsed and
- drained
- 2½ cups vegetable stock
- ¼ teaspoon salt
- ¼ teaspoon ground black pepper

1. Press the Sauté button on the Instant Pot® and heat oil. Add scallions and cook until just tender, 2 minutes. Add rice, millet, and quinoa and cook for 3 minutes to toast. Add stock and stir well. Press the Cancel button. 2. Close lid, set steam release to Sealing, press the Manual button, and set time to 4 minutes. When the timer beeps, quick-release the pressure until the float valve drops and open the lid. Fluff pilaf with a fork and stir in salt and pepper. Serve warm.

Per Serving:
calories: 346 | fat: 7g | protein: 8g | carbs: 61g | fiber: 4g | sodium: 341mg

Brown Rice Vegetable Bowl with Roasted Red Pepper Dressing

Prep time: 10 minutes | Cook time: 22 minutes | Serves 2

- ¼ cup chopped roasted red bell pepper
- 2 tablespoons extra-virgin olive oil
- 1 tablespoon red wine vinegar
- 1 teaspoon honey
- 2 tablespoons light olive oil
- 2 cloves garlic, peeled and minced
- ½ teaspoon ground black pepper
- ¼ teaspoon salt
- 1 cup brown rice
- 1 cup vegetable broth
- ¼ cup chopped fresh flat-leaf parsley
- 2 tablespoons chopped fresh chives
- 2 tablespoons chopped fresh dill
- ½ cup diced tomato
- ½ cup chopped red onion
- ½ cup diced cucumber
- ½ cup chopped green bell pepper

1. Place roasted red pepper, extra-virgin olive oil, red wine vinegar, and honey in a blender. Purée until smooth, about 1 minute. Refrigerate until ready to serve. 2. Press the Sauté button on the Instant Pot® and heat light olive oil. Add garlic and cook until fragrant, about 30 seconds. Add black pepper, salt, and rice and stir well. Press the Cancel button. 3. Stir in broth. Close lid, set steam release to Sealing, press the Manual button, and set time to 22 minutes.

Per Serving:
calories: 561 | fat: 23g | protein: 10g | carbs: 86g | fiber: 5g | sodium: 505mg

Moroccan Vegetables and Chickpeas

Prep time: 25 minutes | Cook time: 6 hours | Serves 6

- 1 large carrot, cut into ¼-inch rounds
- 2 large baking potatoes, peeled and cubed
- 1 large bell pepper, any color, chopped
- 6 ounces (170 g) green beans, trimmed and cut into bite-size pieces
- 1 large yellow onion, chopped
- 2 garlic cloves, minced
- 1 teaspoon peeled, grated fresh ginger
- 1 (15-ounce / 425-g) can diced tomatoes, with the
- juice
- 3 cups canned chickpeas, rinsed and drained
- 1¾ cups vegetable stock
- 1 tablespoon ground coriander
- 1 teaspoon ground cumin
- ¼ teaspoon ground red pepper
- Sea salt
- Black pepper
- 8 ounces (227 g) fresh baby spinach
- ¼ cup diced dried apricots
- ¼ cup diced dried figs
- 1 cup plain greek yogurt

1. Put the carrot, potatoes, bell pepper, green beans, onion, garlic, and ginger in the slow cooker. Stir in the diced tomatoes, chickpeas, and vegetable stock. Sprinkle with coriander, cumin, red pepper, salt, and black pepper. 2. Cover and cook on high for 6 hours or until the vegetables are tender. 3. Add the spinach, apricots, figs, and Greek yogurt, and cook and stir until the spinach wilts, about 4 minutes. Serve hot.

Per Serving:
calories: 307 | fat: 5g | protein: 13g | carbs: 57g | fiber: 12g | sodium: 513mg

White Bean Soup with Kale and Lemon

Prep time: 15 minutes | Cook time: 27 minutes | Serves 8

- 1 tablespoon light olive oil
- 2 stalks celery, chopped
- 1 medium yellow onion, peeled and chopped
- 2 cloves garlic, peeled and minced
- 1 tablespoon chopped fresh oregano
- 4 cups chopped kale
- 1 pound (454 g) dried Great Northern beans, soaked overnight and drained
- 8 cups vegetable broth
- ¼ cup lemon juice
- 1 tablespoon extra-virgin olive oil
- 1 teaspoon ground black pepper

1. Press the Sauté button on the Instant Pot® and heat light olive oil. Add celery and onion and cook 5 minutes. Add garlic and oregano and sauté 30 seconds. Add kale and turn to coat, then cook until just starting to wilt, about 1 minute. Press the Cancel button. 2. Add beans, broth, lemon juice, extra-virgin olive oil, and pepper to the Instant Pot® and stir well. Close lid, set steam release to Sealing, press the Manual button, and set time to 20 minutes. When the timer beeps, let pressure release naturally, about 20 minutes. Open lid and stir well. Serve hot.

Per Serving:
calories: 129 | fat: 3g | protein: 7g | carbs: 22g | fiber: 6g | sodium: 501mg

Herbed Polenta

Prep time: 10 minutes | Cook time: 3 to 5 hours | Serves 4

- 1 cup stone-ground polenta
- 4 cups low-sodium vegetable stock or low-sodium chicken stock
- 1 tablespoon extra-virgin olive oil
- 1 small onion, minced
- 2 garlic cloves, minced
- 1 teaspoon sea salt
- 1 teaspoon dried parsley
- 1 teaspoon dried oregano
- 1 teaspoon dried thyme
- ½ teaspoon freshly ground black pepper
- ½ cup grated Parmesan cheese

1. In a slow cooker, combine the polenta, vegetable stock, olive oil, onion, garlic, salt, parsley, oregano, thyme, and pepper. Stir to mix well. 2. Cover the cooker and cook for 3 to 5 hours on Low heat. 3. Stir in the Parmesan cheese for serving.

Per Serving:
calories: 191 | fat: 9g | protein: 11g | carbs: 18g | fiber: 1g | sodium: 796mg

Bulgur with Red Pepper and Goat Cheese

Prep time: 10 minutes | Cook time: 16 minutes | Serves 4

- 1 tablespoon light olive oil
- 1 medium red bell pepper, seeded and chopped
- ½ medium yellow onion, peeled and chopped
- 1 clove garlic, peeled and minced
- ½ teaspoon ground black pepper
- ¼ teaspoon salt
- 1 cup bulgur wheat
- 2 cups water
- ¼ cup chopped fresh chives
- ¼ cup chopped fresh flat-leaf parsley
- 2 ounces (57 g) crumbled goat cheese

1. Press the Sauté button on the Instant Pot® and heat oil. Add bell pepper and onion, and cook until just softened, about 3 minutes. Add garlic, black pepper, and salt. Cook until garlic is fragrant, about 30 seconds. Press the Cancel button. 2. Add bulgur and water to the Instant Pot® and stir well. Close lid, set steam release to Sealing, press the Rice button, adjust pressure to Low, and set time to 12 minutes. When the timer beeps, quick-release the pressure until the float valve drops. Open lid and fluff bulgur with a fork. 3. Add chives and parsley to pot and toss. Transfer rice mixture to a serving dish and top with goat cheese. Serve warm.

Per Serving:
calories: 123 | fat: 7g | protein: 4g | carbs: 12g | fiber: 4g | sodium: 227mg

Garlicky Split Chickpea Curry

Prep time: 10 minutes | Cook time: 4 to 6 hours | Serves 6

- 1½ cups split gram
- 1 onion, finely chopped
- 2 tomatoes, chopped
- 1 tablespoon freshly grated ginger
- 1 teaspoon cumin seeds, ground or crushed with a mortar and pestle
- 2 teaspoons turmeric
- 2 garlic cloves, crushed
- 1 hot green Thai or other fresh chile, thinly sliced
- 3 cups hot water
- 1 teaspoon salt
- 2 tablespoons rapeseed oil
- 1 teaspoon cumin seeds, crushed
- 1 garlic clove, sliced
- 1 fresh green chile, sliced

1. Heat the slow cooker to high. Add the split gram, onion, tomatoes, ginger, crushed cumin seeds, turmeric, crushed garlic, hot chile, water, and salt, and then stir. 2. Cover and cook on high for 4 hours, or on low for 6 hours, until the split gram is tender. 3. Just before serving, heat the oil in a saucepan. When the oil is hot, add the cumin seeds with the sliced garlic. Cook until the garlic is golden brown, and then pour it over the dhal. 4. To serve, top with the sliced green chile.

Per Serving:
calories: 119 | fat: 5g | protein: 4g | carbs: 15g | fiber: 3g | sodium: 503mg

Black-Eyed Peas with Olive Oil and Herbs

Prep time: 15 minutes | Cook time: 20 minutes | Serves 8

- ¼ cup extra-virgin olive oil
- 4 sprigs oregano, leaves minced and stems reserved
- 2 sprigs thyme, leaves stripped and stems reserved
- 4 sprigs dill, fronds chopped and stems reserved
- 1 pound (454 g) dried black-eyed peas, soaked overnight and drained
- ¼ teaspoon salt
- 1 teaspoon ground black pepper
- 4 cups water

1. In a small bowl, combine oil, oregano leaves, thyme leaves, and dill fronds, and mix to combine. Cover and set aside. 2. Tie herb stems together with butcher's twine. Add to the Instant Pot® along with black-eyed peas, salt, pepper, and water. Close lid, set steam release to Sealing, press the Manual button, and set time to 20 minutes. When the timer beeps, let pressure release naturally, about 20 minutes. 3. Open lid, remove and discard herb stem bundle, and drain off any excess liquid. Stir in olive oil mixture. Serve hot.

Per Serving:
calories: 119 | fat: 7g | protein: 6g | carbs: 9g | fiber: 3g | sodium: 76mg

Vegetarian Dinner Loaf

Prep time: 10 minutes | Cook time: 45 minutes | Serves 6

- 1 cup dried pinto beans, soaked overnight and drained
- 8 cups water, divided
- 1 tablespoon vegetable oil
- 1 teaspoon salt
- 1 cup diced onion
- 1 cup chopped walnuts
- ½ cup rolled oats
- 1 large egg, beaten
- ¾ cup ketchup
- 1 teaspoon garlic powder
- 1 teaspoon dried basil
- 1 teaspoon dried parsley
- ½ teaspoon salt
- ½ teaspoon ground black pepper

1. Add beans and 4 cups water to the Instant Pot®. Close lid, set steam release to Sealing, press the Manual button, and set time to 1 minute. When the timer beeps, quick-release the pressure until the float valve drops. Press the Cancel button. 2. Open lid, then drain and rinse beans and return to the pot with remaining 4 cups water. Soak for 1 hour. 3. Preheat oven to 350°F. 4. Add the oil and salt to pot. Close lid, set steam release to Sealing, press the Manual button, and set time to 11 minutes. When the timer beeps, let pressure release naturally, about 25 minutes, and open lid. Drain beans and pour into a large mixing bowl. 5. Stir in onion, walnuts, oats, egg, ketchup, garlic powder, basil, parsley, salt, and pepper. Spread the mixture into a loaf pan and bake for 30–35 minutes. Cool for 20 minutes in pan before slicing and serving.

Per Serving:
calories: 278 | fat: 17g | protein: 9g | carbs: 27g | fiber: 6g | sodium: 477mg

Sea Salt Soybeans

Prep time: 5 minutes | Cook time: 12 minutes | Serves 4

- 1 cup shelled edamame
- 8 cups water, divided
- 1 tablespoon vegetable oil
- 1 teaspoon coarse sea salt
- 2 tablespoons soy sauce

1. Add edamame and 4 cups water to the Instant Pot®. Close lid, set steam release to Sealing, and set time to 1 minute. When the timer beeps, quick-release the pressure until the float valve drops. Press the Cancel button. 2. Open lid, drain and rinse edamame, and return to pot with the remaining 4 cups water. Soak for 1 hour. 3. Add oil. Close lid, set steam release to Sealing, press the Manual button, and set time to 11 minutes. When the timer beeps, let pressure release naturally, about 25 minutes, then open lid. 4. Drain edamame and transfer to a serving bowl. Sprinkle with salt and serve with soy sauce on the side for dipping.

Per Serving:
calories: 76 | fat: 5g | protein: 4g | carbs: 5g | fiber: 2g | sodium: 768mg

Herbed Barley

Prep time: 10 minutes | Cook time: 30 minutes | Serves 4

- 2 tablespoons olive oil
- ½ cup diced onion
- ½ cup diced celery
- 1 carrot, peeled and diced
- 3 cups water or chicken broth
- 1 cup barley
- 1 bay leaf
- ½ teaspoon thyme
- ½ teaspoon rosemary
- ¼ cup walnuts or pine nuts
- Sea salt and freshly ground pepper, to taste

1. Heat the olive oil in a medium saucepan over medium-high heat. Sauté the onion, celery, and carrot over medium heat until they are tender. 2. Add the water or chicken broth, barley, and seasonings, and bring to a boil. Reduce the heat and simmer for 25 minutes, or until tender. 3. Stir in the nuts and season to taste.

Per Serving:
calories: 283 | fat: 11g | protein: 6g | carbs: 43g | fiber: 9g | sodium: 26mg

Amaranth Salad

Prep time: 5 minutes | Cook time: 6 minutes | Serves 4

- 2 cups water
- 1 cup amaranth
- 1 teaspoon dried Greek oregano
- ½ teaspoon salt
- ½ teaspoon ground black
- pepper
- 1 tablespoon extra-virgin olive oil
- 2 teaspoons red wine vinegar

1. Add water and amaranth to the Instant Pot®. Close lid, set

steam release to Sealing, press the Manual button, and set time to 6 minutes. When the timer beeps, quick-release the pressure until the float valve drops. 2. Open lid and fluff amaranth with a fork. Add oregano, salt, and pepper. Mix well. Drizzle with olive oil and wine vinegar. Serve hot.

Per Serving:
calories: 93 | fat: 5g | protein: 3g | carbs: 12g | fiber: 3g | sodium: 299mg

Greek-Style Pea Casserole

Prep time: 5 minutes | Cook time: 45 minutes | Serves 3

- ⅓ cup extra virgin olive oil
- 1 medium onion (any variety), diced
- 1 medium carrot, peeled and sliced
- 1 medium white potato, peeled and cut into bite-sized pieces
- 1 pound (454 g) peas (fresh or frozen)
- 3 tablespoons chopped fresh dill
- 2 medium tomatoes, grated, or 12 ounces (340 g) canned crushed tomatoes
- ½ teaspoon fine sea salt
- ¼ teaspoon freshly ground black pepper
- ½ cup hot water
- Salt to taste

1. Add the olive oil to a medium pot over medium heat. When the oil starts to shimmer, add the onions and sauté for 2 minutes. Add the carrots and potatoes, and sauté for 3 more minutes. 2. Add the peas and dill. Stir until the peas are coated in the olive oil. 3. Add the tomatoes, sea salt, black pepper, and hot water. Mix well. Bring to the mixture to a boil, then cover, reduce the heat to low, and simmer for 40 minutes or until the peas and carrots are soft and the casserole has thickened. (Check the water levels intermittently, adding more hot water if the mixture appears to be getting too dry.) 4. Remove the casserole from the heat, uncover, and set aside for 20 minutes. Add salt to taste before serving. Store covered in the refrigerator for up to 3 days.

Per Serving:
calories: 439 | fat: 26g | protein: 12g | carbs: 45g | fiber: 13g | sodium: 429mg

Apple Couscous with Curry

Prep time: 10 minutes | Cook time: 10 minutes | Serves 4

- 2 teaspoons olive oil
- 2 leeks, white parts only, sliced
- 1 Granny Smith apple, diced
- 2 cups cooked whole-wheat couscous
- 2 tablespoons curry powder
- ½ cup chopped pecans

1. Heat the olive oil in a large skillet on medium heat and add leeks. Cook until soft and tender, about 5 minutes. 2. Add diced apple and cook until soft. 3. Add couscous and curry powder, then stir to combine. Remove from heat, mix in nuts, and serve.

Per Serving:
calories: 255 | fat: 12g | protein: 5g | carbs: 34g | fiber: 6g | sodium: 15mg

Domatorizo (Greek Tomato Rice)

Prep time: 10 minutes | Cook time: 12 minutes | Serves 6

- 2 tablespoons extra-virgin olive oil
- 1 large onion, peeled and diced
- 1 cup Arborio rice
- 1 cup tomato juice
- 3 tablespoons dry white wine
- 2 cups water

- 1 tablespoon tomato paste
- ½ teaspoon salt
- ½ teaspoon ground black pepper
- ½ cup crumbled or cubed feta cheese
- ⅛ teaspoon dried Greek oregano
- 1 scallion, thinly sliced

1. Press the Sauté button on the Instant Pot® and heat oil. Add onion and cook until just tender, about 3 minutes. Stir in rice and cook for 2 minutes. 2. Add tomato juice and wine to rice. Cook, stirring often, until the liquid is absorbed, about 1 minute. 3. In a small bowl, whisk together water and tomato paste. Add to pot along with salt and pepper and stir well. Press the Cancel button. 4. Close lid, set steam release to Sealing, press the Manual button, and set time to 5 minutes. When the timer beeps, let pressure release naturally for 10 minutes, then quick-release any remaining pressure until the float valve drops. 5. Open lid and stir well. Spoon rice into bowls and top with feta, oregano, and scallion. Serve immediately.

Per Serving:
calories: 184 | fat: 9g | protein: 6g | carbs: 20g | fiber: 1g | sodium: 537mg

Lebanese Rice and Broken Noodles with Cabbage

Prep time: 5 minutes |Cook time: 25 minutes| Serves: 6

- 1 tablespoon extra-virgin olive oil
- 1 cup (about 3 ounces / 85 g) uncooked vermicelli or thin spaghetti, broken into 1- to 1½-inch pieces
- 3 cups shredded cabbage (about half a 14-ounce package of coleslaw mix or half a small head of cabbage)
- 3 cups low-sodium or no-salt-added vegetable broth
- ½ cup water

- 1 cup instant brown rice
- 2 garlic cloves
- ¼ teaspoon kosher or sea salt
- ⅛ to ¼ teaspoon crushed red pepper
- ½ cup loosely packed, coarsely chopped cilantro
- Fresh lemon slices, for serving (optional)

1. In a large saucepan over medium-high heat, heat the oil. Add the pasta and cook for 3 minutes to toast, stirring often. Add the cabbage and cook for 4 minutes, stirring often. Add the broth, water, rice, garlic, salt, and crushed red pepper, and bring to a boil over high heat. Stir, cover, and reduce the heat to medium-low. Simmer for 10 minutes. 2. Remove the pan from the heat, but do not lift the lid. Let sit for 5 minutes. Fish out the garlic cloves, mash them with a fork, then stir the garlic back into the rice. Stir in the cilantro. Serve with the lemon slices (if using).

Per Serving:
calories: 150 | fat: 4g | protein: 3g | carbs: 27g | fiber: 3g | sodium: 664mg

Mediterranean Lentil Casserole

Prep time: 15 minutes | Cook time: 8 to 10 hours | Serves 6

- 1 pound (454 g) lentils, rinsed well under cold water and picked over to remove debris
- 4 cups low-sodium vegetable broth
- 3 carrots, diced
- 3 cups chopped kale
- 1 small onion, diced

- 2 garlic cloves, minced
- 1 teaspoon sea salt
- 1 teaspoon dried basil
- 1 teaspoon dried oregano
- ½ teaspoon dried parsley
- 1 lemon, thinly sliced

1. In a slow cooker, combine the lentils, vegetable broth, carrots, kale, onion, garlic, salt, basil, oregano, and parsley. Stir to mix well. 2. Cover the cooker and cook for 8 to 10 hours on Low heat, or until the lentils are tender. 3. Garnish with lemon slices for serving.

Per Serving:
calories: 302 | fat: 2g | protein: 22g | carbs: 54g | fiber: 26g | sodium: 527mg

Chapter

4

Poultry

Chapter 4 Poultry

Chicken with Lemon Asparagus

Prep time: 10 minutes | Cook time: 13 minutes | Serves 4

- 2 tablespoons olive oil
- 4 (6-ounce / 170-g) boneless, skinless chicken breasts
- ½ teaspoon ground black pepper
- ¼ teaspoon salt
- ¼ teaspoon smoked paprika
- 2 cloves garlic, peeled and minced
- 2 sprigs thyme
- 2 sprigs oregano
- 1 tablespoon grated lemon zest
- ¼ cup lemon juice
- ¼ cup low-sodium chicken broth
- 1 bunch asparagus, trimmed
- ¼ cup chopped fresh parsley
- 4 lemon wedges

1. Press Sauté on the Instant Pot® and heat oil. Season chicken with pepper, salt, and smoked paprika. Brown chicken on both sides, about 4 minutes per side. Add garlic, thyme, oregano, lemon zest, lemon juice, and chicken broth. Press the Cancel button. 2. Close lid, set steam release to Sealing, press the Manual button, and set time to 5 minutes. 3. When the timer beeps, quick-release the pressure until the float valve drops. Press the Cancel button and open lid. Transfer chicken breasts to a serving platter. Tent with foil to keep warm. 4. Add asparagus to the Instant Pot®. Close lid, set steam release to Sealing, press the Manual button, and set time to 0. When the timer beeps, quick-release the pressure until the float valve drops. Open lid and remove asparagus. Arrange asparagus around chicken and garnish with parsley and lemon wedges. Serve immediately.

Per Serving:
calories: 227 | fat: 11g | protein: 35g | carbs: 0g | fiber: 0g | sodium: 426mg

Skillet Greek Turkey and Rice

Prep time: 20 minutes | Cook time: 30 minutes | Serves 2

- 1 tablespoon olive oil
- ½ medium onion, minced
- 2 garlic cloves, minced
- 8 ounces (227 g) ground turkey breast
- ½ cup roasted red peppers, chopped (about 2 jarred peppers)
- ¼ cup sun-dried tomatoes,
- minced
- 1 teaspoon dried oregano
- ½ cup brown rice
- 1¼ cups low-sodium chicken stock
- Salt
- 2 cups lightly packed baby spinach

1. Heat the olive oil in a sauté pan over medium heat. Add the onion and sauté for 5 minutes. Add the garlic and cook for another 30 seconds. 2. Add the turkey breast and cook for 7 minutes, breaking the turkey up with a spoon, until no longer pink. 3. Add the roasted red peppers, sun-dried tomatoes, and oregano and stir to combine. Add the rice and chicken stock and bring the mixture to a boil. 4. Cover the pan and reduce the heat to medium-low. Simmer for 30 minutes, or until the rice is cooked and tender. Season with salt. 5. Add the spinach to the pan and stir until it wilts slightly.

Per Serving:
calories: 446 | fat: 17g | protein: 30g | carbs: 49g | fiber: 5g | sodium: 663mg

Chicken and Mushroom Marsala

Prep time: 10 minutes | Cook time: 25 minutes | Serves 4

- 3 tablespoons all-purpose flour
- ½ teaspoon ground black pepper
- ¼ teaspoon salt
- 2 (6-ounce / 170-g) boneless, skinless chicken breasts
- 2 tablespoons olive oil
- 1 medium white onion, peeled and diced
- 1 pound (454 g) sliced button mushrooms
- 2 cloves garlic, peeled and minced
- 2 sprigs thyme
- 2 sprigs oregano
- ¼ cup marsala wine
- ¼ cup low-sodium chicken broth
- ¼ cup chopped fresh parsley

1. Combine flour, pepper, and salt in a shallow dish. Dredge chicken breasts in flour, shaking to remove excess. Press the Sauté button on the Instant Pot® and heat oil. Brown chicken on both sides, about 4 minutes per side. Transfer chicken to a plate and set aside. 2. Add onion to the pot and cook until just tender, about 3 minutes. Add mushrooms and cook, stirring often, until mushrooms are tender, about 8 minutes. Add garlic, thyme, and oregano, and cook until fragrant, about 30 seconds. 3. Stir in wine and chicken broth, and scrape bottom of pot to release any browned bits. Top with chicken. Press the Cancel button, close lid, set steam release to Sealing, press the Manual button, and set time to 5 minutes. 4. When the timer beeps, let pressure release naturally, about 20 minutes. Press the Cancel button and open lid. Transfer chicken breasts to a cutting board and slice into ½" pieces. Arrange on serving platter. Pour mushrooms and cooking liquid over chicken. Sprinkle with parsley and serve hot.

Per Serving:
calories: 525 | fat: 14g | protein: 37g | carbs: 9g | fiber: 8g | sodium: 218mg

Chicken with Dates and Almonds

Prep time: 15 minutes | Cook time: 6 to 8 hours | Serves 4

- 1 onion, sliced
- 1 (15-ounce / 425-g) can reduced-sodium chickpeas, drained and rinsed
- 2½ pounds (1.1 kg) bone-in, skin-on chicken thighs
- ½ cup low-sodium chicken broth
- 2 garlic cloves, minced
- 1 teaspoon sea salt
- 1 teaspoon ground cumin
- ½ teaspoon ground ginger
- ½ teaspoon ground coriander
- ¼ teaspoon ground cinnamon
- ¼ teaspoon freshly ground black pepper
- ½ cup dried dates
- ¼ cup sliced almonds

1. In a slow cooker, gently toss together the onion and chickpeas. 2. Place the chicken on top of the chickpea mixture and pour the chicken broth over the chicken. 3. In a small bowl, stir together the garlic, salt, cumin, ginger, coriander, cinnamon, and pepper. Sprinkle the spice mix over everything. 4. Top with the dates and almonds. 5. Cover the cooker and cook for 6 to 8 hours on Low heat.

Per Serving:

calories: 841 | fat: 48g | protein: 57g | carbs: 41g | fiber: 9g | sodium: 812mg

Roast Chicken

Prep time: 20 minutes | Cook time: 55 minutes | Serves 4

- ¼ cup white wine
- 2 tablespoons olive oil, divided
- 1 tablespoon Dijon mustard
- 1 garlic clove, minced
- 1 teaspoon dried rosemary
- Juice and zest of 1 lemon
- Sea salt and freshly ground pepper, to taste
- 1 large roasting chicken, giblets removed
- 3 large carrots, peeled and cut into chunks
- 1 fennel bulb, peeled and cut into ½-inch cubes
- 2 celery stalks, cut into chunks

1. Preheat the oven to 400ºF (205ºC). 2. Combine the white wine, 1 tablespoon of olive oil, mustard, garlic, rosemary, lemon juice and zest, sea salt, and freshly ground pepper in a small bowl. 3. Place the chicken in a shallow roasting pan on a roasting rack. 4. Rub the entire chicken, including the cavity, with the wine and mustard mixture. 5. Place the chicken in the oven and roast for 15 minutes. 6. Toss the vegetables with the remaining tablespoon of olive oil, and place around the chicken. 7. Turn the heat down to 375ºF (190ºC). 8. Roast an additional 40–60 minutes, basting the chicken every 15 minutes with the drippings in the bottom of the pan. 9. Cook chicken until internal temperature reaches 180ºF (82ºC) in between the thigh and the body of the chicken. When you remove the instant-read thermometer, the juices should run clear. 10. Let the chicken rest for at least 10–15 minutes before serving.

Per Serving:

calories: 387 | fat: 14g | protein: 50g | carbs: 12g | fiber: 4g | sodium: 306mg

Chicken and Broccoli Casserole

Prep time: 5 minutes | Cook time: 20 to 25 minutes | Serves 4

- ½ pound (227 g) broccoli, chopped into florets
- 2 cups shredded cooked chicken
- 4 ounces (113 g) cream cheese
- ⅓ cup heavy cream
- 1½ teaspoons Dijon mustard
- ½ teaspoon garlic powder
- Salt and freshly ground black pepper, to taste
- 2 tablespoons chopped fresh basil
- 1 cup shredded Cheddar cheese

1. Preheat the air fryer to 390ºF (199ºC). Lightly coat a casserole dish that will fit in air fryer, with olive oil and set aside. 2. Place the broccoli in a large glass bowl with 1 tablespoon of water and cover with a microwavable plate. Microwave on high for 2 to 3 minutes until the broccoli is bright green but not mushy. Drain if necessary and add to another large bowl along with the shredded chicken. 3. In the same glass bowl used to microwave the broccoli, combine the cream cheese and cream. Microwave for 30 seconds to 1 minute on high and stir until smooth. Add the mustard and garlic powder and season to taste with salt and freshly ground black pepper. Whisk until the sauce is smooth. 4. Pour the warm sauce over the broccoli and chicken mixture and then add the basil. Using a silicone spatula, gently fold the mixture until thoroughly combined. 5. Transfer the chicken mixture to the prepared casserole dish and top with the cheese. Air fry for 20 to 25 minutes until warmed through and the cheese has browned.

Per Serving:

calories: 503 | fat: 39g | protein: 32g | carbs: 7g | fiber: 2g | sodium: 391mg

Hoisin Turkey Burgers

Prep time: 30 minutes | Cook time: 20 minutes | Serves 4

- Olive oil
- 1 pound (454 g) lean ground turkey
- ¼ cup whole-wheat bread
- crumbs
- ¼ cup hoisin sauce
- 2 tablespoons soy sauce
- 4 whole-wheat buns

1. Spray the air fryer basket lightly with olive oil. 2. In a large bowl, mix together the turkey, bread crumbs, hoisin sauce, and soy sauce. 3. Form the mixture into 4 equal patties. Cover with plastic wrap and refrigerate the patties for 30 minutes. 4. Place the patties in the air fryer basket in a single layer. Spray the patties lightly with olive oil. 5. Air fry at 370ºF (188ºC) for 10 minutes. Flip the patties over, lightly spray with olive oil, and cook until golden brown, an additional 5 to 10 minutes. 6. Place the patties on buns and top with your choice of low-calorie burger toppings like sliced tomatoes, onions, and cabbage slaw.

Per Serving:

calories: 330 | fat: 13g | protein: 26g | carbs: 29g | fiber: 3g | sodium: 631mg

Grilled Chicken and Vegetables with Lemon-Walnut Sauce

Prep time: 20 minutes | Cook time: 16 minutes | Serves 4

- 1 cup chopped walnuts, toasted
- 1 small shallot, very finely chopped
- ½ cup olive oil, plus more for brushing
- Juice and zest of 1 lemon
- 4 boneless, skinless chicken breasts
- Sea salt and freshly ground pepper, to taste
- 2 zucchini, sliced diagonally ¼-inch thick
- ½ pound (227 g) asparagus
- 1 red onion, sliced ⅓-inch thick
- 1 teaspoon Italian seasoning

1. Preheat a grill to medium-high. 2. Put the walnuts, shallots, olive oil, lemon juice, and zest in a food processor and process until smooth and creamy. 3. Season the chicken with sea salt and freshly ground pepper, and grill on an oiled grate until cooked through, about 7–8 minutes a side or until an instant-read thermometer reaches 180°F (82°C) in the thickest part. 4. When the chicken is halfway done, put the vegetables on the grill. Sprinkle Italian seasoning over the chicken and vegetables to taste. 5. To serve, lay the grilled veggies on a plate, place the chicken breast on the grilled vegetables, and spoon the lemon-walnut sauce over the chicken and vegetables.

Per Serving:
calories: 800 | fat: 54g | protein: 68g | carbs: 13g | fiber: 5g | sodium: 134mg

Cashew Chicken and Snap Peas

Prep time: 15 minutes | Cook time: 6 hours | Serves 2

- 16 ounces (454 g) boneless, skinless chicken breasts, cut into 2-inch pieces
- 2 cups sugar snap peas, strings removed
- 1 teaspoon grated fresh ginger
- 1 teaspoon minced garlic
- 2 tablespoons low-sodium
- soy sauce
- 1 tablespoon ketchup
- 1 tablespoon rice vinegar
- 1 teaspoon honey
- Pinch red pepper flakes
- ¼ cup toasted cashews
- 1 scallion, white and green parts, sliced thin

1. Put the chicken and sugar snap peas into the slow cooker. 2. In a measuring cup or small bowl, whisk together the ginger, garlic, soy sauce, ketchup, vinegar, honey, and red pepper flakes. Pour the mixture over the chicken and snap peas. 3. Cover and cook on low for 6 hours. The chicken should be cooked through, and the snap peas should be tender, but not mushy. 4. Just before serving, stir in the cashews and scallions.

Per Serving:
calories: 463 | fat: 14g | protein: 59g | carbs: 23g | fiber: 5g | sodium: 699mg

Garlic Chicken with Couscous

Prep time: 10 minutes | Cook time: 3½ hours | Serves 4

- 1 whole chicken, 3½ to 4 pounds(1.6 to 1.8 kg), cut into 6 to 8 pieces and patted dry
- Coarse sea salt
- Black pepper
- 1 tablespoon extra-virgin olive oil
- 1 medium yellow onion, halved and thinly sliced
- 6 cloves garlic, halved
- 2 teaspoons dried thyme
- 1 cup dry white wine
- ⅓ cup all-purpose flour
- 1 cup uncooked couscous
- ¼ chopped fresh parsley

1. Season the chicken with salt and pepper. 2. In a large skillet, heat the oil over medium-high heat. Add the chicken skin-side down and cook in batches until the skin is golden brown, about 4 minutes. Turn and cook an additional 2 minutes. 3. Add the onion, garlic, and thyme to the slow cooker. 4. Top the contents of slow cooker with chicken, skin-side up, in a tight layer. 5. In a small bowl, whisk together the wine and the flour until smooth, and add to the slow cooker. 6. Cover and cook until the chicken is tender, about 3½ hours on high or 7 hours on low. 7. Cook the couscous according to package instructions. 8. Serve the chicken and sauce hot over the couscous, sprinkled with parsley.

Per Serving:
calories: 663 | fat: 38g | protein: 46g | carbs: 21g | fiber: 1g | sodium: 166mg

Pomegranate-Glazed Chicken

Prep time: 10 minutes | Cook time: 30 minutes | Serves 6

- 1 teaspoon cumin
- 1 clove garlic, minced
- Sea salt and freshly ground pepper, to taste
- 6 tablespoons olive oil, divided
- 6 boneless, skinless chicken breasts
- 1 cup pomegranate juice (no sugar added)
- 2 tablespoons honey
- 1 tablespoon Dijon mustard
- ½ teaspoon dried thyme
- 1 fresh pomegranate, seeds removed

1. Mix the cumin, garlic, sea salt, and freshly ground pepper with 2 tablespoons of olive oil, and rub into the chicken. 2. Heat the remaining olive oil in a large skillet over medium heat. 3. Add the chicken breasts and sauté for 10 minutes, turning halfway through the cooking time, so the chicken breasts are golden brown on each side. 4. Add the pomegranate juice, honey, Dijon mustard, and thyme. 5. Lower the heat and simmer for 20 minutes, or until the chicken is cooked through and the sauce reduces by half. 6. Transfer the chicken and sauce to a serving platter, and top with fresh pomegranate seeds.

Per Serving:
calories: 532 | fat: 21g | protein: 62g | carbs: 20g | fiber: 2g | sodium: 157mg

Chicken and Spiced Freekeh with Cilantro and Preserved Lemon

Prep time: 20 minutes | Cook time: 11 minutes | Serves 4

- 2 tablespoons extra-virgin olive oil, plus extra for drizzling
- 1 onion, chopped fine
- 4 garlic cloves, minced
- 1½ teaspoons smoked paprika
- ¼ teaspoon ground cardamom
- ¼ teaspoon red pepper flakes
- 2¼ cups chicken broth
- 1½ cups cracked freekeh, rinsed
- 2 (12-ounce / 340-g) bone-in split chicken breasts, halved crosswise and trimmed
- ½ teaspoon table salt
- ¼ teaspoon pepper
- ¼ cup chopped fresh cilantro
- 2 tablespoons sesame seeds, toasted
- ½ preserved lemon, pulp and white pith removed, rind rinsed and minced (2 tablespoons)

1. Using highest sauté function, heat oil in Instant Pot until shimmering. Add onion and cook until softened, about 5 minutes. Stir in garlic, paprika, cardamom, and pepper flakes and cook until fragrant, about 30 seconds. Stir in broth and freekeh. Sprinkle chicken with salt and pepper. Nestle skin side up into freekeh mixture. Lock lid in place and close pressure release valve. Select high pressure cook function and cook for 5 minutes. 2. Turn off Instant Pot and quick-release pressure. Carefully remove lid, allowing steam to escape away from you. Transfer chicken to serving dish and discard skin, if desired. Tent with aluminum foil and let rest while finishing freekeh. 3. Gently fluff freekeh with fork. Lay clean dish towel over pot, replace lid, and let sit for 5 minutes. Season with salt and pepper to taste. Transfer freekeh to serving dish with chicken and sprinkle with cilantro, sesame seeds, and preserved lemon. Drizzle with extra oil and serve.

Per Serving:
calories: 346 | fat: 15g | protein: 43g | carbs: 10g | fiber: 2g | sodium: 418mg

Lebanese Grilled Chicken

Prep time: 10 minutes | Cook time: 14 minutes | Serves 4

- ½ cup olive oil
- ¼ cup apple cider vinegar
- Zest and juice of 1 lemon
- 4 cloves garlic, minced
- 1 teaspoon sea salt
- 1 teaspoon Arabic 7 spices (baharaat)
- ½ teaspoon cinnamon
- 1 chicken, cut into 8 pieces

1. Combine all the ingredients except the chicken in a shallow dish or plastic bag. 2. Place the chicken in the bag or dish and marinate overnight, or at least for several hours. 3. Drain, reserving the marinade. Heat the grill to medium-high. 4. Cook the chicken pieces for 10–14 minutes, brushing them with the marinade every 5 minutes or so. 5. The chicken is done when the crust is golden brown and an instant-read thermometer reads 180ºF (82ºC) in the thickest parts. Remove skin before eating.

Per Serving:
calories: 518 | fat: 34g | protein: 49g | carbs: 4g | fiber: 0g | sodium: 613mg

Blackened Cajun Chicken Tenders

Prep time: 10 minutes | Cook time: 17 minutes | Serves 4

- 2 teaspoons paprika
- 1 teaspoon chili powder
- ½ teaspoon garlic powder
- ½ teaspoon dried thyme
- ¼ teaspoon onion powder
- ⅛ teaspoon ground cayenne pepper
- 2 tablespoons coconut oil
- 1 pound (454 g) boneless, skinless chicken tenders
- ¼ cup full-fat ranch dressing

1. In a small bowl, combine all seasonings. 2. Drizzle oil over chicken tenders and then generously coat each tender in the spice mixture. Place tenders into the air fryer basket. 3. Adjust the temperature to 375ºF (191ºC) and air fry for 17 minutes. 4. Tenders will be 165ºF (74ºC) internally when fully cooked. Serve with ranch dressing for dipping.

Per Serving:
calories: 266 | fat: 17g | protein: 26g | carbs: 2g | fiber: 1g | sodium: 207mg

Brazilian Tempero Baiano Chicken Drumsticks

Prep time: 30 minutes | Cook time: 20 minutes | Serves 4

- 1 teaspoon cumin seeds
- 1 teaspoon dried oregano
- 1 teaspoon dried parsley
- 1 teaspoon ground turmeric
- ½ teaspoon coriander seeds
- 1 teaspoon kosher salt
- ½ teaspoon black peppercorns
- ½ teaspoon cayenne pepper
- ¼ cup fresh lime juice
- 2 tablespoons olive oil
- 1½ pounds (680 g) chicken drumsticks

1. In a clean coffee grinder or spice mill, combine the cumin, oregano, parsley, turmeric, coriander seeds, salt, peppercorns, and cayenne. Process until finely ground. 2. In a small bowl, combine the ground spices with the lime juice and oil. Place the chicken in a resealable plastic bag. Add the marinade, seal, and massage until the chicken is well coated. Marinate at room temperature for 30 minutes or in the refrigerator for up to 24 hours. 3. When you are ready to cook, place the drumsticks skin side up in the air fryer basket. Set the air fryer to 400ºF (204ºC) for 20 to 25 minutes, turning the legs halfway through the cooking time. Use a meat thermometer to ensure that the chicken has reached an internal temperature of 165ºF (74ºC). 4. Serve with plenty of napkins.

Per Serving:
calories: 267 | fat: 13g | protein: 33g | carbs: 2g | fiber: 1g | sodium: 777mg

Niçoise Chicken

Prep time: 20 minutes | Cook time: 50 minutes | Serves 6

- ¼ cup olive oil
- 3 medium onions, coarsely chopped
- 3 cloves garlic, minced
- 4 pounds (1.8 kg) chicken breast from 1 cut-up chicken
- 5 Roma tomatoes, peeled and chopped
- ½ cup white wine
- 1 (14½-ounce / 411-g) can
- chicken broth
- ½ cup black Niçoise olives, pitted
- Juice of 1 lemon
- ¼ cup flat-leaf parsley, chopped
- 1 tablespoon fresh tarragon leaves, chopped
- Sea salt and freshly ground pepper, to taste

1. Heat the olive oil in a deep saucepan or stew pot over medium heat. Cook the onions and garlic 5 minutes, or until tender and translucent. 2. Add the chicken and cook an additional 5 minutes to brown slightly. 3. Add the tomatoes, white wine, and chicken broth, cover, and simmer 30–45 minutes on medium-low heat, or until the chicken is tender and the sauce is thickened slightly. 4. Remove the lid and add the olives and lemon juice. 5. Cook an additional 10–15 minutes to thicken the sauce further. 6. Stir in the parsley and tarragon, and season to taste. Serve immediately with noodles or potatoes and a dark leafy salad.

Per Serving:
calories: 501 | fat: 15g | protein: 74g | carbs: 11g | fiber: 2g | sodium: 451mg

Jerk Chicken Thighs

Prep time: 30 minutes | Cook time: 15 to 20 minutes | Serves 6

- 2 teaspoons ground coriander
- 1 teaspoon ground allspice
- 1 teaspoon cayenne pepper
- 1 teaspoon ground ginger
- 1 teaspoon salt
- 1 teaspoon dried thyme
- ½ teaspoon ground cinnamon
- ½ teaspoon ground nutmeg
- 2 pounds (907 g) boneless chicken thighs, skin on
- 2 tablespoons olive oil

1. In a small bowl, combine the coriander, allspice, cayenne, ginger, salt, thyme, cinnamon, and nutmeg. Stir until thoroughly combined. 2. Place the chicken in a baking dish and use paper towels to pat dry. Thoroughly coat both sides of the chicken with the spice mixture. Cover and refrigerate for at least 2 hours, preferably overnight. 3. Preheat the air fryer to 360°F (182°C). 4. Working in batches if necessary, arrange the chicken in a single layer in the air fryer basket and lightly coat with the olive oil. Pausing halfway through the cooking time to flip the chicken, air fry for 15 to 20 minutes, until a thermometer inserted into the thickest part registers 165°F (74°C).

Per Serving:
calories: 227 | fat: 11g | protein: 30g | carbs: 1g | fiber: 0g | sodium: 532mg

Ginger Turmeric Chicken Thighs

Prep time: 5 minutes | Cook time: 25 minutes | Serves 4

- 4 (4 ounces / 113 g) boneless, skin-on chicken thighs
- 2 tablespoons coconut oil, melted
- ½ teaspoon ground turmeric
- ½ teaspoon salt
- ½ teaspoon garlic powder
- ½ teaspoon ground ginger
- ¼ teaspoon ground black pepper

1. Place chicken thighs in a large bowl and drizzle with coconut oil. Sprinkle with remaining ingredients and toss to coat both sides of thighs. 2. Place thighs skin side up into ungreased air fryer basket. Adjust the temperature to 400°F (204°C) and air fry for 25 minutes. After 10 minutes, turn thighs. When 5 minutes remain, flip thighs once more. Chicken will be done when skin is golden brown and the internal temperature is at least 165°F (74°C). Serve warm.

Per Serving:
calories: 392 | fat: 31g | protein: 25g | carbs: 1g | fiber: 0g | sodium: 412mg

Moroccan Chicken with Apricots, Almonds, and Olives

Prep time: 10 minutes | Cook time: 2 hours | Serves 4

- 3 pounds (1.4 kg) skinless chicken thighs
- 1 yellow onion, cut into ½-inch wedges
- 1 teaspoon ground cumin
- ½ teaspoon ground ginger
- ½ teaspoon ground coriander
- ¼ teaspoon ground cinnamon
- ¼ teaspoon cayenne pepper
- Sea salt
- Black pepper
- 1 bay leaf
- ⅓ cup chicken stock
- 1 (15-ounce / 425-g) can chickpeas, drained and rinsed
- ½ cup green olives
- ½ cup dried turkish apricots
- ⅓ cup sliced almonds, toasted

1. In a large bowl, mix the chicken thighs and the onion. Add the cumin, coriander, ginger, cinnamon, and cayenne and toss to coat. Season the spiced chicken and onion with salt and pepper. 2. Transfer the chicken and onion to the slow cooker. Add the bay leaf and chicken stock to the slow cooker. 3. Cover and cook on high for 2 hours. 4. Stir in the chickpeas, olives, and apricots. Cover and cook until the chicken is tender and cooked through and the apricots are plump, about 1 hour more. 5. Remove the bay leaf and season the juices with salt and pepper. 6. Meanwhile, preheat the oven to 350°F(180°C). Spread the almonds in a pie plate and toast for about 7 minutes, until fragrant and lightly golden. Watch them so they don't burn. 7. Spoon the hot chicken, vegetables, and juices into shallow bowls, sprinkle with the toasted almonds, and serve.

Per Serving:
calories: 625 | fat: 22g | protein: 75g | carbs: 31g | fiber: 8g | sodium: 597mg

Sheet Pan Pesto Chicken with Crispy Garlic Potatoes

Prep time: 15 minutes | Cook time: 50 minutes | Serves 2

- 12 ounces (340 g) small red potatoes (3 or 4 potatoes)
- 1 tablespoon olive oil
- ¼ teaspoon salt
- ½ teaspoon garlic powder
- 1 (8-ounce / 227-g) boneless, skinless chicken breast
- 3 tablespoons prepared pesto

1. Preheat the oven to 425°F (220°C) and set the rack to the bottom position. Line a baking sheet with parchment paper. (Do not use foil, as the potatoes will stick.) 2. Scrub the potatoes and dry them well, then dice into 1-inch pieces. 3. In a medium bowl, combine the potatoes, olive oil, salt, and garlic powder. Toss well to coat. 4. Place the potatoes on the parchment paper and roast for 10 minutes. Flip the potatoes and return to the oven for another 10 minutes. 5. While the potatoes are roasting, place the chicken in the same bowl and toss with the pesto, coating the chicken evenly. 6. Check the potatoes to make sure they are golden brown on the top and bottom. Toss them again and add the chicken breast to the pan. 7. Turn the heat down to 350°F (180°C) and let the chicken and potatoes roast for 30 minutes. Check to make sure the chicken reaches an internal temperature of 165°F (74°C) and the potatoes are tender inside.

Per Serving:
calories: 377 | fat: 16g | protein: 30g | carbs: 31g | fiber: 4g | sodium: 426mg

Chicken Breasts Stuffed with Feta and Spinach

Prep time: 10 minutes | Cook time: 14 minutes | Serves 4

- 1 cup chopped frozen spinach, thawed and drained well
- ½ cup crumbled feta cheese
- 4 (6-ounce / 170-g) boneless, skinless chicken breasts
- ¼ teaspoon salt
- ¼ teaspoon ground black pepper
- 2 tablespoons light olive oil, divided
- 1 cup water

1. In a small bowl, combine spinach and feta. Slice a pocket into each chicken breast along one side. Stuff one-quarter of the spinach and feta mixture into the pocket of each breast. Season chicken on all sides with salt and pepper. Set aside. 2. Press the Sauté button on the Instant Pot® and add 1 tablespoon oil. Add two chicken breasts and brown on both sides, about 3 minutes per side. Transfer to a plate and repeat with remaining 1 tablespoon oil and chicken. 3. Add water to pot and place rack inside. Place chicken breasts on rack. Close lid, set steam release to Sealing, press the Manual button, and set time to 8 minutes. 4. When the timer beeps, quick-release the pressure until the float valve drops. Press the Cancel button and open lid. Transfer chicken to a serving platter. Serve hot.

Per Serving:
calories: 304 | fat: 17g | protein: 40g | carbs: 2g | fiber: 1g | sodium: 772mg

Herb-Marinated Chicken Breasts

Prep time: 10 minutes | Cook time: 10 minutes | Serves 4

- ½ cup fresh lemon juice
- ¼ cup extra-virgin olive oil
- 4 cloves garlic, minced
- 2 tablespoons chopped fresh basil
- 1 tablespoon chopped fresh oregano
- 1 tablespoon chopped fresh
- mint
- 2 pounds (907 g) chicken breast tenders
- ½ teaspoon unrefined sea salt or salt
- ¼ teaspoon freshly ground black pepper

1. In a small bowl, whisk the lemon juice, olive oil, garlic, basil, oregano, and mint well to combine. Place the chicken breasts in a large shallow bowl or glass baking pan, and pour dressing over the top. 2. Cover, place in the refrigerator, and allow to marinate for 1 to 2 hours. Remove from the refrigerator, and season with salt and pepper. 3. Heat a large, wide skillet over medium-high heat. Using tongs, place chicken tenders evenly in the bottom of the skillet. Pour the remaining marinade over the chicken. 4. Allow to cook for 3 to 5 minutes each side, or until chicken is golden, juices have been absorbed, and meat is cooked to an internal temperature of 160°F (71°C).

Per Serving:
calories: 521 | fat: 35g | protein: 48g | carbs: 3g | fiber: 0g | sodium: 435mg

Punjabi Chicken Curry

Prep time: 20 minutes | Cook time: 4 to 6 hours | Serves 6

- 2 tablespoons vegetable oil
- 3 onions, finely diced
- 6 garlic cloves, finely chopped
- 1 heaped tablespoon freshly grated ginger
- 1 (14-ounce / 397-g) can plum tomatoes
- 1 teaspoon salt
- 1 teaspoon turmeric
- 1 teaspoon chili powder
- Handful coriander stems, finely chopped
- 3 fresh green chiles, finely chopped
- 12 pieces chicken, mixed thighs and drumsticks, or a whole chicken, skinned, trimmed, and chopped
- 2 teaspoons garam masala
- Handful fresh coriander leaves, chopped

1. Heat the oil in a frying pan (or in the slow cooker if you have a sear setting). Add the diced onions and cook for 5 minutes. Add the garlic and continue to cook for 10 minutes until the onions are brown. 2. Heat the slow cooker to high and add the onion-and-garlic mixture. Stir in the ginger, tomatoes, salt, turmeric, chili powder, coriander stems, and chiles. 3. Add the chicken pieces. Cover and cook on low for 6 hours, or on high for 4 hours. 4. Once cooked, check the seasoning, and then stir in the garam masala and coriander leaves.

Per Serving:
calories: 298 | fat: 9g | protein: 35g | carbs: 19g | fiber: 3g | sodium: 539mg

Citrus Chicken with Pecan Wild Rice

Prep time: 15 minutes | Cook time: 10 minutes | Serves 4

- 4 boneless, skinless chicken breasts
- Sea salt and freshly ground pepper, to taste
- 2 tablespoons olive oil
- Juice and zest of 1 orange
- 2 cups wild rice, cooked
- 2 green onions, sliced
- 1 cup pecans, toasted and chopped

1. Season chicken breasts with sea salt and freshly ground pepper. 2. Heat a large skillet over medium heat. Add the oil and sear the chicken until browned on 1 side. 3. Flip the chicken and brown other side. 4. Add the orange juice to the skillet and let cook down. 5. In a large bowl, combine the rice, onions, pecans, and orange zest. Season with sea salt and freshly ground pepper to taste. 6. Serve the chicken alongside the rice and a green salad for a complete meal.

Per Serving:

calories: 870 | fat: 34g | protein: 76g | carbs: 66g | fiber: 8g | sodium: 128mg

Personal Cauliflower Pizzas

Prep time: 10 minutes | Cook time: 25 minutes | Serves 2

- 1 (12-ounce / 340-g) bag frozen riced cauliflower
- ⅓ cup shredded Mozzarella cheese
- ¼ cup almond flour
- ¼ grated Parmesan cheese
- 1 large egg
- ½ teaspoon salt
- 1 teaspoon garlic powder
- 1 teaspoon dried oregano
- 4 tablespoons no-sugar-added marinara sauce, divided
- 4 ounces (113 g) fresh Mozzarella, chopped, divided
- 1 cup cooked chicken breast, chopped, divided
- ½ cup chopped cherry tomatoes, divided
- ¼ cup fresh baby arugula, divided

1. Preheat the air fryer to 400°F (204°C). Cut 4 sheets of parchment paper to fit the basket of the air fryer. Brush with olive oil and set aside. 2. In a large glass bowl, microwave the cauliflower according to package directions. Place the cauliflower on a clean towel, draw up the sides, and squeeze tightly over a sink to remove the excess moisture. Return the cauliflower to the bowl and add the shredded Mozzarella along with the almond flour, Parmesan, egg, salt, garlic powder, and oregano. Stir until thoroughly combined. 3. Divide the dough into two equal portions. Place one piece of dough on the prepared parchment paper and pat gently into a thin, flat disk 7 to 8 inches in diameter. Air fry for 15 minutes until the crust begins to brown. Let cool for 5 minutes. 4. Transfer the parchment paper with the crust on top to a baking sheet. Place a second sheet of parchment paper over the crust. While holding the edges of both sheets together, carefully lift the crust off the baking sheet, flip it, and place it back in the air fryer basket. The new sheet of parchment paper is now on the bottom. Remove the top piece of paper and air fry the crust for another 15 minutes until the top begins to brown. Remove the basket from the air fryer. 5. Spread 2 tablespoons of the marinara sauce on top of the crust, followed by half the fresh Mozzarella, chicken, cherry tomatoes, and arugula. Air fry for 5 to 10 minutes longer, until the cheese is melted and beginning to brown. Remove the pizza from the oven and let it sit for 10 minutes before serving. Repeat with the remaining ingredients to make a second pizza.

Per Serving:

calories: 655 | fat: 35g | protein: 67g | carbs: 20g | fiber: 7g | sodium: 741mg

Pesto-Glazed Chicken Breasts

Prep time: 5 minutes | Cook time: 20 minutes | Serves 4

- ¼ cup plus 1 tablespoon extra-virgin olive oil, divided
- 4 boneless, skinless chicken breasts
- ½ teaspoon salt
- ¼ teaspoon freshly ground
- black pepper
- 1 packed cup fresh basil leaves
- 1 garlic clove, minced
- ¼ cup grated Parmesan cheese
- ¼ cup pine nuts

1. In a large, heavy skillet, heat 1 tablespoon of the olive oil over medium-high heat. 2. Season the chicken breasts on both sides with salt and pepper and place in the skillet. Cook for 10 minutes on the first side, then turn and cook for 5 minutes. 3. Meanwhile, in a blender or food processor, combine the basil, garlic, Parmesan cheese, and pine nuts, and blend on high. Gradually pour in the remaining ¼ cup olive oil and blend until smooth. 4. Spread 1 tablespoon pesto on each chicken breast, cover the skillet, and cook for 5 minutes. Serve the chicken pesto side up.

Per Serving:

calories: 531 | fat: 28g | protein: 64g | carbs: 2g | fiber: 0g | sodium: 572mg

Yogurt-Marinated Chicken Kebabs

Prep time: 10 minutes | Cook time: 20 minutes | Serves 4

- ½ cup plain Greek yogurt
- 1 tablespoon lemon juice
- ½ teaspoon ground cumin
- ½ teaspoon ground coriander
- ½ teaspoon kosher salt
- ¼ teaspoon cayenne pepper
- 1½ pounds (680 g) skinless, boneless chicken breast, cut into 1-inch cubes

1. In a large bowl or zip-top bag, combine the yogurt, lemon juice, cumin, coriander, salt, and cayenne pepper. Mix together thoroughly and then add the chicken. Marinate for at least 30 minutes, and up to overnight in the refrigerator. 2. Preheat the oven to 425°F (220°C). Line a baking sheet with parchment paper or foil. Remove the chicken from the marinade and thread it on 4 bamboo or metal skewers. 3. Bake for 20 minutes, turning the chicken over once halfway through the cooking time.

Per Serving:

calories: 170 | fat: 4g | protein: 31g | carbs: 1g | fiber: 0g | sodium: 390mg

Greek Turkey Burger

Prep time: 10 minutes | Cook time: 10 minutes | Serves 4

- 1 pound (454 g) ground turkey
- 1 medium zucchini, grated
- ¼ cup whole-wheat bread crumbs
- ¼ cup red onion, minced
- ¼ cup crumbled feta cheese
- 1 large egg, beaten

- 1 garlic clove, minced
- 1 tablespoon fresh oregano, chopped
- 1 teaspoon kosher salt
- ¼ teaspoon freshly ground black pepper
- 1 tablespoon extra-virgin olive oil

1. In a large bowl, combine the turkey, zucchini, bread crumbs, onion, feta cheese, egg, garlic, oregano, salt, and black pepper, and mix well. Shape into 4 equal patties. 2. Heat the olive oil in a large nonstick grill pan or skillet over medium-high heat. Add the burgers to the pan and reduce the heat to medium. Cook on one side for 5 minutes, then flip and cook the other side for 5 minutes more.

Per Serving:
calories: 285 | fat: 16g | protein: 26g | carbs: 9g | fiber: 2g | sodium: 465mg

Fiesta Chicken Plate

Prep time: 15 minutes | Cook time: 12 to 15 minutes | Serves 4

- 1 pound (454 g) boneless, skinless chicken breasts (2 large breasts)
- 2 tablespoons lime juice
- 1 teaspoon cumin
- ½ teaspoon salt
- ½ cup grated Pepper Jack cheese
- 1 (16-ounce / 454-g) can refried beans

- ½ cup salsa
- 2 cups shredded lettuce
- 1 medium tomato, chopped
- 2 avocados, peeled and sliced
- 1 small onion, sliced into thin rings
- Sour cream
- Tortilla chips (optional)

1. Split each chicken breast in half lengthwise. 2. Mix lime juice, cumin, and salt together and brush on all surfaces of chicken breasts. 3. Place in air fryer basket and air fry at 390°F (199°C) for 12 to 15 minutes, until well done. 4. Divide the cheese evenly over chicken breasts and cook for an additional minute to melt cheese. 5. While chicken is cooking, heat refried beans on stovetop or in microwave. 6. When ready to serve, divide beans among 4 plates. Place chicken breasts on top of beans and spoon salsa over. Arrange the lettuce, tomatoes, and avocados artfully on each plate and scatter with the onion rings. 7. Pass sour cream at the table and serve with tortilla chips if desired.

Per Serving:
calories: 497 | fat: 27g | protein: 38g | carbs: 26g | fiber: 12g | sodium: 722mg

Lemon and Paprika Herb-Marinated Chicken

Prep time: 10 minutes | Cook time: 15 minutes | Serves 2

- 2 tablespoons olive oil
- 4 tablespoons freshly squeezed lemon juice
- ¼ teaspoon salt
- 1 teaspoon paprika

- 1 teaspoon dried basil
- ½ teaspoon dried thyme
- ¼ teaspoon garlic powder
- 2 (4-ounce / 113-g) boneless, skinless chicken breasts

1. In a bowl with a lid, combine the olive oil, lemon juice, salt, paprika, basil, thyme, and garlic powder. 2. Add the chicken and marinate for at least 30 minutes, or up to 4 hours. 3. When ready to cook, heat the grill to medium-high and oil the grill grate. Alternately, you can also cook these in a nonstick sauté pan over medium-high heat. 4. Grill the chicken for 6 to 7 minutes, or until it lifts away from the grill easily. Flip it over and grill for another 6 to 7 minutes, or until it reaches an internal temperature of 165°F(74°C).

Per Serving:
calories: 252 | fat: 16g | protein: 27g | carbs: 2g | fiber: 1g | sodium: 372mg

Chapter
5

Beef, Pork, and Lamb

Chapter 5 Beef, Pork, and Lamb

Seasoned Beef Kebabs

Prep time: 15 minutes | Cook time: 10 minutes | Serves 6

- 2 pounds beef fillet
- 1½ teaspoons salt
- 1 teaspoon freshly ground black pepper
- ½ teaspoon ground allspice
- ½ teaspoon ground nutmeg
- ⅓ cup extra-virgin olive oil
- 1 large onion, cut into 8 quarters
- 1 large red bell pepper, cut into 1-inch cubes

1. Preheat a grill, grill pan, or lightly oiled skillet to high heat. 2. Cut the beef into 1-inch cubes and put them in a large bowl. 3. In a small bowl, mix together the salt, black pepper, allspice, and nutmeg. 4. Pour the olive oil over the beef and toss to coat the beef. Then evenly sprinkle the seasoning over the beef and toss to coat all pieces. 5. Skewer the beef, alternating every 1 or 2 pieces with a piece of onion or bell pepper. 6. To cook, place the skewers on the grill or skillet, and turn every 2 to 3 minutes until all sides have cooked to desired doneness, 6 minutes for medium-rare, 8 minutes for well done. Serve warm.

Per Serving:
calories: 326 | fat: 21g | protein: 32g | carbs: 4g | fiber: 1g | sodium: 714mg

Stewed Pork with Greens

Prep time: 10 minutes | Cook time: 1 hour 40 minutes | Serves 3

- ¾ teaspoon fine sea salt, divided
- ½ teaspoon freshly ground black pepper, divided
- 1¼ pounds (567g) pork shoulder, trimmed and cut into 1½-inch chunks
- 6 tablespoons extra virgin olive oil, divided
- 1 bay leaf
- 3 allspice berries
- 2 tablespoons dry red wine
- 1 medium onion (any variety), chopped
- 2 spring onions, sliced (white parts only)
- 1 leek, sliced (white parts only)
- ¼ cup chopped fresh dill
- 1 pound (454 g) Swiss chard, roughly chopped
- 3 tablespoons fresh lemon juice plus more for serving

1. Sprinkle ¼ teaspoon of the sea salt and ¼ teaspoon of the black pepper over the pork. Rub the seasonings into the meat. 2. Add 1 tablespoon of the olive oil to a heavy pan over medium-high heat. Add the bay leaf and allspice berries, then add the meat and brown for 2–3 minutes per side. 3. Add the red wine and let it bubble, then use a wooden spatula to scrape the browned bits from the pan. Continue simmering until the liquid has evaporated, about 3 minutes, then transfer the meat and juices to a plate. Set aside. 4. Heat 4 tablespoons of the olive oil in a large pot placed over medium heat. Add the onion, spring onions, and leeks, and sauté until soft, about 5 minutes, then add the dill and sauté for 1–2 minutes more. 5. Add the meat and juices to the pot and sprinkle another ¼ teaspoon sea salt and ¼ teaspoon black pepper over the meat. Add just enough hot water to cover the meat halfway (start with less water), then cover and reduce the heat to low. Simmer for about 1 hour or until the meat is tender. 6. Remove the lid and add the chard and lemon juice. Use tongs to toss the chard and mix well. Continue simmering for about 5 minutes, then drizzle in the last tablespoon of olive oil and mix again. Cover and simmer for another 20 minutes, mixing occasionally, until the greens are wilted, then remove the pot from the heat. 7. Let stand covered for 10 minutes, then add a squeeze of lemon before serving. Allow to cool completely before covering and storing in the refrigerator for up to 2 days.

Per Serving:
calories: 565 | fat: 38g | protein: 39g | carbs: 15g | fiber: 4g | sodium: 592mg

Italian Pot Roast

Prep time: 15 minutes | Cook time: 6 hours | Serves 8

- 1 (3-pound / 1.4-kg)beef chuck roast, trimmed and halved crosswise
- 4 cloves garlic, halved lengthwise
- 1½ teaspoons coarse sea salt
- 1 teaspoon black pepper
- 1 tablespoon olive oil
- 1 large yellow onion, cut
- into 8 wedges
- 1¼ pounds (567 g) small white potatoes
- 1 (28-ounce / 794-g) can whole tomatoes in purée
- 1 tablespoon chopped fresh rosemary leaves (or 1 teaspoon dried and crumbled rosemary)

1. With a sharp paring knife, cut four slits in each of the beef roast halves, and stuff the slits with one-half of the garlic halves. Generously season the beef with the salt and pepper. 2. In a large skillet, heat the olive oil over medium-high heat, swirling to coat the bottom of the pan. Cook the beef until browned on all sides, about 5 minutes. 3. Combine the beef, onion, potatoes, tomatoes, rosemary, and the remaining garlic in the slow cooker. 4. Cover and cook until the meat is fork-tender, on high for about 6 hours. 5. Transfer the meat to a cutting board. Thinly slice, and discard any fat or gristle. 6. Skim the fat from the top of the sauce in the slow cooker. 7. Serve hot, dividing the beef and vegetables among the eight bowls, and generously spooning the sauce over the top.

Per Serving:
calories: 317 | fat: 12g | protein: 37g | carbs: 17g | fiber: 4g | sodium: 605mg

Smothered Pork Chops with Leeks and Mustard

Prep time: 15 minutes | Cook time: 35 minutes | Serves 4

- 4 (8- to 10-ounce/ 227- to 283-g) bone-in blade-cut pork chops, about ¾ inch thick, trimmed
- ½ teaspoon table salt
- ½ teaspoon pepper
- 4 teaspoons extra-virgin olive oil, divided
- 2 ounces (57 g) pancetta, chopped fine
- 1 tablespoon all-purpose flour
- ¾ cup dry white wine
- 1½ pounds (680 g) leeks, ends trimmed, halved lengthwise, sliced into 3-inch lengths, and washed thoroughly
- 1 tablespoon Dijon mustard
- 2 tablespoons chopped fresh parsley

1. Pat pork chops dry with paper towels. Using sharp knife, cut 2 slits, about 2 inches apart, through fat on edge of each chop. Sprinkle with salt and pepper. Using highest sauté function, heat 2 teaspoons oil in Instant Pot for 5 minutes (or until just smoking). Brown 2 chops on both sides, 6 to 8 minutes; transfer to plate. Repeat with remaining 2 teaspoons oil and remaining chops; transfer to plate. 2. Add pancetta to fat left in pot and cook, using highest sauté function, until softened and lightly browned, about 2 minutes. Stir in flour and cook for 30 seconds. Stir in wine, scraping up any browned bits and smoothing any lumps. Stir in leeks and cook until softened, about 3 minutes. Nestle chops into pot (chops will overlap) and add any accumulated juices. Lock lid in place and close pressure release valve. Select high pressure cook function and cook for 10 minutes. 3. Turn off Instant Pot and let pressure release naturally for 15 minutes. Quick-release any remaining pressure, then carefully remove lid, allowing steam to escape away from you. Transfer chops to serving platter, tent with aluminum foil, and let rest while finishing leeks. 4. Using highest sauté function, bring leek mixture to simmer. Stir in mustard and cook until slightly thickened, about 5 minutes. Season with salt and pepper to taste. Spoon leek mixture over chops and sprinkle with parsley. Serve.

Per Serving:
calories: 390 | fat: 17g | protein: 35g | carbs: 13g | fiber: 1g | sodium: 780mg

Roast Pork Tenderloin with Cherry-Balsamic Sauce

Prep timePrep Time: 20 minutes | Cook Time: 20 minutes | Serves 2

- 1 cup frozen cherries, thawed
- ⅓ cup balsamic vinegar
- 1 fresh rosemary sprig
- 1 (8-ounce/ 227-g) pork tenderloin
- ¼ teaspoon salt
- ⅛ teaspoon freshly ground black pepper
- 1 tablespoon olive oil

1. Combine the cherries and vinegar in a blender and purée until smooth. 2. Pour into a saucepan, add the rosemary sprig, and bring the mixture to a boil. Reduce the heat to medium-low and simmer for 15 minutes, or until it's reduced by half. 3. While the sauce is simmering, preheat the oven to 425°F (220°C) and set the rack in the middle position. 4. Season the pork on all sides with the salt and pepper. 5. Heat the oil in a sauté pan over medium-high heat. Add the pork and sear for 3 minutes, turning often, until it's golden on all sides. 6. Transfer the pork to an oven-safe baking dish and roast for 15 minutes, or until the internal temperature is 145°F(63°C). 7. Let the pork rest for 5 minutes before serving. Serve sliced and topped with the cherry-balsamic sauce.

Per Serving:
calories: 328 | fat: 11g | protein: 21g | carbs: 30g | fiber: 1g | sodium: 386mg

Spiced Oven-Baked Meatballs with Tomato Sauce

Prep time: 25 minutes | Cook time: 1 hour 5 minutes | Serves 4

For the Meatballs:
- 1 pound (454 g) ground chuck
- ¼ cup unseasoned breadcrumbs
- 2 garlic cloves, minced
- 1 teaspoon salt
- ½ teaspoon black pepper
- 1 teaspoon ground cumin
- 3 tablespoons chopped fresh parsley
- 1 egg, lightly beaten
- 3 tablespoons extra virgin olive oil
- 1 teaspoon tomato paste
- 1 teaspoon red wine vinegar
- 2 tablespoons dry red wine
- 1 teaspoon fresh lemon juice

For the sauce
- 3 medium tomatoes, chopped, or 1 (15-ounce / 425-g) can chopped tomatoes
- 1 tablespoon plus 1 teaspoon tomato paste
- ¼ cup extra virgin olive oil
- 1 teaspoon fine sea salt
- ¼ teaspoon black pepper
- ¼ teaspoon granulated sugar
- 1¾ cups hot water

1. Begin making the meatballs by combining all the ingredients in a large bowl. Knead the mixture for 3 minutes or until all the ingredients are well incorporated. Cover the bowl with plastic wrap and transfer the mixture to the refrigerator to rest for at least 20 minutes. 2. While the meatball mixture is resting, preheat the oven to 350°F (180°C) and begin making the sauce by placing all the ingredients except the hot water in a food processor. Process until smooth and then transfer the mixture to a small pan over medium heat. Add the hot water and mix well. Let the mixture come to a boil and then reduce the heat to low and simmer for 10 minutes. 3. Remove the meatball mixture from the refrigerator and shape it into 24 oblong meatballs. 4. Spread 3 tablespoons of the sauce into the bottom of a large baking dish and place the meatballs in a single layer on top of the sauce. Pour the remaining sauce over the top of the meatballs. 5. Bake for 45 minutes or until the meatballs are lightly brown and then turn the meatballs and bake for an additional 10 minutes. (If the sauce appears to be drying out, add another ¼ cup hot water to the baking dish.) 6. Transfer the meatballs to a serving platter. Spoon the sauce over the meatballs before serving. Store covered in the refrigerator for up to 3 days or in an airtight container in the freezer for up to 3 months.

Per Serving:
calories: 221 | fat: 16g | protein: 14g | carbs: 5g | fiber: 1g | sodium: 661mg

Ground Beef Taco Rolls

Prep time: 20 minutes | Cook time: 10 minutes | Serves 4

- ½ pound (227 g) ground beef
- ⅓ cup water
- 1 tablespoon chili powder
- 2 teaspoons cumin
- ½ teaspoon garlic powder
- ¼ teaspoon dried oregano
- ¼ cup canned diced tomatoes and chiles, drained
- 2 tablespoons chopped cilantro
- 1½ cups shredded Mozzarella cheese
- ½ cup blanched finely ground almond flour
- 2 ounces (57 g) full-fat cream cheese
- 1 large egg

1. In a medium skillet over medium heat, brown the ground beef about 7 to 10 minutes. When meat is fully cooked, drain. 2. Add water to skillet and stir in chili powder, cumin, garlic powder, oregano, and tomatoes with chiles. Add cilantro. Bring to a boil, then reduce heat to simmer for 3 minutes. 3. In a large microwave-safe bowl, place Mozzarella, almond flour, cream cheese, and egg. Microwave for 1 minute. Stir the mixture quickly until smooth ball of dough forms. 4. Cut a piece of parchment for your work surface. Press the dough into a large rectangle on the parchment, wetting your hands to prevent the dough from sticking as necessary. Cut the dough into eight rectangles. 5. On each rectangle place a few spoons of the meat mixture. Fold the short ends of each roll toward the center and roll the length as you would a burrito. 6. Cut a piece of parchment to fit your air fryer basket. Place taco rolls onto the parchment and place into the air fryer basket. 7. Adjust the temperature to 360ºF (182ºC) and air fry for 10 minutes. 8. Flip halfway through the cooking time. 9. Allow to cool 10 minutes before serving.

Per Serving:
calories: 411 | fat: 31g | protein: 27g | carbs: 7g | fiber: 3g | sodium: 176mg

Beef Sliders with Pepper Slaw

Prep time: 10 minutes |Cook time: 10 minutes| Serves: 4

- Nonstick cooking spray
- 1 (8-ounce / 227-g) package white button mushrooms
- 2 tablespoons extra-virgin olive oil, divided
- 1 pound (454 g) ground beef (93% lean)
- 2 garlic cloves, minced (about 1 teaspoon)
- ½ teaspoon kosher or sea salt, divided
- ¼ teaspoon freshly ground black pepper
- 1 tablespoon balsamic vinegar
- 2 bell peppers of different colors, sliced into strips
- 2 tablespoons torn fresh basil or flat-leaf (Italian) parsley
- Mini or slider whole-grain rolls, for serving (optional)

1. Set one oven rack about 4 inches below the broiler element. Preheat the oven broiler to high. 2. Line a large, rimmed baking sheet with aluminum foil. Place a wire cooling rack on the aluminum foil, and spray the rack with nonstick cooking spray. Set aside. 3. Put half the mushrooms in the bowl of a food processor and pulse about 15 times, until the mushrooms are finely chopped but not puréed, similar to the texture of ground meat. Repeat with the remaining mushrooms. 4. In a large skillet over medium-high heat, heat 1 tablespoon of oil. Add the mushrooms and cook for 2 to 3 minutes, stirring occasionally, until the mushrooms have cooked down and some of their liquid has evaporated. Remove from the heat. 5. In a large bowl, combine the ground beef with the cooked mushrooms, garlic, ¼ teaspoon of salt, and pepper. Mix gently using your hands. Form the meat into 8 small (½-inch-thick) patties, and place on the prepared rack, making two lines of 4 patties down the center of the pan. 6. Place the pan in the oven so the broiler heating element is directly over as many burgers as possible. Broil for 4 minutes. Flip the burgers and rearrange them so any burgers not getting brown are nearer to the heat source. Broil for 3 to 4 more minutes, or until the internal temperature of the meat is 160ºF (71ºC) on a meat thermometer. Watch carefully to prevent burning. 7. While the burgers are cooking, in a large bowl, whisk together the remaining 1 tablespoon of oil, vinegar, and remaining ¼ teaspoon of salt. Add the peppers and basil, and stir gently to coat with the dressing. Serve the sliders with the pepper slaw as a topping or on the side. If desired, serve with the rolls, burger style.

Per Serving:
calories: 252 | fat: 13g | protein: 27g | carbs: 9g | fiber: 2g | sodium: 373mg

Red Curry Flank Steak

Prep time: 30 minutes | Cook time: 12 to 18 minutes | Serves 4

- 3 tablespoons red curry paste
- ¼ cup olive oil
- 2 teaspoons grated fresh ginger
- 2 tablespoons soy sauce
- 2 tablespoons rice wine
- vinegar
- 3 scallions, minced
- 1½ pounds (680 g) flank steak
- Fresh cilantro (or parsley) leaves

1. Mix the red curry paste, olive oil, ginger, soy sauce, rice vinegar and scallions together in a bowl. Place the flank steak in a shallow glass dish and pour half the marinade over the steak. Pierce the steak several times with a fork or meat tenderizer to let the marinade penetrate the meat. Turn the steak over, pour the remaining marinade over the top and pierce the steak several times again. Cover and marinate the steak in the refrigerator for 6 to 8 hours. 2. When you are ready to cook, remove the steak from the refrigerator and let it sit at room temperature for 30 minutes. 3. Preheat the air fryer to 400ºF (204ºC). 4. Cut the flank steak in half so that it fits more easily into the air fryer and transfer both pieces to the air fryer basket. Pour the marinade over the steak. Air fry for 12 to 18 minutes, depending on your preferred degree of doneness of the steak (12 minutes = medium rare). Flip the steak over halfway through the cooking time. 5. When your desired degree of doneness has been reached, remove the steak to a cutting board and let it rest for 5 minutes before slicing. Thinly slice the flank steak against the grain of the meat. Transfer the slices to a serving platter, pour any juice from the bottom of the air fryer over the sliced flank steak and sprinkle the fresh cilantro on top.

Per Serving:
calories: 397 | fat: 24g | protein: 38g | carbs: 6g | fiber: 3g | sodium: 216mg

Beef Bourguignon with Egg Noodles

Prep time: 15 minutes | Cook time: 8 hours | Serves 8

- 2 pounds (907 g) lean beef stew meat
- 6 tablespoons all-purpose flour
- 2 large carrots, cut into 1-inch slices
- 16 ounces (454 g) pearl onions, peeled fresh or frozen, thawed
- 8 ounces (227 g) mushrooms, stems removed
- 2 garlic cloves, minced
- ¾ cup beef stock
- ½ cup dry red wine
- ¼ cup tomato paste
- 1½ teaspoons sea salt
- ½ teaspoon dried rosemary
- ¼ teaspoon dried thyme
- ½ teaspoon black pepper
- 8 ounces (227 g) uncooked egg noodles
- ¼ cup chopped fresh thyme leaves

1. Place the beef in a medium bowl, sprinkle with the flour, and toss well to coat. 2. Place the beef mixture, carrots, onions, mushrooms, and garlic in the slow cooker. 3. Combine the stock, wine, tomato paste, salt, rosemary, thyme, and black pepper in a small bowl. Stir into the beef mixture. 4. Cover and cook on low for 8 hours. 5. Cook the noodles according to package directions, omitting any salt. 6. Serve the beef mixture over the noodles, sprinkled with the thyme.

Per Serving:
calories: 397 | fat: 6g | protein: 34g | carbs: 53g | fiber: 6g | sodium: 592mg

Braised Short Ribs with Fennel and Pickled Grapes

Prep time: 20 minutes | Cook time: 55 minutes | Serves 4

- 1½ pounds (680 g) boneless beef short ribs, trimmed and cut into 2-inch pieces
- 1 teaspoon table salt, divided
- 1 tablespoon extra-virgin olive oil
- 1 fennel bulb, 2 tablespoons fronds chopped, stalks discarded, bulb halved, cored, and sliced into
- 1-inch-thick wedges
- 1 onion, halved and sliced ½ inch thick
- 4 garlic cloves, minced
- 2 teaspoons fennel seeds
- ½ cup chicken broth
- 1 sprig fresh rosemary
- ¼ cup red wine vinegar
- 1 tablespoon sugar
- 4 ounces (113 g) seedless red grapes, halved (½ cup)

1. Pat short ribs dry with paper towels and sprinkle with ½ teaspoon salt. Using highest sauté function, heat oil in Instant Pot for 5 minutes (or until just smoking). Brown short ribs on all sides, 6 to 8 minutes; transfer to plate. 2. Add fennel wedges, onion, and ¼ teaspoon salt to fat left in pot and cook, using highest sauté function, until vegetables are softened and lightly browned, about 5 minutes. Stir in garlic and fennel seeds and cook until fragrant, about 30 seconds. Stir in broth and rosemary sprig, scraping up any browned bits. Nestle short ribs into vegetable mixture and add any accumulated juices. Lock lid in place and close pressure release valve. Select high pressure cook function and cook for 35 minutes. 3. Meanwhile, microwave vinegar, sugar, and remaining ¼ teaspoon salt in bowl until simmering, about 1 minute. Add grapes and let sit, stirring occasionally, for 20 minutes. Drain grapes and return to now-empty bowl. (Drained grapes can be refrigerated for up to 1 week.) 4. Turn off Instant Pot and let pressure release naturally for 15 minutes. Quick-release any remaining pressure, then carefully remove lid, allowing steam to escape away from you. Transfer short ribs to serving dish, tent with aluminum foil, and let rest while finishing sauce. 5. Strain braising liquid through fine-mesh strainer into fat separator. Discard rosemary sprig and transfer vegetables to serving dish with beef. Let braising liquid settle for 5 minutes, then pour ¾ cup defatted liquid over short ribs and vegetables; discard remaining liquid. Sprinkle with grapes and fennel fronds. Serve.

Per Serving:
calories: 310 | fat: 17g | protein: 24g | carbs: 15g | fiber: 3g | sodium: 750mg

Herbs and Lamb Stew

Prep time: 25 minutes | Cook time: 55 minutes | Serves 8

- 1 pound (454 g) boneless lamb shoulder, trimmed and cut into 1" pieces
- 2 tablespoons all-purpose flour
- ¼ teaspoon salt
- ¼ teaspoon ground black pepper
- 2 tablespoons olive oil, divided
- 2 medium carrots, peeled and sliced
- 2 stalks celery, sliced
- 1 medium onion, peeled and
- chopped
- 3 cloves garlic, peeled and minced
- 4 thyme sprigs
- 1 sprig rosemary
- 2 tablespoons chopped fresh oregano
- 1 bay leaf
- 2 cups low-sodium chicken broth
- 1 cup tomato sauce
- 1 medium russet potato, cut into 1" pieces
- ¼ cup chopped fresh parsley

1. In a medium bowl, add lamb, flour, salt, and pepper. Toss until lamb is thoroughly coated. Set aside. 2. Press the Sauté button on the Instant Pot® and heat 1 tablespoon oil. Add half of the lamb pieces in a single layer, leaving space between each piece to prevent steaming, and brown well on all sides, about 3 minutes per side. Transfer lamb to a large bowl and repeat with remaining 1 tablespoon oil and lamb. 3. Add carrots, celery, and onion to the pot. Cook until tender, about 8 minutes. Add garlic and cook until fragrant, about 30 seconds. Add thyme, rosemary, oregano, and bay leaf. Stir well. 4. Slowly add chicken broth, scraping the bottom of the pot well to release any brown bits. Add tomato sauce, potato, and browned lamb along with any juices. Press the Cancel button. 5. Close lid, set steam release to Sealing, press the Stew button, and set time to 40 minutes. When the timer beeps, quick-release the pressure until the float valve drops, open lid, and stir well. Remove and discard thyme, rosemary, and bay leaf. Sprinkle with parsley and serve hot.

Per Serving:
calories: 222 | fat: 11g | protein: 18g | carbs: 11g | fiber: 2g | sodium: 285mg

Ground Pork and Eggplant Casserole

Prep time: 20 minutes | Cook time: 18 minutes | Serves 8

- 2 pounds (907 g) lean ground pork
- 1 large yellow onion, peeled and diced
- 1 stalk celery, diced
- 1 medium green bell pepper, seeded and diced
- 2 medium eggplants, cut into ½" pieces
- 4 cloves garlic, peeled and minced
- ⅛ teaspoon dried thyme
- 1 tablespoon freeze-dried parsley
- 3 tablespoons tomato paste
- ½ teaspoon hot sauce
- 2 teaspoons Worcestershire sauce
- 1 teaspoon salt
- ½ teaspoon ground black pepper
- 1 large egg, beaten
- ½ cup low-sodium chicken broth

1. Press the Sauté button on the Instant Pot® and add pork, onion, celery, and bell pepper to the pot. Cook until pork is no longer pink, breaking it apart as it cooks, about 8 minutes. 2. Drain and discard any fat rendered from pork. Add eggplant, garlic, thyme, parsley, tomato paste, hot sauce, Worcestershire sauce, salt, pepper, and egg. Stir well, then press the Cancel button. 3. Pour in chicken broth. Close lid, set steam release to Sealing, press the Manual button, and set time to 10 minutes. When the timer beeps, let pressure release naturally, about 25 minutes. Open lid and serve hot.

Per Serving:
calories: 292 | fat: 18g | protein: 22g | carbs: 10g | fiber: 4g | sodium: 392mg

Smoked Paprika and Lemon Marinated Pork Kabobs

Prep time: 10 minutes | Cook time: 10 minutes | Serves 4

- ⅓ cup finely chopped flat-leaf parsley
- ¼ cup olive oil
- 2 tablespoons minced red onion
- 1 tablespoon lemon juice
- 1 tablespoon smoked paprika
- 2 teaspoons ground cumin
- 1 clove garlic, minced
- ¼ teaspoon cayenne pepper
- ½ teaspoon salt
- 2 pork tenderloins, each about 1 pound (454 g), trimmed of silver skin and any excess fat, cut into 1¼-inch cubes
- 1 lemon, cut into wedges, for serving

1. In a large bowl, whisk together the parsley, olive oil, onion, lemon juice, smoked paprika, cumin, garlic, cayenne, and salt. Add the pork and toss to coat well. Cover and refrigerate, stirring occasionally, for at least 4 hours (or as long as overnight). 2. Soak bamboo skewers in water for 30 minutes. 3. Preheat the grill to high heat. 4. Remove the meat from the marinade, discarding the marinade. Thread the meat onto the soaked skewers and place the skewers on the grill. Cook, with the lid closed, turning occasionally, until the pork is cooked through and browned on all sides, about 8 to 10 minutes total. 5. Transfer the skewers to a serving platter and serve immediately with the lemon wedges.

Per Serving:
calories: 447 | fat: 21g | protein: 60g | carbs: 3g | fiber: 1g | sodium: 426mg

Pork Casserole with Fennel and Potatoes

Prep time: 20 minutes | Cook time: 6 to 8 hours | Serves 6

- 2 large fennel bulbs
- 3 pounds (1.4 kg) pork tenderloin, cut into 1½-inch pieces
- 2 pounds (907 g) red potatoes, quartered
- 1 cup low-sodium chicken broth
- 4 garlic cloves, minced
- 1½ teaspoons dried thyme
- 1 teaspoon dried parsley
- 1 teaspoon sea salt
- Freshly ground black pepper
- ⅓ cup shredded Parmesan cheese

1. Cut the stalks off the fennel bulbs. Trim a little piece from the bottom of the bulbs to make them stable, then cut straight down through the bulbs to halve them. Cut the halves into quarters. Peel off and discard any wilted outer layers. Cut the fennel pieces crosswise into slices. 2. In a slow cooker, combine the fennel, pork, and potatoes. Stir to mix well. 3. In a small bowl, whisk together the chicken broth, garlic, thyme, parsley, and salt until combined. Season with pepper and whisk again. Pour the sauce over the pork. 4. Cover the cooker and cook for 6 to 8 hours on Low heat. 5. Top with Parmesan cheese for serving.

Per Serving:
calories: 412 | fat: 7g | protein: 55g | carbs: 31g | fiber: 5g | sodium: 592mg

Beef, Mushroom, and Green Bean Soup

Prep time: 10 minutes | Cook time: 45 minutes | Serves 4

2 tablespoons olive oil

- 1 pound (454 g) chuck or round beef roast, cut into 2-inch pieces
- 1 large onion, diced
- ½ teaspoon sea salt
- ¼ teaspoon freshly ground black pepper
- ½ cup white wine
- 8 cups chicken broth
- 1 pound (454 g) green beans
- 8 ounces (227 g) cremini (baby bella) mushrooms, chopped
- 3 tablespoons tomato paste
- ½ teaspoon dried oregano

1. In a large stockpot, heat the olive oil over medium-high heat. Add the beef and brown, 5 to 7 minutes. Add the onion, salt, and pepper and cook for 5 minutes. Add the wine and cook for 4 minutes. Add the broth, green beans, mushrooms, tomato paste, and oregano and stir to combine. 2. Bring to a boil, reduce the heat to low, cover, and simmer for 35 to 45 minutes, until the meat is cooked through. Serve.

Per Serving:
calories: 307 | fat: 14g | protein: 28g | carbs: 17g | fiber: 5g | sodium: 265mg

Lamb Couscous

Prep time: 25 minutes | Cook time: 30 minutes | Serves 8 to 10

- 2 pounds (907 g) boneless lamb meat, cut into 2-inch pieces
- ½ teaspoon dried thyme
- ½ teaspoon dried marjoram
- Sea salt and freshly ground pepper, to taste
- ¼ cup olive oil
- 1 onion, peeled and coarsely chopped
- 1 bulb celeriac, cut in chunks
- 5 cups chicken broth
- 2 zucchini, cut into 1-inch pieces
- 1 cup cooked chickpeas
- 1 cup raisins (optional)
- ¼ teaspoon ground ginger
- ¼ teaspoon ground cinnamon
- ¼ teaspoon ground cardamom
- ¼ teaspoon ground cloves
- ¼ teaspoon ground nutmeg
- 5 cups cooked whole-wheat couscous
- ½ cup fresh cilantro, chopped
- ½ cup fresh mint, chopped
- ½ cup green onions, chopped

1. Season the lamb meat with the thyme, marjoram, sea salt, and freshly ground pepper, and grill in a grill basket for 8–10 minutes, stirring frequently. 2. If you don't have a grill basket, you can also cook the lamb in a heavy skillet. 3. Set aside, but keep warm. 4. Heat the olive oil in a large skillet. 5. Add the onion and celeriac, and cook until tender, stirring frequently. 6. Add the chicken broth, zucchini, chickpeas, raisins, and spices, and simmer 10–20 minutes. 7. To serve, mound the couscous in the middle of a serving platter and arrange the vegetables and meat around the couscous. Garnish with the fresh cilantro, mint, and green onions.

Per Serving:
calories: 442 | fat: 13g | protein: 31g | carbs: 53g | fiber: 9g | sodium: 118mg

Pork Milanese

Prep time: 10 minutes | Cook time: 12 minutes | Serves 4

- 4 (1-inch) boneless pork chops
- Fine sea salt and ground black pepper, to taste
- 2 large eggs
- ¾ cup powdered Parmesan cheese
- Chopped fresh parsley, for garnish
- Lemon slices, for serving

1. Spray the air fryer basket with avocado oil. Preheat the air fryer to 400°F (204°C). 2. Place the pork chops between 2 sheets of plastic wrap and pound them with the flat side of a meat tenderizer until they're ¼ inch thick. Lightly season both sides of the chops with salt and pepper. 3. Lightly beat the eggs in a shallow bowl. Divide the Parmesan cheese evenly between 2 bowls and set the bowls in this order: Parmesan, eggs, Parmesan. Dredge a chop in the first bowl of Parmesan, then dip it in the eggs, and then dredge it again in the second bowl of Parmesan, making sure both sides and all edges are well coated. Repeat with the remaining chops. 4. Place the chops in the air fryer basket and air fry for 12 minutes, or until the internal temperature reaches 145°F (63°C), flipping halfway through. 5. Garnish with fresh parsley and serve immediately

with lemon slices. Store leftovers in an airtight container in the refrigerator for up to 3 days. Reheat in a preheated 390°F (199°C) air fryer for 5 minutes, or until warmed through.

Per Serving:
calories: 349 | fat: 14g | protein: 50g | carbs: 3g | fiber: 0g | sodium: 464mg

Mediterranean Chimichurri Skirt Steak

Prep time: 10 minutes | Cook time: 15 minutes | Serves 4

- ¾ cup fresh mint
- ¾ cup fresh parsley
- ⅔ cup extra-virgin olive oil
- ⅓ cup lemon juice
- Zest of 1 lemon
- 2 tablespoons dried oregano
- 4 garlic cloves, peeled
- ½ teaspoon red pepper flakes
- ½ teaspoon kosher salt
- 1 to 1½ pounds (454 to 680 g) skirt steak, cut in half if longer than grill pan

1. In a food processor or blender, add the mint, parsley, olive oil, lemon juice, lemon zest, oregano, garlic, red pepper flakes, and salt. Process until the mixture reaches your desired consistency—anywhere from a slightly chunky to smooth purée. Remove a half cup of the chimichurri mixture and set aside. 2. Pour the remaining chimichurri mixture into a medium bowl or zip-top bag and add the steak. Mix together well and marinate for at least 30 minutes, and up to 8 hours in the refrigerator. 3. In a grill pan over medium-high heat, add the steak and cook 4 minutes on each side (for medium rare). Cook an additional 1 to 2 minutes per side for medium. 4. Place the steak on a cutting board, tent with foil to keep it warm, and let it rest for 10 minutes. Thinly slice the steak crosswise against the grain and serve with the reserved sauce.

Per Serving:
calories: 460 | fat: 38g | protein: 28g | carbs: 5g | fiber: 2g | sodium: 241mg

Grilled Kefta

Prep time: 10 minutes | Cook time: 5 minutes | Serves 4

- 1 medium onion
- ⅓ cup fresh Italian parsley
- 1 pound (454 g) ground beef
- ¼ teaspoon ground cumin
- ¼ teaspoon cinnamon
- 1 teaspoon salt
- ½ teaspoon freshly ground black pepper

1. Preheat a grill or grill pan to high. 2. Mince the onion and parsley in a food processor until finely chopped. 3. In a large bowl, using your hands, combine the beef with the onion mix, ground cumin, cinnamon, salt, and pepper. 4. Divide the meat into 6 portions. Form each portion into a flat oval. 5. Place the patties on the grill or grill pan and cook for 3 minutes on each side.

Per Serving:
calories: 203 | fat: 10g | protein: 24g | carbs: 3g | fiber: 1g | sodium: 655mg

Beef Stew with Red Wine

Prep time: 15 minutes | Cook time: 46 minutes | Serves 8

- 1 pound (454 g) beef stew meat, cut into 1" pieces
- 2 tablespoons all-purpose flour
- ¼ teaspoon salt
- ¼ teaspoon ground black pepper
- 2 tablespoons olive oil, divided
- 1 pound (454 g) whole crimini mushrooms
- 2 cloves garlic, peeled and minced
- 4 sprigs thyme
- 2 bay leaves
- 8 ounces (227 g) baby carrots
- 8 ounces (227 g) frozen pearl onions, thawed
- 1 cup red wine
- ½ cup beef broth
- ¼ cup chopped fresh parsley

1. In a medium bowl, toss beef with flour, salt, and pepper until thoroughly coated. Set aside. 2. Press the Sauté button on the Instant Pot® and heat 1 tablespoon oil. Add half of the beef pieces in a single layer, leaving space between each piece to prevent steaming, and brown well on all sides, about 3 minutes per side. Transfer beef to a medium bowl and repeat with remaining 1 tablespoon oil and beef. Press the Cancel button. 3. Add mushrooms, garlic, thyme, bay leaves, carrots, onions, wine, and broth to the Instant Pot®. Stir well. Close lid, set steam release to Sealing, press the Stew button, and set time to 40 minutes. When the timer beeps, quick-release the pressure until the float valve drops, open lid, and stir well. Remove and discard thyme and bay leaves. Sprinkle with parsley and serve hot.

Per Serving:
calories: 206 | fat: 13g | protein: 12g | carbs: 6g | fiber: 1g | sodium: 186mg

Pork Tenderloin with Vegetable Ragu

Prep time: 25 minutes | Cook time: 18 minutes | Serves 6

- 2 tablespoons light olive oil, divided
- 1 (1½-pound / 680-g) pork tenderloin
- ¼ teaspoon salt
- ¼ teaspoon ground black pepper
- 1 medium zucchini, trimmed and sliced
- 1 medium yellow squash, sliced
- 1 medium onion, peeled and chopped
- 1 medium carrot, peeled and
- grated
- 1 (14½-ounce / 411-g) can diced tomatoes, drained
- 2 cloves garlic, peeled and minced
- ¼ teaspoon crushed red pepper flakes
- 1 tablespoon chopped fresh basil
- 1 tablespoon chopped fresh oregano
- 1 sprig fresh thyme
- ½ cup red wine

1. Press the Sauté button on the Instant Pot® and heat 1 tablespoon oil. Season pork with salt and black pepper. Brown pork lightly on all sides, about 2 minutes per side. Transfer pork to a plate and set aside. 2. Add remaining 1 tablespoon oil to the pot. Add zucchini and squash, and cook until tender, about 5 minutes. Add onion and carrot, and cook until just softened, about 5 minutes. Add tomatoes, garlic, crushed red pepper flakes, basil, oregano, thyme, and red wine to pot, and stir well. Press the Cancel button. 3. Top vegetable mixture with browned pork. Close lid, set steam release to Sealing, press the Manual button, and set time to 3 minutes. When the timer beeps, quick-release the pressure until the float valve drops and open lid. Transfer pork to a cutting board and cut into 1" slices. Pour sauce on a serving platter and arrange pork slices on top. Serve immediately.

Per Serving:
calories: 190 | fat: 7g | protein: 23g | carbs: 9g | fiber: 2g | sodium: 606mg

Lamb and Onion Tagine

Prep time: 10 minutes | Cook time: 2 hours 15 minutes | Serves 4

- 2 tablespoons finely chopped fresh flat-leaf parsley
- 2 tablespoons finely chopped fresh cilantro
- 2 cloves garlic, minced
- ½ teaspoon ground turmeric
- ½ teaspoon ground ginger
- 1 teaspoon ground cinnamon, divided
- 1 teaspoon plus a pinch kosher salt
- ½ teaspoon ground black pepper
- 2 tablespoons plus ⅓ cup
- water
- 3 tablespoons extra-virgin olive oil
- 4 bone-in leg of lamb steaks, ½' thick (about 2½ pounds / 1.1 kg)
- 1 can (28 ounces / 794-g) whole peeled plum tomatoes, drained
- 2 large red onions, 1 finely chopped, the other sliced in ⅛' rounds
- 2 teaspoons honey, divided
- 1 tablespoon toasted sesame seeds

1. In a large bowl, combine the parsley, cilantro, garlic, turmeric, ginger, ¼ teaspoon of the cinnamon, 1 teaspoon of the salt, and the pepper. Add 2 tablespoons of the water and the oil and mix. Add the lamb steaks and turn to coat each one. Cover and refrigerate, turning the steaks occasionally, for at least 1 hour. 2. Make a small cut into each tomato and squeeze out the seeds and excess juices. 3. In a 12' tagine or a deep heavy-bottom skillet, scatter the chopped onion. Arrange the lamb steaks snugly in a single layer. Drizzle the remaining marinade over the top. Add the tomatoes around the lamb. Drizzle 1 teaspoon of the honey and ¼ teaspoon of the cinnamon over the top. 4. Lay the onion rounds on top of the lamb. Drizzle the remaining 1 teaspoon honey. Sprinkle the remaining ½ teaspoon cinnamon and the pinch of salt. Turn the heat on to medium (medium-low if using a pot) and cook, uncovered, nudging the lamb occasionally, until the chopped onion below is translucent, about 15 minutes. 5. Pour in the ⅓ cup water around the outer edges of the food. Cover with a lid, slightly askew to keep air flowing in and out of the tagine or skillet. Reduce the heat to low and simmer gently, nudging the lamb occasionally to prevent sticking. Cook until the lamb is very tender, adding water as needed to keep the sauce moist, about 2 hours. 6. Sprinkle with the sesame seeds and serve.

Per Serving:
calories: 537 | fat: 25g | protein: 63g | carbs: 19g | fiber: 6g | sodium: 791mg

Greek Lamb Burgers

Prep time: 10 minutes | Cook time: 10 minutes | Serves 4

- 1 pound (454 g) ground lamb
- ½ teaspoon salt
- ½ teaspoon freshly ground black pepper
- 4 tablespoons feta cheese, crumbled
- Buns, toppings, and tzatziki, for serving (optional)

1. Preheat a grill, grill pan, or lightly oiled skillet to high heat. 2. In a large bowl, using your hands, combine the lamb with the salt and pepper. 3. Divide the meat into 4 portions. Divide each portion in half to make a top and a bottom. Flatten each half into a 3-inch circle. Make a dent in the center of one of the halves and place 1 tablespoon of the feta cheese in the center. Place the second half of the patty on top of the feta cheese and press down to close the 2 halves together, making it resemble a round burger. 4. Cook the stuffed patty for 3 minutes on each side, for medium-well. Serve on a bun with your favorite toppings and tzatziki sauce, if desired.

Per Serving:
calories: 345 | fat: 29g | protein: 20g | carbs: 1g | fiber: 0g | sodium: 462mg

Lamb Tagine

Prep time: 15 minutes | Cook time: 7 hours | Serves 6

- 1 navel orange
- 2 tablespoons all-purpose flour
- 2 pounds (907 g) boneless leg of lamb, trimmed and cut into 1½-inch cubes
- ½ cup chicken stock
- 2 large white onions, chopped
- 1 teaspoon pumpkin pie spice
- 1 teaspoon ground cumin
- ½ teaspoon sea salt
- ¼ teaspoon saffron threads, crushed in your palm
- ¼ teaspoon ground red pepper
- 1 cup pitted dates
- 2 tablespoons honey
- 3 cups hot cooked couscous, for serving
- 2 tablespoons toasted slivered almonds, for serving

1. Grate 2 teaspoons of zest from the orange into a small bowl. Squeeze ¼ cup juice from the orange into another small bowl. 2. Add the flour to the orange juice, stirring with a whisk until smooth. Stir in the orange zest. 3. Heat a large nonstick skillet over medium-high heat. Add the lamb and sauté 7 minutes or until browned. Stir in the stock, scraping the bottom of the pan with a wooden spoon to loosen the flavorful brown bits. Stir in the orange juice mixture. 4. Stir the onions into the lamb mixture. Add the pumpkin pie spice, cumin, salt, saffron, and ground red pepper. 5. Pour the lamb mixture into the slow cooker. Cover and cook on low for 6 hours or until the lamb is tender. 6. Stir the dates and honey into the lamb mixture. Cover and cook on low for 1 hour or until thoroughly heated. 7. Serve the lamb tagine over the couscous and sprinkle with the almonds.

Per Serving:
calories: 451 | fat: 11g | protein: 37g | carbs: 53g | fiber: 5g | sodium: 329mg

Spiced Lamb Stew with Fennel and Dates

Prep time: 10 minutes | Cook time: 3 hours | Serves 4

- 2 tablespoons olive oil, divided
- 1 fennel bulb, trimmed, cored, and thinly sliced
- 1 red onion, thinly sliced
- 2 cloves garlic, thinly sliced
- 1½ pounds (680 g) lamb shoulder, cut into 1½-inch cubes and dried with paper towels
- 1 teaspoon ground ginger
- 2 teaspoons ground cumin
- 2 teaspoons ground coriander
- ¼ teaspoon cayenne pepper
- 1 teaspoon salt
- 1 cup pitted chopped dates
- 2 cups water, divided
- ¼ cup chopped cilantro, for garnish

1. Heat 1 tablespoon of olive oil in a Dutch oven. Add the fennel, onion, and garlic and cook, stirring frequently, until softened and beginning to brown, about 7 minutes. Transfer the vegetables to a plate. 2. Add the remaining 1 tablespoon of olive oil to the pot and cook the lamb, turning every couple of minutes, until browned on all sides. 3. In a small bowl, combine the ginger, cumin, coriander, cayenne, and salt and mix well. Sprinkle the spice mixture over the meat in the pot and cook, stirring, for 1 minute. 4. Return the vegetables to the pot and add the dates and 1 cup of water. Reduce the heat to medium-low, cover, and cook, stirring occasionally and adding the remaining 1 cup of water as needed, for 2½ hours, until the lamb is very tender and the sauce has thickened. Serve immediately, garnished with cilantro.

Per Serving:
calories: 539 | fat: 20g | protein: 50g | carbs: 52g | fiber: 6g | sodium: 749mg

Rosemary Roast Beef

Prep time: 30 minutes | Cook time: 30 to 35 minutes | Serves 8

- 1 (2-pound / 907-g) top round beef roast, tied with kitchen string
- Sea salt and freshly ground black pepper, to taste
- 2 teaspoons minced garlic
- 2 tablespoons finely chopped fresh rosemary
- ¼ cup avocado oil

1. Season the roast generously with salt and pepper. 2. In a small bowl, whisk together the garlic, rosemary, and avocado oil. Rub this all over the roast. Cover loosely with aluminum foil or plastic wrap and refrigerate for at least 12 hours or up to 2 days. 3. Remove the roast from the refrigerator and allow to sit at room temperature for about 1 hour. 4. Set the air fryer to 325°F (163°C). Place the roast in the air fryer basket and roast for 15 minutes. Flip the roast and cook for 15 to 20 minutes more, until the meat is browned and an instant-read thermometer reads 120°F (49°C) at the thickest part (for medium-rare). 5. Transfer the meat to a cutting board, and let it rest for 15 minutes before thinly slicing and serving.

Per Serving:
calories: 208 | fat: 12g | protein: 25g | carbs: 0g | fiber: 0g | sodium: 68mg

Beef Whirls

Prep time: 30 minutes | Cook time: 18 minutes | Serves 6

- 3 cube steaks (6 ounces / 170 g each)
- 1 (16-ounce / 454-g) bottle Italian dressing
- 1 cup Italian-style bread crumbs
- ½ cup grated Parmesan
- cheese
- 1 teaspoon dried basil
- 1 teaspoon dried oregano
- 1 teaspoon dried parsley
- ¼ cup beef broth
- 1 to 2 tablespoons oil

1. In a large resealable bag, combine the steaks and Italian dressing. Seal the bag and refrigerate to marinate for 2 hours. 2. In a medium bowl, whisk the bread crumbs, cheese, basil, oregano, and parsley until blended. Stir in the beef broth. 3. Place the steaks on a cutting board and cut each in half so you have 6 equal pieces. Sprinkle with the bread crumb mixture. Roll up the steaks, jelly roll-style, and secure with toothpicks. 4. Preheat the air fryer to 400°F (204°C). 5. Place 3 roll-ups in the air fryer basket. 6. Cook for 5 minutes. Flip the roll-ups and spritz with oil. Cook for 4 minutes more until the internal temperature reaches 145°F (63°C). Repeat with the remaining roll-ups. Let rest for 5 to 10 minutes before serving.

Per Serving:
calories: 307 | fat: 15g | protein: 24g | carbs: 17g | fiber: 1g | sodium: 236mg

Moroccan Lamb Roast

Prep time: 15 minutes | Cook time: 6 to 8 hours | Serves 6

- ¼ cup low-sodium beef broth or low-sodium chicken broth
- 1 teaspoon dried ginger
- 1 teaspoon dried cumin
- 1 teaspoon ground turmeric
- 1 teaspoon paprika
- 1 teaspoon garlic powder
- 1 teaspoon red pepper flakes
- ½ teaspoon ground cinnamon
- ½ teaspoon ground
- coriander
- ½ teaspoon ground nutmeg
- ½ teaspoon ground cloves
- ½ teaspoon sea salt
- ½ teaspoon freshly ground black pepper
- 1 (3-pound/ 1.4-kg) lamb roast
- 4 ounces (113 g) carrots, chopped
- ¼ cup sliced onion
- ¼ cup chopped fresh mint

1. Pour the broth into a slow cooker. 2. In a small bowl, stir together the ginger, cumin, turmeric, paprika, garlic powder, red pepper flakes, cinnamon, coriander, nutmeg, cloves, salt, and black pepper. Rub the spice mix firmly all over the lamb roast. Put the lamb in the slow cooker and add the carrots and onion. 3. Top everything with the mint. 4. Cover the cooker and cook for 6 to 8 hours on Low heat.

Per Serving:
calories: 601 | fat: 39g | protein: 56g | carbs: 4g | fiber: 1g | sodium: 398mg

Braised Pork with Broccoli Rabe and Sage

Prep time: 15 minutes | Cook time: 50 minutes | Serves 4

- 1½ pounds (680 g) boneless pork butt roast, trimmed and cut into 2-inch pieces
- ½ teaspoon table salt
- ½ teaspoon pepper
- 1 tablespoon extra-virgin olive oil
- 2 tablespoons minced fresh sage, divided
- 5 garlic cloves, peeled and
- smashed
- 1 tablespoon all-purpose flour
- ¼ cup chicken broth
- ¼ cup dry white wine
- 1 pound (454 g) broccoli rabe, trimmed and cut into 1-inch pieces
- ½ teaspoon grated orange zest

1. Pat pork dry with paper towels and sprinkle with salt and pepper. Using highest sauté function, heat oil in Instant Pot for 5 minutes (or until just smoking). Brown pork on all sides, 6 to 8 minutes; transfer to plate. 2. Add 1 tablespoon sage, garlic, and flour to fat left in pot and cook, using highest sauté function, until fragrant, about 1 minute. Stir in broth and wine, scraping up any browned bits. Return pork to pot along with any accumulated juices. Lock lid in place and close pressure release valve. Select high pressure cook function and cook for 30 minutes. 3. Turn off Instant Pot and let pressure release naturally for 15 minutes. Quick-release any remaining pressure, then carefully remove lid, allowing steam to escape away from you. Transfer pork to serving dish, tent with aluminum foil, and let rest while preparing broccoli rabe. 4. Whisk sauce until smooth and bring to simmer using highest sauté function. Stir in broccoli rabe and cook, partially covered, until tender and bright green, about 3 minutes. Stir in orange zest and remaining 1 tablespoon sage. Serve pork with broccoli rabe mixture.

Per Serving:
calories: 340 | fat: 16g | protein: 37g | carbs: 7g | fiber: 3g | sodium: 490mg

Chapter 6

Fish and Seafood

Chapter 6 Fish and Seafood

Sicilian Kale and Tuna Bowl

Prep time: 5 minutes |Cook time: 15 minutes| Serves: 6

- 1 pound (454 g) kale, chopped, center ribs removed (about 12 cups)
- 3 tablespoons extra-virgin olive oil
- 1 cup chopped onion (about ½ medium onion)
- 3 garlic cloves, minced (about 1½ teaspoons)
- 1 (2¼-ounce / 35-g) can sliced olives, drained (about ½ cup)
- ¼ cup capers
- ¼ teaspoon crushed red pepper
- 2 teaspoons sugar
- 2 (6-ounce / 170-g) cans tuna in olive oil, undrained
- 1 (15-ounce / 425-g) can cannellini beans or great northern beans, drained and rinsed
- ¼ teaspoon freshly ground black pepper
- ¼ teaspoon kosher or sea salt

1. Fill a large stockpot three-quarters full of water, and bring to a boil. Add the kale and cook for 2 minutes. (This is to make the kale less bitter.) Drain the kale in a colander and set aside. 2. Set the empty pot back on the stove over medium heat, and pour in the oil. Add the onion and cook for 4 minutes, stirring often. Add the garlic and cook for 1 minute, stirring often. Add the olives, capers, and crushed red pepper, and cook for 1 minute, stirring often. Add the partially cooked kale and sugar, stirring until the kale is completely coated with oil. Cover the pot and cook for 8 minutes. 3. Remove the kale from the heat, mix in the tuna, beans, pepper, and salt, and serve.

Per Serving:
calories: 323 | fat: 14g | protein: 26g | carbs: 26g | fiber: 7g | sodium: 653mg

Poached Octopus

Prep time: 10 minutes | Cook time: 16 minutes | Serves 8

- 2 pounds (907 g) potatoes (about 6 medium)
- 3 teaspoons salt, divided
- 1 (2-pound / 907-g) frozen octopus, thawed, cleaned, and rinsed
- 3 cloves garlic, peeled, divided
- 1 bay leaf
- 2 teaspoons whole peppercorns
- ½ cup olive oil
- ¼ cup white wine vinegar
- ½ teaspoon ground black pepper
- ½ cup chopped fresh parsley

1. Place potatoes in the Instant Pot® with 2 teaspoons salt and enough water to just cover the potatoes halfway. Close lid, set steam release to Sealing, press the Manual button, and set time to 6 minutes. When the timer beeps, quick-release the pressure until the float valve drops and open lid. Press the Cancel button. 2. Remove potatoes with tongs (reserve the cooking water), and peel them as soon as you can handle them. Dice potatoes into bite-sized pieces. Set aside. 3. Add octopus to potato cooking water in the pot and add more water to cover if needed. Add 1 garlic clove, bay leaf, and peppercorns. Close lid, set steam release to Sealing, press the Manual button, and set time to 10 minutes. When the timer beeps, quick-release the pressure until the float valve drops and open lid. Remove and discard bay leaf. 4. Check octopus for tenderness by seeing if a fork will sink easily into the thickest part of the flesh. If not, close the top and bring it to pressure for another minute or two and check again. 5. Remove octopus and drain. Chop head and tentacles into small, bite-sized chunks. 6. Crush remaining 2 garlic cloves and place in a small jar or plastic container. Add olive oil, vinegar, remaining 1 teaspoon salt, and pepper. Close the lid and shake well. 7. In a large serving bowl, mix potatoes with octopus, cover with vinaigrette, and sprinkle with parsley.

Per Serving:
calories: 301 | fat: 15g | protein: 15g | carbs: 30g | fiber: 2g | sodium: 883mg

Dilly Baked Salmon

Prep time: 5 minutes | Cook time: 15 minutes | Serves 4

- 4 (6-ounce / 170-g) salmon filets
- 2 tablespoons extra-virgin olive oil
- ½ teaspoon salt
- ¼ teaspoon freshly ground black pepper
- Juice of large Valencia orange or tangerine
- 4 teaspoons orange or tangerine zest
- 4 tablespoons chopped fresh dill

1. Preheat the oven to 375°F(190°C). Prepare four 10-inch-long pieces of aluminum foil. 2. Rub each salmon filet on both sides with the olive oil. Season each with salt and pepper and place one in the center of each piece of foil. 3. Drizzle the orange juice over each piece of fish and top with 1 teaspoon orange zest and 1 tablespoon dill. 4. For each packet, fold the two long sides of the foil together and then fold the short ends in to make a packet. Make sure to leave about 2 inches of air space within the foil so the fish can steam. Place the packets on a baking sheet. 5. Bake for 15 minutes. Open the packets carefully (they will be very steamy), transfer the fish to 4 serving plates, and pour the sauce over the top of each.

Per Serving:
calories: 297 | fat: 15g | protein: 36g | carbs: 4g | fiber: 1g | sodium: 420mg

Summer Mackerel Niçoise Platter

Prep time: 10 minutes | Cook time: 15 minutes | Serves 2

For the Dressing:
- 3 tablespoons red wine vinegar
- 4 tablespoons olive oil
- 1 teaspoon Dijon mustard
- ¼ teaspoon salt
- Pinch freshly ground black pepper

For the Salad:
- 2 teaspoons salt
- 2 small red potatoes
- 1 cup tender green beans
- 2 cups baby greens
- 2 hard-boiled eggs
- ½ cup cherry tomatoes, halved
- ⅓ cup Niçoise olives
- 2 (4-ounce / 113-g) tins of mackerel fillets, drained

Make the Dressing: Combine the vinegar, olive oil, Dijon mustard, salt, and pepper in a lidded jar. Shake or whisk the dressing until thoroughly combined. Taste and add more salt and pepper to taste, if needed. Make the Salad: 1. Fill a large saucepan with about 3 inches of water, add salt, and bring to a boil. Add the potatoes and cook for 10 to 15 minutes, or until you can pierce them with a sharp knife, but they are still firm. 2. Remove the potatoes and add the green beans to the water. Reduce the heat and let the beans simmer for 5 minutes. 3. Place both the potatoes and green beans in a colander and run it under cold water until vegetables are cool. 4. Lay the baby greens on a large platter. 5. Slice the potatoes and arrange them on one section of the platter. Add the green beans to another section of the platter. Slice the hard-boiled eggs and arrange them in another section. 6. Continue with the tomatoes, olives, and mackerel fillets. Pour the dressing over the salad.

Per Serving:
calories: 657 | fat: 47g | protein: 25g | carbs: 38g | fiber: 7g | sodium: 355mg

Mediterranean Spice-Crusted Salmon over White Beans

Prep time: 10 minutes | Cook time: 25 minutes | Serves 6

- ¼ cup olive oil, divided
- 1 large bulb fennel, cored and thinly sliced
- 1 yellow onion, diced
- 2 cloves garlic, minced
- ½ cup white wine
- 3 cans (15 ounces / 425 g each) no-salt-added cannellini beans, drained and rinsed
- 1 (14½-ounce / 411-g) can
- diced fire-roasted tomatoes
- 1 teaspoon Dijon mustard
- ⅛ teaspoon red-pepper flakes
- 1 tablespoon fennel seeds
- 2 teaspoons ground black pepper
- 1 teaspoon kosher salt
- 6 wild salmon fillets (6 ounces / 170 g each)
- ¼ cup thinly sliced basil

1. In a large skillet over medium heat, warm 2 tablespoons of the oil until shimmering. Cook the sliced fennel, onion, and garlic, stirring, until tender, about 8 minutes. Stir in the wine and cook until reduced by half, about 5 minutes. Add the beans and tomatoes and cook, stirring occasionally, to meld all the flavors, about 10 minutes. Stir in the mustard and pepper flakes. 2. Meanwhile, in a small bowl, combine the fennel seeds, black pepper, and salt. Sprinkle all over the salmon fillets. 3. In a large nonstick skillet over medium heat, warm the remaining 2 tablespoons oil. Cook the salmon, skin side up, until golden brown, about 5 minutes. Flip and cook until your desired doneness, about 3 minutes for medium. 4. Stir the basil into the bean mixture just before serving, divide among 6 shallow bowls, and top each with a salmon fillet.

Per Serving:
calories: 488 | fat: 22g | protein: 42g | carbs: 30g | fiber: 9g | sodium: 745mg

Crispy Fish Sticks

Prep time: 15 minutes | Cook time: 10 minutes | Serves 4

- 1 ounce (28 g) pork rinds, finely ground
- ¼ cup blanched finely ground almond flour
- ½ teaspoon Old Bay
- seasoning
- 1 tablespoon coconut oil
- 1 large egg
- 1 pound (454 g) cod fillet, cut into ¾-inch strips

1. Place ground pork rinds, almond flour, Old Bay seasoning, and coconut oil into a large bowl and mix together. In a medium bowl, whisk egg. 2. Dip each fish stick into the egg and then gently press into the flour mixture, coating as fully and evenly as possible. Place fish sticks into the air fryer basket. 3. Adjust the temperature to 400°F (204°C) and air fry for 10 minutes or until golden. 4. Serve immediately.

Per Serving:
calories: 223 | fat: 14g | protein: 21g | carbs: 2g | fiber: 1g | sodium: 390mg

Garlicky Broiled Sardines

Prep time: 5 minutes | Cook time: 3 minutes | Serves 4

- 4 (3¼-ounce / 92-g) cans sardines (about 16 sardines), packed in water or olive oil
- 2 tablespoons extra-virgin olive oil (if sardines are packed in water)
- 4 garlic cloves, minced
- ½ teaspoon red pepper flakes
- ½ teaspoon salt
- ¼ teaspoon freshly ground black pepper

1. Preheat the broiler. Line a baking dish with aluminum foil. Arrange the sardines in a single layer on the foil. 2. Combine the olive oil (if using), garlic, and red pepper flakes in a small bowl and spoon over each sardine. Season with salt and pepper. 3. Broil just until sizzling, 2 to 3 minutes. 4. To serve, place 4 sardines on each plate and top with any remaining garlic mixture that has collected in the baking dish.

Per Serving:
calories: 197 | fat: 11g | protein: 23g | carbs: 1g | fiber: 0g | sodium: 574mg

Shrimp Salad

Prep time: 30 minutes | Cook time: 5 minutes | Serves 4

For the Vinaigrette:
- ⅛ cup red wine vinegar
- Juice of 1 lemon
- 1 small shallot, finely minced
- 1 tablespoon fresh mint, chopped
- ¼ teaspoon dried oregano
- ¼ cup olive oil
- Sea salt and freshly ground pepper, to taste

For the Salad:
- 1 pound (454 g) shrimp, deveined and shelled
- Juice and zest of 1 lemon
- 1 clove garlic, minced
- 2 cups baby spinach leaves
- 1 cup romaine lettuce, chopped
- ½ cup grape tomatoes
- 1 medium cucumber, peeled, seeded, and diced
- ½ cup low-salt olives, pitted
- ¼ cup low-fat feta cheese

Make the vinaigrette: 1. Combine the wine vinegar, lemon juice, shallot, chopped mint, and oregano in a bowl. 2. Add the olive oil, whisking constantly for up to 1 minute, or until you create a smooth emulsion, then season with sea salt and freshly ground pepper. 3. Refrigerate for 1 hour and whisk before serving if separated. Make the salad: 1. Combine the shrimp with the lemon juice and garlic in a shallow bowl or bag. Marinate for at least 2 hours. 2. Grill the shrimp in a grill basket or sauté in a frying pan 2–3 minutes until pink. 3. In a large bowl, toss the greens, tomatoes, cucumber, olives, and feta cheese together. 4. Toss the shrimp with the salad mixture, and drizzle with the vinaigrette. Serve immediately.

Per Serving:
calories: 284 | fat: 18g | protein: 26g | carbs: 6g | fiber: 2g | sodium: 339mg

Seafood Paella

Prep time: 20 minutes | Cook time: 13 minutes | Serves 4

- ½ teaspoon saffron threads
- 2 cups vegetable broth
- 2 tablespoons olive oil
- 1 medium yellow onion, peeled and diced
- 1 cup diced carrot
- 1 medium green bell pepper, seeded and diced
- 1 cup fresh or frozen green peas
- 2 cloves garlic, peeled and minced
- 1 cup basmati rice
- ¼ cup chopped fresh flat-leaf parsley
- ½ pound (227 g) medium shrimp, peeled and deveined
- ½ pound (227 g) mussels, scrubbed and beards removed
- ½ pound (227 g) clams, rinsed
- ¼ teaspoon ground black pepper

1. Add saffron and broth to a medium microwave-safe bowl and stir well. Microwave for 30 seconds on High to just warm broth. Set aside. 2. Press the Sauté button on the Instant Pot® and heat oil. Add onion, carrot, bell pepper, and peas, and cook until they begin to soften, about 5 minutes. Add garlic and rice. Stir until well coated. Add saffron broth and parsley. Press the Cancel button. 3. Close lid, set steam release to Sealing, press the Manual button, and set time to 7 minutes. When the timer beeps, quick-release the pressure until the float valve drops and open lid. Press the Cancel button. 4. Stir rice mixture, then top with shrimp, mussels, and clams. Close lid, set steam release to Sealing, press the Manual button, and set time to 1 minute. When the timer beeps, let pressure release naturally for 10 minutes. Quick-release the remaining pressure until the float valve drops and open lid. Discard any mussels that haven't opened. Season with black pepper before serving.

Per Serving:
calories: 434 | fat: 11g | protein: 33g | carbs: 52g | fiber: 5g | sodium: 633mg

Moroccan Crusted Sea Bass

Prep time: 15 minutes | Cook time: 40 minutes | Serves 4

- 1½ teaspoons ground turmeric, divided
- ¾ teaspoon saffron
- ½ teaspoon ground cumin
- ¼ teaspoon kosher salt
- ¼ teaspoon freshly ground black pepper
- 1½ pounds (680 g) sea bass fillets, about ½ inch thick
- 8 tablespoons extra-virgin olive oil, divided
- 8 garlic cloves, divided (4 minced cloves and 4 sliced)
- 6 medium baby portobello mushrooms, chopped
- 1 large carrot, sliced on an angle
- 2 sun-dried tomatoes, thinly sliced (optional)
- 2 tablespoons tomato paste
- 1 (15-ounce / 425-g) can chickpeas, drained and rinsed
- 1½ cups low-sodium vegetable broth
- ¼ cup white wine
- 1 tablespoon ground coriander (optional)
- 1 cup sliced artichoke hearts marinated in olive oil
- ½ cup pitted kalamata olives
- ½ lemon, juiced
- ½ lemon, cut into thin rounds
- 4 to 5 rosemary sprigs or 2 tablespoons dried rosemary
- Fresh cilantro, for garnish

1. In a small mixing bowl, combine 1 teaspoon turmeric and the saffron and cumin. Season with salt and pepper. Season both sides of the fish with the spice mixture. Add 3 tablespoons of olive oil and work the fish to make sure it's well coated with the spices and the olive oil. 2. In a large sauté pan or skillet, heat 2 tablespoons of olive oil over medium heat until shimmering but not smoking. Sear the top side of the sea bass for about 1 minute, or until golden. Remove and set aside. 3. In the same skillet, add the minced garlic and cook very briefly, tossing regularly, until fragrant. Add the mushrooms, carrot, sun-dried tomatoes (if using), and tomato paste. Cook for 3 to 4 minutes over medium heat, tossing frequently, until fragrant. Add the chickpeas, broth, wine, coriander (if using), and the sliced garlic. Stir in the remaining ½ teaspoon ground turmeric. Raise the heat, if needed, and bring to a boil, then lower heat to simmer. Cover part of the way and let the sauce simmer for about 20 minutes, until thickened. 4. Carefully add the seared fish to the skillet. Ladle a bit of the sauce on top of the fish. Add the artichokes, olives, lemon juice and slices, and rosemary sprigs. Cook another 10 minutes or until the fish is fully cooked and flaky. Garnish with fresh cilantro.

Per Serving:
calories: 696 | fat: 41g | protein: 48g | carbs: 37g | fiber: 9g | sodium: 810mg

Steamed Clams

Prep time: 10 minutes | Cook time: 8 minutes | Serves 4

- 2 pounds (907 g) fresh clams, rinsed
- 1 tablespoon olive oil
- 1 small white onion, peeled and diced
- 1 clove garlic, peeled and quartered
- ½ cup Chardonnay
- ½ cup water

1. Place clams in the Instant Pot® steamer basket. Set aside. 2. Press the Sauté button and heat oil. Add onion and cook until tender, about 3 minutes. Add garlic and cook about 30 seconds. Pour in Chardonnay and water. Insert steamer basket with clams. Press the Cancel button. 3. Close lid, set steam release to Sealing, press the Manual button, and set time to 4 minutes. When the timer beeps, quick-release the pressure until the float valve drops. Open lid. 4. Transfer clams to four bowls and top with a generous scoop of cooking liquid.

Per Serving:
calories: 205 | fat: 6g | protein: 30g | carbs: 7g | fiber: 0g | sodium: 135mg

Salmon with Garlicky Broccoli Rabe and White Beans

Prep time: 20 minutes | Cook time: 10 minutes | Serves 4

- 2 tablespoons extra-virgin olive oil, plus extra for drizzling
- 4 garlic cloves, sliced thin
- ½ cup chicken or vegetable broth
- ¼ teaspoon red pepper flakes
- 1 lemon, sliced ¼ inch thick, plus lemon wedges for serving
- 4 (6-ounce / 170-g) skinless salmon fillets, 1½ inches thick
- ½ teaspoon table salt
- ¼ teaspoon pepper
- 1 pound (454 g) broccoli rabe, trimmed and cut into 1-inch pieces
- 1 (15-ounce / 425-g) can cannellini beans, rinsed

1. Using highest sauté function, cook oil and garlic in Instant Pot until garlic is fragrant and light golden brown, about 3 minutes. Using slotted spoon, transfer garlic to paper towel–lined plate and season with salt to taste; set aside for serving. Turn off Instant Pot, then stir in broth and pepper flakes. 2. Fold sheet of aluminum foil into 16 by 6-inch sling. Arrange lemon slices widthwise in 2 rows across center of sling. Sprinkle flesh side of salmon with salt and pepper, then arrange skinned side down on top of lemon slices. Using sling, lower salmon into Instant Pot; allow narrow edges of sling to rest along sides of insert. Lock lid in place and close pressure release valve. Select high pressure cook function and cook for 3 minutes. 3. Turn off Instant Pot and quick-release pressure. Carefully remove lid, allowing steam to escape away from you. Using sling, transfer salmon to large plate. Tent with foil and let rest while preparing broccoli rabe mixture. 4. Stir broccoli rabe and beans into cooking liquid, partially cover, and cook, using highest sauté function, until broccoli rabe is tender, about 5 minutes. Season with salt and pepper to taste. Gently lift and tilt salmon fillets with

spatula to remove lemon slices. Serve salmon with broccoli rabe mixture and lemon wedges, sprinkling individual portions with garlic chips and drizzling with extra oil.

Per Serving:
calories: 510 | fat: 30g | protein: 43g | carbs: 15g | fiber: 6g | sodium: 650mg

Rosemary Salmon

Prep time: 5 minutes | Cook time: 5 minutes | Serves 4

- 1 cup water
- 4 (4-ounce / 113-g) salmon fillets
- ½ teaspoon salt
- ½ teaspoon ground black pepper
- 1 sprig rosemary, leaves
- stripped off and minced
- 2 tablespoons chopped fresh thyme
- 2 tablespoons extra-virgin olive oil
- 4 lemon wedges

1. Add water to the Instant Pot® and place rack inside. 2. Season fish fillets with salt and pepper. Measure out four pieces of foil large enough to wrap around fish fillets. Lay fish fillets on foil. Top with rosemary and thyme, then drizzle each with olive oil. Carefully wrap loosely in foil. 3. Place foil packets on rack. Close lid, set steam release to Sealing, press the Steam button, and set time to 5 minutes. 4. When the timer beeps, quick-release the pressure until the float valve drops. Press the Cancel button and open lid. Carefully remove packets to plates. Serve immediately with lemon wedges.

Per Serving:
calories: 160 | fat: 8g | protein: 24g | carbs: 0g | fiber: 0g | sodium: 445mg

Wild Cod Oreganata

Prep time: 10 minutes | Cook time: 20 minutes | Serves 2

- 10 ounces (283 g) wild cod (1 large piece or 2 smaller ones)
- ⅓ cup panko bread crumbs
- 1 tablespoon dried oregano
- Zest of 1 lemon
- ½ teaspoon salt
- Pinch freshly ground black
- pepper
- 1 tablespoon olive oil
- 2 tablespoons freshly squeezed lemon juice
- 2 tablespoons white wine
- 1 tablespoon minced fresh parsley

1. Preheat the oven to 350°F(180°C). Place the cod in a baking dish and pat it dry with a paper towel. 2. In a small bowl, combine the panko, oregano, lemon zest, salt, pepper, and olive oil and mix well. Pat the panko mixture onto the fish. 3. Combine the lemon juice and wine in a small bowl and pour it around the fish. 4. Bake the fish for 20 minutes, or until it flakes apart easily and reaches an internal temperature of 145°F(63°C). 5. Garnish with fresh minced parsley.

Per Serving:
calories: 203 | fat: 8g | protein: 23g | carbs: 9g | fiber: 2g | sodium: 149mg

Mediterranean Cod Stew

Prep time: 10 minutes |Cook time: 20 minutes| Serves: 6

- 2 tablespoons extra-virgin olive oil
- 2 cups chopped onion (about 1 medium onion)
- 2 garlic cloves, minced (about 1 teaspoon)
- ¾ teaspoon smoked paprika
- 1 (14½-ounce / 411-g) can diced tomatoes, undrained
- 1 (12-ounce / 340-g) jar roasted red peppers, drained and chopped
- 1 cup sliced olives, green or black
- ⅓ cup dry red wine
- ¼ teaspoon freshly ground black pepper
- ¼ teaspoon kosher or sea salt
- 1½ pounds (680 g) cod fillets, cut into 1-inch pieces
- 3 cups sliced mushrooms (about 8 ounces / 227 g)

1. In a large stockpot over medium heat, heat the oil. Add the onion and cook for 4 minutes, stirring occasionally. Add the garlic and smoked paprika and cook for 1 minute, stirring often. 2. Mix in the tomatoes with their juices, roasted peppers, olives, wine, pepper, and salt, and turn the heat up to medium-high. Bring to a boil. Add the cod and mushrooms, and reduce the heat to medium. 3. Cover and cook for about 10 minutes, stirring a few times, until the cod is cooked through and flakes easily, and serve.

Per Serving:
calories: 209 | fat: 8g | protein: 23g | carbs: 12g | fiber: 4g | sodium: 334mg

Southern Italian Seafood Stew in Tomato Broth

Prep time: 15 minutes | Cook time: 1 hour 20 minutes | Serves 6

- ½ cup olive oil
- 1 fennel bulb, cored and finely chopped
- 2 stalks celery, finely chopped
- 1 medium onion, finely chopped
- 1 tablespoon dried oregano
- ½ teaspoon crushed red pepper flakes
- 1½ pounds (680 g) cleaned squid, bodies cut into ½-inch rings, tentacles halved
- 2 cups dry white wine
- 1 (28-ounce / 794-g) can tomato purée
- 1 bay leaf
- 1 teaspoon salt
- ½ teaspoon freshly ground black pepper
- 1 cup bottled clam juice
- 1 pound (454 g) whole head-on prawns
- 1½ pounds (680 g) mussels, scrubbed
- 1 lemon, cut into wedges, for serving

1. In a large Dutch oven, heat the olive oil over medium-high heat. Add the fennel, celery, onion, oregano, and red pepper flakes and reduce the heat to medium. Cook, stirring occasionally, for about 15 minutes, until the vegetables soften. Stir in the squid, reduce the heat to low, and simmer for 15 minutes. 2. Add the wine to the pot, raise the heat to medium-high, and bring to a boil. Cook, stirring occasionally, until the wine has evaporated. Reduce the heat again to low and add the tomato purée, bay leaf, salt, and pepper. Cook gently, stirring every once in a while, for about 40 minutes, until

the mixture becomes very thick. 3. Stir in 2 cups of water and the clam juice, raise the heat again to medium-high, and bring to a boil. 4. Add the shrimp and mussels and cook, covered, for 5 minutes or so, until the shells of the mussels have opened and the prawns are pink and cooked through. 5. To serve, ladle the seafood and broth into bowls and garnish with the lemon wedges. Serve hot.

Per Serving:
calories: 490 | fat: 23g | protein: 48g | carbs: 22g | fiber: 5g | sodium: 899mg

Paprika-Spiced Fish

Prep time: 5 minutes | Cook time: 10 minutes | Serves 4

- 4 (5-ounce / 142-g) sea bass fillets
- ½ teaspoon salt
- 1 tablespoon smoked
- paprika
- 3 tablespoons unsalted butter
- Lemon wedges

1. Season the fish on both sides with the salt. Repeat with the paprika. 2. Preheat a skillet over high heat. Melt the butter. 3. Once the butter is melted, add the fish and cook for 4 minutes on each side. 4. Once the fish is done cooking, move to a serving dish and squeeze lemon over the top.

Per Serving:
calories: 257 | fat: 34g | protein: 34g | carbs: 1g | fiber: 1g | sodium: 416mg

Red Snapper with Peppers and Potatoes

Prep time: 15 minutes | Cook time: 4 to 6 hours | Serves 4

- 1 pound (454 g) red potatoes, chopped
- 1 green bell pepper, seeded and sliced
- 1 red bell pepper, seeded and sliced
- ½ onion, sliced
- 1 (15-ounce / 425-g) can no-salt-added diced tomatoes
- ⅓ cup whole Kalamata olives, pitted
- 5 garlic cloves, minced
- 1 teaspoon dried thyme
- 1 teaspoon dried rosemary
- Juice of 1 lemon
- Sea salt
- Freshly ground black pepper
- 1½ to 2 pounds (680 to 907 g) fresh red snapper fillets
- 2 lemons, thinly sliced
- ¼ cup chopped fresh parsley

1. In a slow cooker, combine the potatoes, green and red bell peppers, onion, tomatoes, olives, garlic, thyme, rosemary, and lemon juice. Season with salt and black pepper. Stir to mix well. 2. Nestle the snapper into the vegetable mixture in a single layer, cutting it into pieces to fit if needed. Top it with lemon slices. 3. Cover the cooker and cook for 4 to 6 hours on Low heat, or until the potatoes are tender. 4. Garnish with fresh parsley for serving.

Per Serving:
calories: 350 | fat: 5g | protein: 45g | carbs: 41g | fiber: 8g | sodium: 241mg

Trout in Parsley Sauce

Prep time: 10 minutes | Cook time: 3 minutes | Serves 4

- 4 (½-pound / 227-g) river trout, rinsed and patted dry
- ¾ teaspoon salt, divided
- 4 cups torn lettuce leaves, divided
- 1 teaspoon white wine vinegar
- ½ cup water
- ½ cup minced fresh flat-leaf
- parsley
- 1 small shallot, peeled and minced
- 2 tablespoons olive oil mayonnaise
- ½ teaspoon lemon juice
- ¼ teaspoon sugar
- 2 tablespoons toasted sliced almonds

1. Season trout with ½ teaspoon salt inside and out. Put 3 cups lettuce leaves in the bottom of the Instant Pot®. Arrange trout over lettuce and top trout with remaining 1 cup lettuce. Stir vinegar into water and pour into pot. 2. Close lid, set steam release to Sealing, press the Manual button, and set time to 3 minutes. When the timer beeps, quick-release the pressure until the float valve drops and open lid. 3. Use a spatula to move fish to a serving plate. Peel and discard skin from fish. Remove and discard fish heads if desired. 4. In a small bowl, mix together parsley, shallot, mayonnaise, lemon juice, sugar, and remaining ¼ teaspoon salt. Evenly divide among the fish, spreading it over them. Sprinkle toasted almonds over the sauce. Serve immediately.

Per Serving:
calories: 159 | fat: 9g | protein: 15g | carbs: 4g | fiber: 1g | sodium: 860mg

Fish Tagine

Prep time: 25 minutes | Cook time: 12 minutes | Serves 4

- 2 tablespoons extra-virgin olive oil, plus extra for drizzling
- 1 large onion, halved and sliced ¼ inch thick
- 1 pound (454 g) carrots, peeled, halved lengthwise, and sliced ¼ inch thick
- 2 (2-inch) strips orange zest, plus 1 teaspoon grated zest
- ¾ teaspoon table salt, divided
- 2 tablespoons tomato paste
- 4 garlic cloves, minced, divided
- 1¼ teaspoons paprika
- 1 teaspoon ground cumin
- ¼ teaspoon red pepper flakes
- ¼ teaspoon saffron threads, crumbled
- 1 (8-ounce / 227-g) bottle clam juice
- 1½ pounds (680 g) skinless halibut fillets, 1½ inches thick, cut into 2-inch pieces
- ¼ cup pitted oil-cured black olives, quartered
- 2 tablespoons chopped fresh parsley
- 1 teaspoon sherry vinegar

1. Using highest sauté function, heat oil in Instant Pot until shimmering. Add onion, carrots, orange zest strips, and ¼ teaspoon salt, and cook until vegetables are softened and lightly browned, 10 to 12 minutes. Stir in tomato paste, three-quarters of garlic, paprika, cumin, pepper flakes, and saffron and cook until fragrant, about 30 seconds. Stir in clam juice, scraping up any browned bits. 2. Sprinkle halibut with remaining ½ teaspoon salt. Nestle halibut into onion mixture and spoon some of cooking liquid on top of

pieces. Lock lid in place and close pressure release valve. Select high pressure cook function and set cook time for 0 minutes. Once Instant Pot has reached pressure, immediately turn off pot and quick-release pressure. 3. Discard orange zest. Gently stir in olives, parsley, vinegar, grated orange zest, and remaining garlic. Season with salt and pepper to taste. Drizzle extra oil over individual portions before serving.

Per Serving:
calories: 310 | fat: 15g | protein: 34g | carbs: 18g | fiber: 4g | sodium: 820mg

Spicy Tomato Basil Mussels

Prep time: 20 minutes | Cook time: 5½ hours | Serves 4

- 3 tablespoons olive oil
- 4 cloves garlic, minced
- 3 shallot cloves, minced
- 8 ounces (227 g) mushrooms, diced
- 1 (28-ounce / 794-g) can diced tomatoes, with the juice
- ¾ cup white wine
- 2 tablespoons dried oregano
- ½ tablespoon dried basil
- ½ teaspoon black pepper
- 1 teaspoon paprika
- ¼ teaspoon red pepper flakes
- 3 pounds (1.4 kg) mussels

1. In a large sauté pan, heat the olive oil over medium-high heat. Cook the garlic, shallots, and mushrooms for 2 to 3 minutes, until the garlic is just a bit brown and fragrant. Scrape the entire contents of the pan into the slow cooker. 2. Add the tomatoes and white wine to the slow cooker. Sprinkle with the oregano, basil, black pepper, paprika, and red pepper flakes. 3. Cover and cook on low for 4 to 5 hours, or on high for 2 to 3 hours. The mixture is done cooking when mushrooms are fork tender. 4. Clean and debeard the mussels. Discard any open mussels. 5. Increase the heat on the slow cooker to high once the mushroom mixture is done. Add the cleaned mussels to the slow cooker and secure the lid tightly. Cook for 30 more minutes. 6. To serve, ladle the mussels into bowls with plenty of broth. Discard any mussels that didn't open up during cooking. Serve hot, with crusty bread for sopping up the sauce.

Per Serving:
calories: 470 | fat: 19g | protein: 44g | carbs: 24g | fiber: 5g | sodium: 897mg

Oregano Tilapia Fingers

Prep time: 15 minutes | Cook time: 9 minutes | Serves 4

- 1 pound (454 g) tilapia fillet
- ½ cup coconut flour
- 2 eggs, beaten
- ½ teaspoon ground paprika
- 1 teaspoon dried oregano
- 1 teaspoon avocado oil

1. Cut the tilapia fillets into fingers and sprinkle with ground paprika and dried oregano. 2. Then dip the tilapia fingers in eggs and coat in the coconut flour. 3. Sprinkle fish fingers with avocado oil and cook in the air fryer at 370ºF (188ºC) for 9 minutes.

Per Serving:
calories: 187 | fat: 9g | protein: 26g | carbs: 2g | fiber: 1g | sodium: 92mg

Lemon-Oregano Grilled Shrimp

Prep time: 10 minutes | Cook time: 6 minutes | Serves 6

- ½ cup oregano leaves
- 1 clove garlic, minced
- 1 teaspoon finely grated lemon zest
- 3 tablespoons lemon juice
- ¾ teaspoon salt, plus more for seasoning shrimp
- ½ teaspoon freshly ground black pepper, plus more for seasoning shrimp
- ½ cup olive oil, plus 2 tablespoons, divided
- 2½ pounds (1.1 kg) large shrimp, peeled and deveined

1. In a small bowl, stir together the oregano, garlic, lemon zest, lemon juice, salt, and pepper. Whisk in ½ cup of olive oil until well combined. 2. Preheat the grill to high heat. 3. Place the shrimp in a large bowl and toss with the remaining 2 tablespoons of olive oil and a pinch or two of salt and pepper. Thread the shrimp onto skewers, 3 to 5 at a time depending on the size of the shrimp. Place the skewers on the grill and cook for 2 to 3 minutes per side, just until the shrimp are cooked through and just beginning to char. As the shrimp are cooked, transfer the skewers to a serving platter. Spoon the sauce over the skewers and serve immediately.

Per Serving:

calories: 389 | fat: 26g | protein: 36g | carbs: 8g | fiber: 3g | sodium: 530mg

Linguine with Clams and White Wine

Prep time: 20 minutes | Cook time: 12 minutes | Serves 4

- 2 tablespoons olive oil
- 4 cups sliced mushrooms
- 1 medium yellow onion, peeled and diced
- 2 tablespoons chopped fresh oregano
- 3 cloves garlic, peeled and minced
- ¼ teaspoon salt
- ¼ teaspoon ground black pepper
- ½ cup white wine
- 1½ cups water
- 8 ounces (227 g) linguine, broken in half
- 1 pound (454 g) fresh clams, rinsed and purged
- 3 tablespoons lemon juice
- ¼ cup grated Parmesan cheese
- 2 tablespoons chopped fresh parsley

1. Press the Sauté button on the Instant Pot® and heat oil. Add mushrooms and onion. Cook until tender, about 5 minutes. Add oregano, garlic, salt, and pepper, and cook until very fragrant, about 30 seconds. Add wine, water, and pasta, pushing pasta down until submerged in liquid. Press the Cancel button. 2. Top pasta with clams and sprinkle lemon juice on top. Close lid, set steam release to Sealing, press the Manual button, and set time to 5 minutes. When the timer beeps, quick-release the pressure until the float valve drops and open lid. Transfer to a serving bowl and top with cheese and parsley. Serve immediately.

Per Serving:

calories: 486 | fat: 11g | protein: 39g | carbs: 52g | fiber: 5g | sodium: 301mg

Shrimp Foil Packets

Prep time: 15 minutes | Cook time: 4 to 6 hours | Serves 4

- 1½ pounds (680 g) whole raw medium shrimp, peeled, deveined, and divided into 4 (6-ounce / 170-g) portions
- Sea salt
- Freshly ground black pepper
- 2 teaspoons extra-virgin olive oil, divided
- 4 teaspoons balsamic
- vinegar, divided
- 4 garlic cloves, minced
- 1 red onion, cut into chunks
- 1 large zucchini, sliced
- 4 Roma tomatoes, chopped
- 4 teaspoons dried oregano, divided
- Juice of 1 lemon

1. Place a large sheet of aluminum foil on a work surface. Lay one-quarter of the shrimp in the center of the foil and season it with salt and pepper. Drizzle with ½ teaspoon of olive oil and 1 teaspoon of vinegar. 2. Top the shrimp with one-quarter each of the garlic, onion, and zucchini, plus 1 tomato and 1 teaspoon of oregano. Place a second sheet of foil on top of the ingredients. Fold the corners over to seal the packet. 3. Repeat to make 3 more foil packets. Place the packets in a slow cooker in a single layer, or stack them if needed. 4. Cover the cooker and cook for 4 to 6 hours on Low heat. 5. Be careful when serving: Very hot steam will release when you open the foil packets. Drizzle each opened packet with lemon juice for serving.

Per Serving:

calories: 210 | fat: 5g | protein: 30g | carbs: 17g | fiber: 3g | sodium: 187mg

Steamed Cod with Capers and Lemon

Prep time: 10 minutes | Cook time: 3 minutes | Serves 4

- 1 cup water
- 4 (4-ounce / 113-g) cod fillets, rinsed and patted dry
- ½ teaspoon ground black pepper
- 1 small lemon, thinly sliced
- 2 tablespoons extra-virgin olive oil
- ¼ cup chopped fresh parsley
- 2 tablespoons capers
- 1 tablespoon chopped fresh chives

1. Add water to the Instant Pot® and place the rack inside. 2. Season fish fillets with pepper. Top each fillet with three slices of lemon. Place fillets on rack. Close lid, set steam release to Sealing, press the Steam button, and set time to 3 minutes. 3. While fish cooks, combine olive oil, parsley, capers, and chives in a small bowl and mix well. Set aside. 4. When the timer beeps, quick-release the pressure until the float valve drops. Press the Cancel button and open lid. Place cod fillets on a serving platter. Remove and discard lemon slices and drizzle fish with olive oil mixture, making sure each fillet has herbs and capers on top. Serve immediately.

Per Serving:

calories: 140 | fat: 10g | protein: 14g | carbs: 0g | fiber: 0g | sodium: 370mg

Braised Striped Bass with Zucchini and Tomatoes

Prep time: 20 minutes | Cook time: 16 minutes | Serves 4

- 2 tablespoons extra-virgin olive oil, divided, plus extra for drizzling
- 3 zucchini (8 ounces / 227 g each), halved lengthwise and sliced ¼ inch thick
- 1 onion, chopped
- ¾ teaspoon table salt, divided
- 3 garlic cloves, minced
- 1 teaspoon minced fresh oregano or ¼ teaspoon dried
- ¼ teaspoon red pepper flakes
- 1 (28-ounce / 794-g) can whole peeled tomatoes, drained with juice reserved, halved
- 1½ pounds (680 g) skinless striped bass, 1½ inches thick, cut into 2-inch pieces
- ¼ teaspoon pepper
- 2 tablespoons chopped pitted kalamata olives
- 2 tablespoons shredded fresh mint

1. Using highest sauté function, heat 1 tablespoon oil in Instant Pot for 5 minutes (or until just smoking). Add zucchini and cook until tender, about 5 minutes; transfer to bowl and set aside. 2. Add remaining 1 tablespoon oil, onion, and ¼ teaspoon salt to now-empty pot and cook, using highest sauté function, until onion is softened, about 5 minutes. Stir in garlic, oregano, and pepper flakes and cook until fragrant, about 30 seconds. Stir in tomatoes and reserved juice. 3. Sprinkle bass with remaining ½ teaspoon salt and pepper. Nestle bass into tomato mixture and spoon some of cooking liquid on top of pieces. Lock lid in place and close pressure release valve. Select high pressure cook function and set cook time for 0 minutes. Once Instant Pot has reached pressure, immediately turn off pot and quick-release pressure. Carefully remove lid, allowing steam to escape away from you. 4. Transfer bass to plate, tent with aluminum foil, and let rest while finishing vegetables. Stir zucchini into pot and let sit until heated through, about 5 minutes. Stir in olives and season with salt and pepper to taste. Serve bass with vegetables, sprinkling individual portions with mint and drizzling with extra oil.

Per Serving:
calories: 302 | fat: 12g | protein: 34g | carbs: 15g | fiber: 6g | sodium: 618mg

Roasted Red Snapper

Prep time: 5 minutes | Cook time: 45 minutes | Serves 4

- 1 (2 to 2½ pounds / 907 g to 1.1 kg) whole red snapper, cleaned and scaled
- 2 lemons, sliced (about 10 slices)
- 3 cloves garlic, sliced
- 4 or 5 sprigs of thyme
- 3 tablespoons cold salted butter, cut into small cubes, divided

1. Preheat the oven to 350°F(180°C). 2. Cut a piece of foil to about the size of your baking sheet; put the foil on the baking sheet. 3. Make a horizontal slice through the belly of the fish to create a pocket. 4. Place 3 slices of lemon on the foil and the fish on top of the lemons. 5. Stuff the fish with the garlic, thyme, 3 lemon slices and butter. Reserve 3 pieces of butter. 6. Place the reserved 3 pieces of butter on top of the fish, and 3 or 4 slices of lemon on top of the butter. Bring the foil together and seal it to make a pocket around the fish. 7. Put the fish in the oven and bake for 45 minutes. Serve with remaining fresh lemon slices.

Per Serving:
calories: 345 | fat: 13g | protein: 54g | carbs: 12g | fiber: 3g | sodium: 170mg

Almond-Encrusted Salmon

Prep time: 10 minutes | Cook time: 12 minutes | Serves 4

- ¼ cup olive oil
- 1 tablespoon honey
- ¼ cup breadcrumbs
- ½ cup finely chopped almonds, lightly toasted
- ½ teaspoon dried thyme
- Sea salt and freshly ground pepper, to taste
- 4 salmon steaks

1. Preheat the oven to 350°F (180°C). 2. Combine the olive oil with the honey. (Soften the honey in the microwave for 15 seconds, if necessary, for easier blending.) 3. In a shallow dish, combine the breadcrumbs, almonds, thyme, sea salt, and freshly ground pepper. 4. Coat the salmon steaks with the olive oil mixture, then the almond mixture. 5. Place on a baking sheet brushed with olive oil and bake 8–12 minutes, or until the almonds are lightly browned and the salmon is firm.

Per Serving:
calories: 634 | fat: 34g | protein: 69g | carbs: 12g | fiber: 2g | sodium: 289mg

Salmon with Wild Rice and Orange Salad

Prep time: 20 minutes | Cook time: 18 minutes | Serves 4

- 1 cup wild rice, picked over and rinsed
- 3 tablespoons extra-virgin olive oil, divided
- 1½ teaspoon table salt, for cooking rice
- 2 oranges, plus ⅛ teaspoon grated orange zest
- 4 (6-ounce / 170-g) skinless salmon fillets, 1½ inches thick
- 1 teaspoon ground dried Aleppo pepper
- ½ teaspoon table salt
- 1 small shallot, minced
- 1 tablespoon red wine vinegar
- 2 teaspoons Dijon mustard
- 1 teaspoon honey
- 2 carrots, peeled and shredded
- ¼ cup chopped fresh mint

1. Combine 6 cups water, rice, 1 tablespoon oil, and 1½ teaspoons salt in Instant Pot. Lock lid in place and close pressure release valve. Select high pressure cook function and cook for 15 minutes. Turn off Instant Pot and let pressure release naturally for 15 minutes. Quick-release any remaining pressure, then carefully remove lid, allowing steam to escape away from you. Drain rice and set aside to cool slightly. Wipe pot clean with paper towels. 2. Add ½ cup water to now-empty Instant Pot. Fold sheet of aluminum foil into 16 by 6-inch sling. Slice 1 orange ¼ inch thick and shingle widthwise in 3 rows across center of sling. Sprinkle flesh side of salmon with Aleppo pepper and ½ teaspoon salt, then arrange skinned side down on top of orange slices. Using sling, lower salmon into Instant Pot; allow narrow edges of sling to rest along sides of insert. Lock lid in place and close pressure release valve. Select high pressure cook function and cook for 3 minutes. 3. Meanwhile, cut away peel and pith from remaining 1 orange. Quarter orange, then slice crosswise into ¼-inch pieces. Whisk remaining 2 tablespoons oil, shallot, vinegar, mustard, honey, and orange zest together in large bowl. Add rice, orange pieces, carrots, and mint, and gently toss to combine. Season with salt and pepper to taste. 4. Turn off Instant Pot and quick-release pressure. Carefully remove lid, allowing steam to escape away from you. Using sling, transfer salmon to large plate. Gently lift and tilt fillets with spatula to remove orange slices. Serve salmon with salad.

Per Serving:
calories: 690 | fat: 34g | protein: 43g | carbs: 51g | fiber: 5g | sodium: 770mg

Chapter 7

Snacks and Appetizers

Chapter 7 Snacks and Appetizers

Garlic-Lemon Hummus

Prep time: 15 minutes | Cook time: 0 minutes | Serves 6

- 1 (15-ounce / 425-g) can chickpeas, drained and rinsed
- 4 to 5 tablespoons tahini (sesame seed paste)
- 4 tablespoons extra-virgin olive oil, divided
- 2 lemons, juice
- 1 lemon, zested, divided
- 1 tablespoon minced garlic
- Pinch salt

1. In a food processor, combine the chickpeas, tahini, 2 tablespoons of olive oil, lemon juice, half of the lemon zest, and garlic and blend for up to 1 minute. After 30 seconds of blending, stop and scrape the sides down with a spatula, before blending for another 30 seconds. At this point, you've made hummus! Taste and add salt as desired. Feel free to add 1 teaspoon of water at a time to help thin the hummus to a better consistency. 2. Scoop the hummus into a bowl, then drizzle with the remaining 2 tablespoons of olive oil and remaining lemon zest.

Per Serving:
calories: 216 | fat: 15g | protein: 5g | carbs: 17g | fiber: 5g | sodium: 12mg

Shrimp and Chickpea Fritters

Prep time: 5 minutes | Cook time: 10 minutes | Serves 6

- 2 tablespoons olive oil, plus ¼ cup, divided
- ½ small yellow onion, finely chopped
- 12 ounces (340 g) raw medium shrimp, peeled, deveined, and finely chopped
- ¼ cup chickpea flour
- 2 tablespoon all-purpose flour
- 2 tablespoons roughly chopped parsley
- 1 teaspoon baking powder
- ½ teaspoon hot or sweet paprika
- ¾ teaspoon salt, plus additional to sprinkle over finished dish
- ½ lemon

1. Heat 2 tablespoons of the olive oil in a large skillet over medium-high heat. Add the onion and cook, stirring frequently, until softened, about 5 minutes. Using a slotted spoon, transfer the cooked onions to a medium bowl. Add the shrimp, chickpea flour, all-purpose flour, parsley, baking powder, paprika, and salt and mix well. Let sit for 10 minutes. 2. Heat the remaining ¼ cup olive oil in the same skillet set over medium-high heat. When the oil is very hot, add the batter, about 2 tablespoons at a time. Cook for about 2 minutes, until the bottom turns golden and the edges are crisp. Flip over and cook for another minute or two until the second side is golden and crisp. Drain on paper towels. Serve hot, with lemon squeezed over the top. Season with salt just before serving.

Per Serving:
calories: 148 | fat: 6g | protein: 15g | carbs: 9g | fiber: 3g | sodium: 435mg

Stuffed Cucumber Cups

Prep time: 5 minutes | Cook time: 0 minutes | Serves 2

- 1 medium cucumber (about 8 ounces / 227 g, 8 to 9 inches long)
- ½ cup hummus (any flavor) or white bean dip
- 4 or 5 cherry tomatoes, sliced in half
- 2 tablespoons fresh basil, minced

1. Slice the ends off the cucumber (about ½ inch from each side) and slice the cucumber into 1-inch pieces. 2. With a paring knife or a spoon, scoop most of the seeds from the inside of each cucumber piece to make a cup, being careful to not cut all the way through. 3. Fill each cucumber cup with about 1 tablespoon of hummus or bean dip. 4. Top each with a cherry tomato half and a sprinkle of fresh minced basil.

Per Serving:
calories: 135 | fat: 6g | protein: 6g | carbs: 16g | fiber: 5g | sodium: 242mg

Salted Almonds

Prep time: 5 minutes | Cook time: 25 minutes | Makes 1 cup

- 1 cup raw almonds
- 1 egg white, beaten
- ½ teaspoon coarse sea salt

1. Preheat oven to 350ºF (180ºC). 2. Spread the almonds in an even layer on a baking sheet. Bake for 20 minutes until lightly browned and fragrant. 3. Coat the almonds with the egg white and sprinkle with the salt. Put back in the oven for about 5 minutes until they have dried. Cool completely before serving.

Per Serving:
calories: 211 | fat: 18g | protein: 8g | carbs: 8g | fiber: 5g | sodium: 305mg

Crispy Spiced Chickpeas

Prep time: 5 minutes | Cook time: 25 minutes | Serves 6

- 3 cans (15 ounces / 425 g each) chickpeas, drained and rinsed
- 1 cup olive oil
- 1 teaspoon paprika
- ½ teaspoon ground cumin
- ½ teaspoon kosher salt
- ¼ teaspoon ground cinnamon
- ¼ teaspoon ground black pepper

1. Spread the chickpeas on paper towels and pat dry. 2. In a large saucepan over medium-high heat, warm the oil until shimmering. Add 1 chickpea; if it sizzles right away, the oil is hot enough to proceed. 3. Add enough chickpeas to form a single layer in the saucepan. Cook, occasionally gently shaking the saucepan until golden brown, about 8 minutes. With a slotted spoon, transfer to a paper towel–lined plate to drain. Repeat with the remaining chickpeas until all the chickpeas are fried. Transfer to a large bowl. 4. In a small bowl, combine the paprika, cumin, salt, cinnamon, and pepper. Sprinkle all over the fried chickpeas and toss to coat. The chickpeas will crisp as they cool.

Per Serving:

calories: 175 | fat: 9g | protein: 6g | carbs: 20g | fiber: 5g | sodium: 509mg

Goat' S Cheese & Hazelnut Dip

Prep time: 10 minutes | Cook time: 0 minutes | Serves 8

- 2 heads yellow chicory or endive
- Enough ice water to cover

Dip:
- 12 ounces (340 g) soft goat's cheese
- 3 tablespoons extra-virgin olive oil
- 1 tablespoon fresh lemon juice

Topping:
- 2 tablespoons chopped fresh chives
- ¼ cup crushed hazelnuts, pecans, or walnuts

- the leaves
- Pinch of salt

- 1 teaspoon lemon zest (about ½ lemon)
- 1 clove garlic, minced
- Freshly ground black pepper, to taste
- Salt, if needed, to taste

- 1 tablespoon extra-virgin olive oil
- Chile flakes or black pepper, to taste

1. Cut off the bottom of the chicory and trim the leaves to get rid of any that are limp or brown. Place the leaves in salted ice water for 10 minutes. This will help the chicory leaves to become crisp. Drain and leave in the strainer. 2. To make the dip: Place the dip ingredients in a bowl and use a fork or spatula to mix until smooth and creamy. 3. Stir in the chives. Transfer to a serving bowl and top with the crushed hazelnuts, olive oil, and chile flakes. Serve with the crisp chicory leaves. Store in a sealed jar in the fridge for up to 5 days.

Per Serving:

calories: 219 | fat: 18g | protein: 10g | carbs: 5g | fiber: 4g | sodium: 224mg

Manchego Crackers

Prep time: 15 minutes | Cook time: 15 minutes | Makes 40 crackers

- 4 tablespoons butter, at room temperature
- 1 cup finely shredded Manchego cheese
- 1 cup almond flour
- 1 teaspoon salt, divided
- ¼ teaspoon freshly ground black pepper
- 1 large egg

1. Using an electric mixer, cream together the butter and shredded cheese until well combined and smooth. 2. In a small bowl, combine the almond flour with ½ teaspoon salt and pepper. Slowly add the almond flour mixture to the cheese, mixing constantly until the dough just comes together to form a ball. 3. Transfer to a piece of parchment or plastic wrap and roll into a cylinder log about 1½ inches thick. Wrap tightly and refrigerate for at least 1 hour. 4. Preheat the oven to 350°F(180ºC). Line two baking sheets with parchment paper or silicone baking mats. 5. To make the egg wash, in a small bowl, whisk together the egg and remaining ½ teaspoon salt. 6. Slice the refrigerated dough into small rounds, about ¼ inch thick, and place on the lined baking sheets. 7. Brush the tops of the crackers with egg wash and bake until the crackers are golden and crispy, 12 to 15 minutes. Remove from the oven and allow to cool on a wire rack. 8. Serve warm or, once fully cooled, store in an airtight container in the refrigerator for up to 1 week.

Per Serving:

2 crackers: calories: 73 | fat: 7g | protein: 3g | carbs: 1g | fiber: 1g | sodium: 154mg

Flatbread with Ricotta and Orange-Raisin Relish

Prep time: 5 minutes | Cook time: 8 minutes | Serves 4 to 6

- ¾ cup golden raisins, roughly chopped
- 1 shallot, finely diced
- 1 tablespoon olive oil
- 1 tablespoon red wine vinegar
- 1 tablespoon honey
- 1 tablespoon chopped flat-leaf parsley
- 1 tablespoon fresh orange zest strips
- Pinch of salt
- 1 oval prebaked whole-wheat flatbread, such as naan or pocketless pita
- 8 ounces (227 g) whole-milk ricotta cheese
- ½ cup baby arugula

1. Preheat the oven to 450°F(235ºC). 2. In a small bowl, stir together the raisins, shallot, olive oil, vinegar, honey, parsley, orange zest, and salt. 3. Place the flatbread on a large baking sheet and toast in the preheated oven until the edges are lightly browned, about 8 minutes. 4. Spoon the ricotta cheese onto the flatbread, spreading with the back of the spoon. Scatter the arugula over the cheese. Cut the flatbread into triangles and top each piece with a dollop of the relish. Serve immediately.

Per Serving:

calories: 195 | fat: 9g | protein: 6g | carbs: 25g | fiber: 1g | sodium: 135mg

Tirokafteri (Spicy Feta and Yogurt Dip)

Prep time: 10 minutes | Cook time: 0 minutes | Serves 8

- 1 teaspoon red wine vinegar
- 1 small green chili, seeded and sliced
- 2 teaspoons extra virgin
- olive oil
- 9 ounces (255 g) full-fat feta
- ¾ cup full-fat Greek yogurt

1. Combine the vinegar, chili, and olive oil in a food processor. Blend until smooth. 2. In a small bowl, combine the feta and Greek yogurt, and use a fork to mash the ingredients until a paste is formed. Add the pepper mixture and stir until blended. 3. Cover and transfer to the refrigerator to chill for at least 1 hour before serving. Store covered in the refrigerator for up to 3 days.

Per Serving:
calories: 109 | fat: 8g | protein: 6g | carbs: 4g | fiber: 0g | sodium: 311mg

Garlic-Parmesan Croutons

Prep time: 3 minutes | Cook time: 12 minutes | Serves 4

- Oil, for spraying
- 4 cups cubed French bread
- 1 tablespoon grated Parmesan cheese
- 3 tablespoons olive oil
- 1 tablespoon granulated garlic
- ½ teaspoon unsalted salt

1. Line the air fryer basket with parchment and spray lightly with oil. 2. In a large bowl, mix together the bread, Parmesan cheese, olive oil, garlic, and salt, tossing with your hands to evenly distribute the seasonings. Transfer the coated bread cubes to the prepared basket. 3. Air fry at 350ºF (177ºC) for 10 to 12 minutes, stirring once after 5 minutes, or until crisp and golden brown.

Per Serving:
calories: 220 | fat: 12g | protein: 5g | carbs: 23g | fiber: 1g | sodium: 285mg

Baked Eggplant Baba Ganoush

Prep time: 10 minutes | Cook time: 1 hour | Makes about 4 cups

- 2 pounds (907 g, about 2 medium to large) eggplant
- 3 tablespoons tahini
- Zest of 1 lemon
- 2 tablespoons lemon juice
- ¾ teaspoon kosher salt
- ½ teaspoon ground sumac,
- plus more for sprinkling (optional)
- ⅓ cup fresh parsley, chopped
- 1 tablespoon extra-virgin olive oil

1. Preheat the oven to 350ºF (180ºC). Place the eggplants directly on the rack and bake for 60 minutes, or until the skin is wrinkly. 2. In a food processor add the tahini, lemon zest, lemon juice, salt, and sumac. Carefully cut open the baked eggplant and scoop the flesh into the food processor. Process until the ingredients are well blended. 3. Place in a serving dish and mix in the parsley. Drizzle with the olive oil and sprinkle with sumac, if desired.

Per Serving:
calories: 50 | fat: 16g | protein: 4g | carbs: 2g | fiber: 1g | sodium: 110mg

No-Mayo Tuna Salad Cucumber Bites

Prep time: 5 minutes | Cook time: 0 minutes | Serves 3

- 1 (5-ounce / 142-g) can water-packed tuna, drained
- ⅓ cup full-fat Greek yogurt
- ½ teaspoon extra virgin olive oil
- 1 tablespoon finely chopped spring onion (white parts only)
- 1 tablespoon chopped fresh dill
- Pinch of coarse sea salt
- ¼ teaspoon freshly ground black pepper
- 1 medium cucumber, cut into 15 (¼-inch) thick slices
- 1 teaspoon red wine vinegar

1. In a medium bowl, combine the tuna, yogurt, olive oil, spring onion, dill, sea salt, and black pepper. Mix well. 2. Arrange the cucumber slices on a plate and sprinkle the vinegar over the slices. 3. Place 1 heaping teaspoon of the tuna salad on top of each cucumber slice 4. Serve promptly. Store the tuna salad mixture covered in the refrigerator for up to 1 day.

Per Serving:
calories: 80 | fat: 3g | protein: 11g | carbs: 4g | fiber: 1g | sodium: 131mg

Black-Eyed Pea "Caviar"

Prep time: 10 minutes | Cook time: 30 minutes | Makes 5 cups

- 1 cup dried black-eyed peas
- 4 cups water
- 1 pound (454 g) cooked corn kernels
- ½ medium red onion, peeled and diced
- ½ medium green bell pepper, seeded and diced
- 2 tablespoons minced pickled jalapeño pepper
- 1 medium tomato, diced
- 2 tablespoons chopped fresh cilantro
- ¼ cup red wine vinegar
- 2 tablespoons extra-virgin olive oil
- 1 teaspoon salt
- ½ teaspoon ground black pepper
- ½ teaspoon ground cumin

1. Add black-eyed peas and water to the Instant Pot®. Close lid, set steam release to Sealing, press the Manual button, and set time to 30 minutes. 2. When the timer beeps, let pressure release naturally, about 25 minutes, and open lid. Drain peas and transfer to a large mixing bowl. Add all remaining ingredients and stir until thoroughly combined. Cover and refrigerate for 2 hours before serving.

Per Serving:
½ cup: calories: 28 | fat: 1g | protein: 1g | carbs: 4 | fiber: 1g | sodium: 51mg

Garlic Edamame

Prep time: 5 minutes | Cook time: 10 minutes | Serves 4

- Olive oil
- 1 (16-ounce / 454-g) bag frozen edamame in pods
- ½ teaspoon salt
- ½ teaspoon garlic salt
- ¼ teaspoon freshly ground black pepper
- ½ teaspoon red pepper flakes (optional)

1. Spray the air fryer basket lightly with olive oil. 2. In a medium bowl, add the frozen edamame and lightly spray with olive oil. Toss to coat. 3. In a small bowl, mix together the salt, garlic salt, black pepper, and red pepper flakes (if using). Add the mixture to the edamame and toss until evenly coated. 4. Place half the edamame in the air fryer basket. Do not overfill the basket. 5. Air fry at 375°F (191°C) for 5 minutes. Shake the basket and cook until the edamame is starting to brown and get crispy, 3 to 5 more minutes. 6. Repeat with the remaining edamame and serve immediately.

Per Serving:
calories: 125 | fat: 5g | protein: 12g | carbs: 10g | fiber: 5g | sodium: 443mg

Cinnamon-Apple Chips

Prep time: 10 minutes | Cook time: 32 minutes | Serves 4

- Oil, for spraying
- 2 Red Delicious or Honeycrisp apples
- ¼ teaspoon ground cinnamon, divided

1. Line the air fryer basket with parchment and spray lightly with oil. 2. Trim the uneven ends off the apples. Using a mandoline on the thinnest setting or a sharp knife, cut the apples into very thin slices. Discard the cores. 3. Place half of the apple slices in a single layer in the prepared basket and sprinkle with half of the cinnamon. 4. Place a metal air fryer trivet on top of the apples to keep them from flying around while they are cooking. 5. Air fry at 300°F (149°C) for 16 minutes, flipping every 5 minutes to ensure even cooking. Repeat with the remaining apple slices and cinnamon. 6. Let cool to room temperature before serving. The chips will firm up as they cool.

Per Serving:
calories: 63 | fat: 0g | protein: 0g | carbs: 15g | fiber: 3g | sodium: 1mg

Sweet-and-Spicy Nuts

Prep time: 5 minutes | Cook time: 20 minutes | Serves 10 to 12

- Nonstick cooking spray
- Zest and juice of 1 lemon
- 2 tablespoons honey
- 2 teaspoons Berbere or
- baharat spice blend
- 1 teaspoon Aleppo pepper
- 1½ cups cashews
- 1½ cups dry-roasted peanuts

1. Preheat the oven to 375°F (190°C). Line a baking sheet with parchment paper and spray the parchment with cooking spray. 2. Spread the nuts in an even layer over the prepared baking sheet. Bake for 8 to 10 minutes, until fragrant. Remove from the oven and let cool slightly. Keep the oven on. 3. In a small bowl, stir together the lemon zest, lemon juice, honey, Berbere, and Aleppo pepper. 4. Transfer the nuts to a large bowl and pour over the honey-spice mixture. Toss to coat evenly. Return the nut mixture to the baking sheet and spread into an even layer. Bake for 8 to 10 minutes, until the nuts are caramelized. Remove from the oven and let cool completely before serving. 5. Can be stored refrigerated for up to 2 weeks.

Per Serving:
calories: 336 | fat: 27g | protein: 11g | carbs: 17g | fiber: 3g | sodium: 7mg

Black Bean Corn Dip

Prep time: 10 minutes | Cook time: 10 minutes | Serves 4

- ½ (15 ounces / 425 g) can black beans, drained and rinsed
- ½ (15 ounces / 425 g) can corn, drained and rinsed
- ¼ cup chunky salsa
- 2 ounces (57 g) reduced-fat
- cream cheese, softened
- ¼ cup shredded reduced-fat Cheddar cheese
- ½ teaspoon ground cumin
- ½ teaspoon paprika
- Salt and freshly ground black pepper, to taste

1. Preheat the air fryer to 325°F (163°C). 2. In a medium bowl, mix together the black beans, corn, salsa, cream cheese, Cheddar cheese, cumin, and paprika. Season with salt and pepper and stir until well combined. 3. Spoon the mixture into a baking dish. 4. Place baking dish in the air fryer basket and bake until heated through, about 10 minutes. 5. Serve hot.

Per Serving:
calories: 119 | fat: 2g | protein: 8g | carbs: 19g | fiber: 6g | sodium: 469mg

Honey-Rosemary Almonds

Prep time: 5 minutes |Cook time: 10 minutes| Serves: 6

- 1 cup raw, whole, shelled almonds
- 1 tablespoon minced fresh rosemary
- ¼ teaspoon kosher or sea salt
- 1 tablespoon honey
- Nonstick cooking spray

1. In a large skillet over medium heat, combine the almonds, rosemary, and salt. Stir frequently for 1 minute. 2. Drizzle in the honey and cook for another 3 to 4 minutes, stirring frequently, until the almonds are coated and just starting to darken around the edges. 3. Remove from the heat. Using a spatula, spread the almonds onto a pan coated with nonstick cooking spray. Cool for 10 minutes or so. Break up the almonds before serving.

Per Serving:
calories: 149 | fat: 12g | protein: 5g | carbs: 8g | fiber: 3g | sodium: 97mg

Classic Hummus with Tahini

Prep time: 5 minutes | Cook time: 0 minutes | Makes about 2 cups

- 2 cups drained canned chickpeas, liquid reserved
- ½ cup tahini
- ¼ cup olive oil, plus more for garnish
- 2 cloves garlic, peeled, or to taste
- Juice of 1 lemon, plus more as needed
- 1 tablespoon ground cumin
- Salt
- Freshly ground black pepper
- 1 teaspoon paprika, for garnish
- 2 tablespoons chopped flat-leaf parsley, for garnish
- 4 whole-wheat pita bread or flatbread rounds, warmed

1. In a food processor, combine the chickpeas, tahini, oil, garlic, lemon juice, and cumin. Season with salt and pepper, and process until puréed. With the food processor running, add the reserved chickpea liquid until the mixture is smooth and reaches the desired consistency. 2. Spoon the hummus into a serving bowl, drizzle with a bit of olive oil, and sprinkle with the paprika and parsley. 3. Serve immediately, with warmed pita bread or flatbread, or cover and refrigerate for up to 2 days. Bring to room temperature before serving.

Per Serving:
¼ cup: calories: 309 | fat: 16g | protein: 9g | carbs: 36g | fiber: 7g | sodium: 341mg

Whole Wheat Pitas

Prep time: 5 minutes | Cook time: 30 minutes | Makes 8 pitas

- 2 cups whole wheat flour
- 1¼ cups all-purpose flour
- 1¼ teaspoons table salt
- 1¼ cup warm water (105°–110°F)
- 1 (¼-ounce / 7-g) package active dry yeast (2½ teaspoons)
- 1 teaspoon olive oil

1. In the bowl of an electric stand mixer (or a large bowl), whisk together the flours and salt. In a small bowl or glass measuring cup, whisk together the water and yeast until the yeast is dissolved. Let sit until foamy, about 5 minutes. Add the yeast mixture to the flour mixture. Fit the mixer with the dough hook and mix on low (or stir) until it forms a shaggy dough. 2. Increase the speed to medium and knead until the dough is smooth and elastic, 2 to 3 minutes. If kneading by hand, turn the dough out onto a lightly floured work surface and knead about 10 minutes. 3. Form the dough into a ball and return it to the bowl. Pour in the oil, turning the dough to coat. Cover the bowl with a kitchen towel and let the dough rise until doubled in size, about 1 hour. 4. Preheat the oven to 475°F(245ºC). Place a baking sheet on the lowest rack of the oven. 5. When the dough has risen, take it out of the bowl and give it a few gentle kneads. Divide the dough into 8 equal portions and shape into balls. Place on a lightly floured surface and cover with the kitchen towel. 6. Roll out each dough ball to form a 6" circle. Place on the heated baking sheet. Bake until puffed up and beginning to turn color, 6 to 7 minutes. Remove with a metal spatula or tongs and place in a bread basket or on a serving platter. Repeat with the remaining dough balls. 7. To make a pocket in the pita, allow it to cool. Slice off ¼ of the pita from 1 edge, and then carefully insert the knife into the pita to cut the pocket. Gently pull the sides apart to make the pocket larger.

Per Serving:
calories: 181 | fat: 2g | protein: 6g | carbs: 37g | fiber: 4g | sodium: 366mg

Black Olive and Lentil Pesto

Prep time: 10 minutes | Cook time: 20 minutes | Serves 10 to 12

- ¾ cup green lentils, rinsed
- ¼ teaspoon salt
- ½ cup pitted Kalamata olives
- 2 tablespoons fresh Greek oregano
- 2 garlic cloves, minced
- 2 tablespoons coarsely chopped fresh parsley
- 3 tablespoons fresh lemon juice
- 5 tablespoons olive oil

1. Place the lentils in a large saucepan and add cold water to cover by 1 inch. Bring the water to a boil; cover and simmer for 20 minutes, or until the lentils are soft but not disintegrating. Drain and let cool. 2. Shake the colander a few times to remove any excess water, then transfer the lentils to a blender or food processor. Add the salt, olives, oregano, garlic, and parsley. With the machine running, add the lemon juice, then the olive oil, and blend until smooth. 3. Serve with pita chips, pita bread, or as a dip for fresh vegetables.

Per Serving:
1 cup: calories: 70 | fat: 7g | protein: 1g | carbs: 2g | fiber: 1g | sodium: 99mg

Pesto Cucumber Boats

Prep time: 10 minutes | Cook time: 0 minutes | Serves 4 to 6

- 3 medium cucumbers
- ¼ teaspoon salt
- 1 packed cup fresh basil leaves
- 1 garlic clove, minced
- ¼ cup walnut pieces
- ¼ cup grated Parmesan cheese
- ¼ cup extra-virgin olive oil
- ½ teaspoon paprika

1. Cut each cucumber in half lengthwise and again in half crosswise to make 4 stocky pieces. Use a spoon to remove the seeds and hollow out a shallow trough in each piece. Lightly salt each piece and set aside on a platter. 2. In a blender or food processor, combine the basil, garlic, walnuts, Parmesan cheese, and olive oil and blend until smooth. 3. Use a spoon to spread pesto into each cucumber "boat" and sprinkle each with paprika. Serve.

Per Serving:
calories: 143 | fat: 14g | protein: 3g | carbs: 4g | fiber: 1g | sodium: 175mg

Chapter

8

Vegetables and Sides

Chapter 8 Vegetables and Sides

Braised Greens with Olives and Walnuts

Prep time: 5 minutes | Cook time: 20 minutes | Serves 4

- 8 cups fresh greens (such as kale, mustard greens, spinach, or chard)
- 2 to 4 garlic cloves, finely minced
- ½ cup roughly chopped pitted green or black olives
- ½ cup roughly chopped

- shelled walnuts
- ¼ cup extra-virgin olive oil
- 2 tablespoons red wine vinegar
- 1 to 2 teaspoons freshly chopped herbs such as oregano, basil, rosemary, or thyme

1. Remove the tough stems from the greens and chop into bite-size pieces. Place in a large rimmed skillet or pot. 2. Turn the heat to high and add the minced garlic and enough water to just cover the greens. Bring to a boil, reduce the heat to low, and simmer until the greens are wilted and tender and most of the liquid has evaporated, adding more if the greens start to burn. For more tender greens such as spinach, this may only take 5 minutes, while tougher greens such as chard may need up to 20 minutes. Once cooked, remove from the heat and add the chopped olives and walnuts. 3. In a small bowl, whisk together olive oil, vinegar, and herbs. Drizzle over the cooked greens and toss to coat. Serve warm.

Per Serving:
calories: 254 | fat: 25g | protein: 4g | carbs: 6g | fiber: 3g | sodium: 137mg

Caramelized Eggplant with Harissa Yogurt

Prep time: 10 minutes | Cook time: 15 minutes | Serves 2

- 1 medium eggplant (about ¾ pound / 340 g), cut crosswise into ½-inch-thick slices and quartered
- 2 tablespoons vegetable oil
- Kosher salt and freshly ground black pepper, to

- taste
- ½ cup plain yogurt (not Greek)
- 2 tablespoons harissa paste
- 1 garlic clove, grated
- 2 teaspoons honey

1. In a bowl, toss together the eggplant and oil, season with salt and pepper, and toss to coat evenly. Transfer to the air fryer and air fry at 400°F (204°C), shaking the basket every 5 minutes, until the eggplant is caramelized and tender, about 15 minutes. 2. Meanwhile, in a small bowl, whisk together the yogurt, harissa, and garlic, then spread onto a serving plate. 3. Pile the warm eggplant over the yogurt and drizzle with the honey just before serving.

Per Serving:
calories: 247 | fat: 16g | protein: 5g | carbs: 25g | fiber: 8g | sodium: 34mg

Roasted Fennel with Parmesan

Prep time: 5 minutes | Cook time: 30 minutes | Serves 4

- 2 fennel bulbs (about 2 pounds / 907 g), cored and cut into 8 wedges each (reserve fronds for garnish)
- ¼ cup olive oil
- Salt

- Freshly ground black pepper
- 1¼ teaspoons red pepper flakes
- ½ cup freshly grated Parmesan cheese

1. Preheat the oven to 350°F (180°C). 2. Arrange the fennel wedges on a large, rimmed baking sheet and drizzle the oil over the top. 3. Sprinkle each wedge with a pinch each of salt, black pepper, and red pepper flakes. Sprinkle the cheese over the top. 4. Bake in the preheated oven for about 30 minutes, until the fennel is tender and the cheese is golden brown. Remove from the oven and let cool in the oil until just warm. Using a slotted metal spatula, transfer the fennel to plates and garnish with the reserved fennel fronds.

Per Serving:
calories: 237 | fat: 19g | protein: 11g | carbs: 10g | fiber: 4g | sodium: 363mg

Crispy Green Beans

Prep time: 5 minutes | Cook time: 8 minutes | Serves 4

- 2 teaspoons olive oil
- ½ pound (227 g) fresh green beans, ends trimmed

- ¼ teaspoon salt
- ¼ teaspoon ground black pepper

1. In a large bowl, drizzle olive oil over green beans and sprinkle with salt and pepper. 2. Place green beans into ungreased air fryer basket. Adjust the temperature to 350°F (177°C) and set the timer for 8 minutes, shaking the basket two times during cooking. Green beans will be dark golden and crispy at the edges when done. Serve warm.

Per Serving:
calories: 33 | fat: 3g | protein: 1g | carbs: 3g | fiber: 1g | sodium: 147mg

Eggplant Caponata

Prep time: 20 minutes | Cook time: 5 minutes | Serves 8

- ¼ cup extra-virgin olive oil
- ¼ cup white wine
- 2 tablespoons red wine vinegar
- 1 teaspoon ground cinnamon
- 1 large eggplant, peeled and diced
- 1 medium onion, peeled and diced
- 1 medium green bell pepper, seeded and diced
- 1 medium red bell pepper, seeded and diced
- 2 cloves garlic, peeled and minced
- 1 (14½-ounce / 411-g) can diced tomatoes
- 3 stalks celery, diced
- ½ cup chopped oil-cured olives
- ½ cup golden raisins
- 2 tablespoons capers, rinsed and drained
- ½ teaspoon salt
- ½ teaspoon ground black pepper

1. Place all ingredients in the Instant Pot®. Stir well to mix. Close lid, set steam release to Sealing, press the Manual button, and set time to 5 minutes. 2. When the timer beeps, quick-release the pressure until the float valve drops. Open the lid and stir well. Serve warm or at room temperature.

Per Serving:
calories: 90 | fat: 1g | protein: 2g | carbs: 17g | fiber: 4g | sodium: 295mg

Braised Whole Cauliflower with North African Spices

Prep time: 15 minutes | Cook time: 10 minutes | Serves 4

- 2 tablespoons extra-virgin olive oil
- 6 garlic cloves, minced
- 3 anchovy fillets, rinsed and minced (optional)
- 2 teaspoons ras el hanout
- ⅛ teaspoon red pepper flakes
- 1 (28-ounce / 794-g) can whole peeled tomatoes,
- drained with juice reserved, chopped coarse
- 1 large head cauliflower (3 pounds / 1.4 kg)
- ½ cup pitted brine-cured green olives, chopped coarse
- ¼ cup golden raisins
- ¼ cup fresh cilantro leaves
- ¼ cup pine nuts, toasted

1. Using highest sauté function, cook oil, garlic, anchovies (if using), ras el hanout, and pepper flakes in Instant Pot until fragrant, about 3 minutes. Turn off Instant Pot, then stir in tomatoes and reserved juice. 2. Trim outer leaves of cauliflower and cut stem flush with bottom florets. Using paring knife, cut 4-inch-deep cross in stem. Nestle cauliflower stem side down into pot and spoon some of sauce over top. Lock lid in place and close pressure release valve. Select high pressure cook function and cook for 3 minutes. 3. Turn off Instant Pot and quick-release pressure. Carefully remove lid, allowing steam to escape away from you. Using tongs and slotted spoon, transfer cauliflower to serving dish and tent with aluminum foil. Stir olives and raisins into sauce and cook, using highest sauté function, until sauce has thickened slightly, about 5 minutes. Season with salt and pepper to taste. Cut cauliflower into wedges and spoon some of sauce over top. Sprinkle with cilantro and pine nuts. Serve, passing remaining sauce separately.

Per Serving:
calories: 265 | fat: 16g | protein: 8g | carbs: 29g | fiber: 9g | sodium: 319mg

Roasted Asparagus and Fingerling Potatoes with Thyme

Prep time: 5 minutes | Cook time: 20 minutes | Serves 4

- 1 pound (454 g) asparagus, trimmed
- 1 pound (454 g) fingerling potatoes, cut into thin rounds
- 2 scallions, thinly sliced
- 3 tablespoons olive oil
- ¾ teaspoon salt
- ¼ teaspoon freshly ground black pepper
- 1 tablespoon fresh thyme leaves

1. Preheat the oven to 450°F (235°C). 2. In a large baking dish, combine the asparagus, potatoes, and scallions and toss to mix. Add the olive oil, salt, and pepper and toss again to coat all of the vegetables in the oil. Spread the vegetables out in as thin a layer as possible and roast in the preheated oven, stirring once, until the vegetables are tender and nicely browned, about 20 minutes. Just before serving, sprinkle with the thyme leaves. Serve hot.

Per Serving:
calories: 197 | fat: 11g | protein: 5g | carbs: 24g | fiber: 5g | sodium: 449mg

White Beans with Rosemary, Sage, and Garlic

Prep time: 10 minutes | Cook time: 10 minutes | Serves 2

- 1 tablespoon olive oil
- 2 garlic cloves, minced
- 1 (15-ounce / 425-g) can white cannellini beans, drained and rinsed
- ¼ teaspoon dried sage
- 1 teaspoon minced fresh
- rosemary (from 1 sprig) plus 1 whole fresh rosemary sprig
- ½ cup low-sodium chicken stock
- Salt

1. Heat the olive oil in a sauté pan over medium-high heat. Add the garlic and sauté for 30 seconds. 2. Add the beans, sage, minced and whole rosemary, and chicken stock and bring the mixture to a boil. 3. Reduce the heat to medium and simmer the beans for 10 minutes, or until most of the liquid is evaporated. If desired, mash some of the beans with a fork to thicken them. 4. Season with salt. Remove the rosemary sprig before serving

Per Serving:
calories: 155 | fat: 7g | protein: 6g | carbs: 17g | fiber: 8g | sodium: 153mg

Caponata (Sicilian Eggplant)

Prep time: 1 hour 5 minutes | Cook time: 40 minutes | Serves 2

- 3 medium eggplant, cut into ½-inch cubes (about 1½ pounds / 680 g)
- ½ teaspoon fine sea salt
- ¼ cup extra virgin olive oil
- 1 medium onion (red or white), chopped
- 1 tablespoon dried oregano
- ½ cup green olives, pitted and halved
- 2 tablespoons capers, rinsed
- 3 medium tomatoes (about 15 ounces / 425 g), chopped
- 3 tablespoons red wine vinegar
- 2 tablespoons granulated sugar
- Salt to taste
- Freshly ground black pepper to taste
- 2 tablespoons chopped fresh basil
- 1 tablespoon toasted pine nuts (optional)

1. Place the eggplant in a large colander. Sprinkle ½ teaspoon sea salt over the top and set the eggplant aside to rest for about an hour. 2. Add the olive oil to a large pan over medium heat. When the oil starts to shimmer, add the eggplant and sauté until it starts to turn golden brown, about 5 minutes. Add the onions and continue sautéing until the onions become soft. 3. Add the oregano, olives, capers, and tomatoes (with juices) to the pan. Reduce the heat to medium-low and simmer for about 20–25 minutes. 4. While the onions and tomatoes are cooking, combine the vinegar and sugar in a small bowl. Stir until the sugar is completely dissolved, then add the mixture to the pan. Continue cooking for 2–3 more minutes or until you can no longer smell the vinegar and then remove the pan from the heat. 5. Season the mixture to taste with salt and black pepper. Just prior to serving, top each serving with a sprinkle of chopped basil and toasted pine nuts, if using. Store in the refrigerator for up to 3 days.

Per Serving:
calories: 473 | fat: 32g | protein: 6g | carbs: 47g | fiber: 15g | sodium: 702mg

Beet and Watercress Salad with Orange and Dill

Prep time: 20 minutes | Cook time: 8 minutes | Serves 4

- 2 pounds (907 g) beets, scrubbed, trimmed, and cut into ¾-inch pieces
- ½ cup water
- 1 teaspoon caraway seeds
- ½ teaspoon table salt
- 1 cup plain Greek yogurt
- 1 small garlic clove, minced to paste
- 5 ounces (142 g) watercress, torn into bite-size pieces
- 1 tablespoon extra-virgin olive oil, divided, plus extra for drizzling
- 1 tablespoon white wine vinegar, divided
- 1 teaspoon grated orange zest plus 2 tablespoons juice
- ¼ cup hazelnuts, toasted, skinned, and chopped
- ¼ cup coarsely chopped fresh dill
- Coarse sea salt

1. Combine beets, water, caraway seeds, and table salt in Instant Pot. Lock lid in place and close pressure release valve. Select high pressure cook function and cook for 8 minutes. Turn off Instant Pot and quick-release pressure. Carefully remove lid, allowing steam to escape away from you. 2. Using slotted spoon, transfer beets to plate; set aside to cool slightly. Combine yogurt, garlic, and 3 tablespoons beet cooking liquid in bowl; discard remaining cooking liquid. In large bowl toss watercress with 2 teaspoons oil and 1 teaspoon vinegar. Season with table salt and pepper to taste. 3. Spread yogurt mixture over surface of serving dish. Arrange watercress on top of yogurt mixture, leaving 1-inch border of yogurt mixture. Add beets to now-empty large bowl and toss with orange zest and juice, remaining 2 teaspoons vinegar, and remaining 1 teaspoon oil. Season with table salt and pepper to taste. Arrange beets on top of watercress mixture. Drizzle with extra oil and sprinkle with hazelnuts, dill, and sea salt. Serve.

Per Serving:
calories: 240 | fat: 15g | protein: 9g | carbs: 19g | fiber: 5g | sodium: 440mg

Roasted Garlic

Prep time: 5 minutes | Cook time: 20 minutes | Makes 12 cloves

- 1 medium head garlic
- 2 teaspoons avocado oil

1. Remove any hanging excess peel from the garlic but leave the cloves covered. Cut off ¼ of the head of garlic, exposing the tips of the cloves. 2. Drizzle with avocado oil. Place the garlic head into a small sheet of aluminum foil, completely enclosing it. Place it into the air fryer basket. 3. Adjust the temperature to 400°F (204°C) and air fry for 20 minutes. If your garlic head is a bit smaller, check it after 15 minutes. 4. When done, garlic should be golden brown and very soft. 5. To serve, cloves should pop out and easily be spread or sliced. Store in an airtight container in the refrigerator up to 5 days. You may also freeze individual cloves on a baking sheet, then store together in a freezer-safe storage bag once frozen.

Per Serving:
calories: 8 | fat: 1g | protein: 0g | carbs: 0g | fiber: 0g | sodium: 0mg

Toasted Pita Wedges

Prep time: 5 minutes | Cook time: 12 minutes | Makes 32 wedges

- 4 whole-wheat pita rounds
- 1 tablespoon olive oil
- 1 teaspoon garlic powder
- ¼ teaspoon paprika
- Sea salt and freshly ground pepper, to taste

1. Preheat oven to 400°F (205°C). 2. Cut the pita rounds into 8 wedges each, and lay on a parchment-lined baking sheet in an even layer. 3. Drizzle with olive oil, and sprinkle with garlic powder and paprika. Season with sea salt and freshly ground pepper. 4. Bake for 10–12 minutes, until wedges are lightly browned and crisp. Allow to cool completely before serving for crisper wedges.

Per Serving:
4 wedges: calories: 102 | fat: 3g | protein: 3g | carbs: 18g | fiber: 2g | sodium: 142mg

Superflax Tortillas

Prep time: 5 minutes | Cook time: 10 minutes | Serves 6

- 1 packed cup flax meal
- ⅓ cup coconut flour
- ¼ cup ground chia seeds
- 2 tablespoons whole psyllium husks
- 1 teaspoon salt, or to taste
- 1 cup lukewarm water
- 2 tablespoons extra-virgin avocado oil or ghee

1. Place all the dry ingredients in a bowl and mix to combine. (For ground chia seeds, simply place whole seeds into a coffee grinder or food processor and pulse until smooth.) Add the water and mix until well combined. Place the dough in the refrigerator to rest for about 30 minutes. 2. When ready, remove the dough from the fridge and cut it into 4 equal pieces. You will make the remaining 2 tortillas using the excess dough. Place one piece of dough between two pieces of parchment paper and roll it out until very thin. Alternatively, use a silicone roller and a silicone mat. Remove the top piece of parchment paper. Press a large 8-inch (20 cm) lid into the dough (or use a piece of parchment paper cut into a circle of the same size). Press the lid into the dough or trace around it with your knife to cut out the tortilla. 3. Repeat for the remaining pieces of dough. Add the cut-off excess dough to the last piece and create the remaining 2 tortillas from it. If you have any dough left over, simply roll it out and cut it into tortilla-chip shapes. 4. Grease a large pan with the avocado oil and cook 1 tortilla at a time for 2 to 3 minutes on each side over medium heat until lightly browned. Don't overcook: the tortillas should be flexible, not too crispy. 5. Once cool, store the tortillas in a sealed container for up to 1 week and reheat them in a dry pan, if needed.

Per Serving:

calories: 182 | fat: 16g | protein: 4g | carbs: 8g | fiber: 7g | sodium: 396mg

Sicilian-Style Roasted Cauliflower with Capers, Currants, and Crispy Breadcrumbs

Prep time: 10 minutes | Cook time: 55 minutes | Serves 4

- 1 large head of cauliflower (2 pounds / 907 g), cut into 2-inch florets
- 6 tablespoons olive oil, divided
- 1 teaspoon salt
- ½ teaspoon freshly ground black pepper
- 3 garlic cloves, thinly sliced
- 2 tablespoons salt-packed capers, soaked, rinsed, and
- patted dry
- ¾ cup fresh whole-wheat breadcrumbs
- ½ cup chicken broth
- 1 teaspoon anchovy paste
- ⅓ cup golden raisins
- 1 tablespoon white wine vinegar
- 2 tablespoons chopped flat-leaf parsley

1. Preheat the oven to 425°F(220°C). 2. In a medium bowl, toss the cauliflower florets with 3 tablespoons olive oil, and the salt and pepper. Spread the cauliflower out in a single layer on a large, rimmed baking sheet and roast in the preheated oven, stirring occasionally, for about 45 minutes, until the cauliflower is golden brown and crispy at the edges. 3. While the cauliflower is roasting, put the remaining 3 tablespoons of olive oil in a small saucepan and heat over medium-low heat. Add the garlic and cook, stirring, for about 5 minutes, until the garlic begins to turn golden. Stir in the capers and cook for 3 minutes more. Add the breadcrumbs, stir to mix well, and cook until the breadcrumbs turn golden brown and are crisp. Use a slotted spoon to transfer the breadcrumbs to a bowl or plate. 4. In the same saucepan, stir together the broth and anchovy paste and bring to a boil over medium-high heat. Stir in the raisins and vinegar and cook, stirring occasionally, for 5 minutes, until the liquid has mostly been absorbed. 5. When the cauliflower is done, transfer it to a large serving bowl. Add the raisin mixture and toss to mix. Top with the breadcrumbs and serve immediately, garnished with parsley.

Per Serving:

calories: 364 | fat: 22g | protein: 8g | carbs: 37g | fiber: 6g | sodium: 657mg

Garlic and Herb Roasted Grape Tomatoes

Prep time: 10 minutes | Cook time: 45 minutes | Serves 2

- 1 pint grape tomatoes
- 10 whole garlic cloves, skins removed
- ¼ cup olive oil
- ½ teaspoon salt
- 1 fresh rosemary sprig
- 1 fresh thyme sprig

1. Preheat oven to 350°F(180°C). 2. Toss tomatoes, garlic cloves, oil, salt, and herb sprigs in a baking dish. 3. Roast tomatoes until they are soft and begin to caramelize, about 45 minutes. 4. Remove herbs before serving.

Per Serving:

calories: 271 | fat: 26g | protein: 3g | carbs: 12g | fiber: 3g | sodium: 593mg

Glazed Sweet Potato Bites

Prep time: 10 minutes | Cook time: 25 minutes | Serves 4

- Oil, for spraying
- 3 medium sweet potatoes, peeled and cut into 1-inch pieces
- 2 tablespoons honey
- 1 tablespoon olive oil
- 2 teaspoons ground cinnamon

1. Line the air fryer basket with parchment and spray lightly with oil. 2. In a large bowl, toss together the sweet potatoes, honey, olive oil, and cinnamon until evenly coated. 3. Place the potatoes in the prepared basket. 4. Air fry at 400°F (204°C) for 20 to 25 minutes, or until crispy and easily pierced with a fork.

Per Serving:

calories: 149 | fat: 3g | protein: 2g | carbs: 29g | fiber: 4g | sodium: 54mg

Couscous-Stuffed Eggplants

Prep time: 10 minutes | Cook time: 45 minutes | Serves 4

- 2 medium eggplants (about 8 ounces / 227 g each)
- 1 tablespoon olive oil
- ⅓ cup whole-wheat couscous
- 3 tablespoons diced dried apricots
- 4 scallions, thinly sliced
- 1 large tomato, seeded and
- diced
- 2 tablespoons chopped fresh mint leaves
- 1 tablespoon chopped, toasted pine nuts
- 1 tablespoon lemon juice
- ½ teaspoon salt
- ¼ teaspoon freshly ground black pepper

1. Preheat the oven to 400°F (205°C). 2. Halve the eggplants lengthwise and score the cut sides with a knife, cutting all the way through the flesh but being careful not to cut through the skin. Brush the cut sides with the olive oil and place the eggplant halves, cut-side up, on a large, rimmed baking sheet. Roast in the preheated oven for about 20 to 30 minutes, until the flesh is softened. 3. While the eggplant is roasting, place the couscous in a small saucepan or heat-safe bowl and cover with boiling water. Cover and let stand until the couscous is tender and has absorbed the water, about 10 minutes. 4. When the eggplants are soft, remove them from the oven (don't turn the oven off) and scoop the flesh into a large bowl, leaving a bit of eggplant inside the skin so that the skin holds its shape. Be cautious not to break the skin. Chop or mash the eggplant flesh and add the couscous, dried apricots, scallions, tomato, mint, pine nuts, lemon juice, salt, and pepper and stir to mix well. 5. Spoon the couscous mixture into the eggplant skins and return them to the baking sheet. Bake in the oven for another 15 minutes or so, until heated through. Serve hot.

Per Serving:
calories: 146 | fat: 5g | protein: 4g | carbs: 22g | fiber: 6g | sodium: 471mg

Artichokes Provençal

Prep time: 15 minutes | Cook time: 10 minutes | Serves 4

- 4 large artichokes
- 1 medium lemon, cut in half
- 2 tablespoons olive oil
- ½ medium white onion, peeled and sliced
- 4 cloves garlic, peeled and chopped
- 2 tablespoons chopped fresh oregano
- 2 tablespoons chopped fresh basil
- 2 sprigs fresh thyme
- 2 medium tomatoes, seeded and chopped
- ¼ cup chopped Kalamata olives
- ¼ cup red wine
- ¼ cup water
- ¼ teaspoon salt
- ¼ teaspoon ground black pepper

1. Run artichokes under running water, making sure water runs between leaves to flush out any debris. Slice off top ⅓ of artichoke, trim stem, and pull away any tough outer leaves. Rub all cut surfaces with lemon. 2. Press the Sauté button on the Instant Pot® and heat oil. Add onion and cook until just tender, about 2 minutes. Add garlic, oregano, basil, and thyme, and cook until fragrant,

about 30 seconds. Add tomatoes and olives and gently mix, then add wine and water and cook for 30 seconds. Press the Cancel button, then add artichokes cut side down to the Instant Pot®. 3. Close lid, set steam release to Sealing, press the Manual button, and set time to 5 minutes. When the timer beeps, quick-release the pressure until the float valve drops. Open lid and transfer artichokes to a serving platter. Pour sauce over top, then season with salt and pepper. Serve warm.

Per Serving:
calories: 449 | fat: 16g | protein: 20g | carbs: 40g | fiber: 12g | sodium: 762mg

Roasted Cherry Tomato Caprese

Prep time: 15 minutes | Cook time: 30 minutes | Serves 4

- 2 pints (about 20 ounces / 567 g) cherry tomatoes
- 6 thyme sprigs
- 6 garlic cloves, smashed
- 2 tablespoons extra-virgin olive oil
- ½ teaspoon kosher salt
- 8 ounces (227 g) fresh, unsalted Mozzarella, cut into bite-size slices
- ¼ cup basil, chopped or cut into ribbons
- Loaf of crusty whole-wheat bread, for serving

1. Preheat the oven to 350°F (180°C). Line a baking sheet with parchment paper or foil. 2. Put the tomatoes, thyme, garlic, olive oil, and salt into a large bowl and mix together. Place on the prepared baking sheet in a single layer. Roast for 30 minutes, or until the tomatoes are bursting and juicy. 3. Place the Mozzarella on a platter or in a bowl. Pour all the tomato mixture, including the juices, over the Mozzarella. Garnish with the basil. 4. Serve with crusty bread.

Per Serving:
calories: 250 | fat: 17g | protein: 17g | carbs: 9g | fiber: 2g | sodium: 157mg

Lemony Orzo

Prep time: 5 minutes | Cook time: 5 minutes | Yield 2 cups

- 1 cup dry orzo
- 1 cup halved grape tomatoes
- 1 (6-ounce / 170-g) bag baby spinach
- 2 tablespoons extra-virgin
- olive oil
- ¼ teaspoon salt
- Freshly ground black pepper
- ¾ cup crumbled feta cheese
- 1 lemon, juiced and zested

1. Bring a medium pot of water to a boil. Stir in the orzo and cook uncovered for 8 minutes. Drain the water, then return the orzo to medium heat. 2. Add in the tomatoes and spinach and cook until the spinach is wilted. Add the oil, salt, and pepper and mix well. Top the dish with feta, lemon juice, and lemon zest, then toss one or two more times and enjoy!

Per Serving:
½ cup: calories: 273 | fat: 13g | protein: 10g | carbs: 32g | fiber: 6g | sodium: 445mg

Summer Squash Ribbons with Lemon and Ricotta

Prep time: 20 minutes | Cook time: 0 minutes | Serves 4

- 2 medium zucchini or yellow squash
- ½ cup ricotta cheese
- 2 tablespoons fresh mint, chopped, plus additional mint leaves for garnish
- 2 tablespoons fresh parsley, chopped
- Zest of ½ lemon
- 2 teaspoons lemon juice
- ½ teaspoon kosher salt
- ¼ teaspoon freshly ground black pepper
- 1 tablespoon extra-virgin olive oil

1. Using a vegetable peeler, make ribbons by peeling the summer squash lengthwise. The squash ribbons will resemble the wide pasta, pappardelle. 2. In a medium bowl, combine the ricotta cheese, mint, parsley, lemon zest, lemon juice, salt, and black pepper. 3. Place mounds of the squash ribbons evenly on 4 plates then dollop the ricotta mixture on top. Drizzle with the olive oil and garnish with the mint leaves.

Per Serving:
calories: 90 | fat: 6g | protein: 5g | carbs: 5g | fiber: 1g | sodium: 180mg

Barley-Stuffed Cabbage Rolls with Pine Nuts and Currants

Prep time: 15 minutes | Cook time: 2 hours | Serves 4

- 1 large head green cabbage, cored
- 1 tablespoon olive oil
- 1 large yellow onion, chopped
- 3 cups cooked pearl barley
- 3 ounces (85 g) feta cheese, crumbled
- ½ cup dried currants
- 2 tablespoons pine nuts, toasted
- 2 tablespoons chopped fresh flat-leaf parsley
- ½ teaspoon sea salt
- ½ teaspoon black pepper
- ½ cup apple juice
- 1 tablespoon apple cider vinegar
- 1 (15-ounce / 425-g) can crushed tomatoes, with the juice

1. Steam the cabbage head in a large pot over boiling water for 8 minutes. Remove to a cutting board and let cool slightly. 2. Remove 16 leaves from the cabbage head (reserve the rest of the cabbage for another use). Cut off the raised portion of the center vein of each cabbage leaf (do not cut out the vein). 3. Heat the oil in a large nonstick lidded skillet over medium heat. Add the onion, cover, and cook 6 minutes, or until tender. Remove to a large bowl. 4. Stir the barley, feta cheese, currants, pine nuts, and parsley into the onion mixture. Season with ¼ teaspoon of the salt and ¼ teaspoon of the pepper. 5. Place cabbage leaves on a work surface. On 1 cabbage leaf, spoon about ⅓ cup of the barley mixture into the center. Fold in the edges of the leaf over the barley mixture and roll the cabbage leaf up as if you were making a burrito. Repeat for the remaining 15 cabbage leaves and filling. 6. Arrange the cabbage rolls in the slow cooker. 7. Combine the remaining ¼ teaspoon salt, ¼ teaspoon

pepper, the apple juice, apple cider vinegar, and tomatoes. Pour the apple juice mixture evenly over the cabbage rolls. 8. Cover and cook on high 2 hours or on low for 6 to 8 hours. Serve hot.

Per Serving:
calories: 394 | fat: 12g | protein: 12g | carbs: 66g | fiber: 16g | sodium: 560mg

Mini Moroccan Pumpkin Cakes

Prep time: 10 minutes | Cook time: 10 minutes | Serves 6

- 2 cups cooked brown rice
- 1 cup pumpkin purée
- ½ cup finely chopped walnuts
- 3 tablespoons olive oil, divided
- ½ medium onion, diced
- ½ red bell pepper, diced
- 1 teaspoon ground cumin
- Sea salt and freshly ground pepper, to taste
- 1 teaspoon hot paprika or a pinch of cayenne

1. Combine the rice, pumpkin, and walnuts in a large bowl; set aside. 2. In a medium skillet, heat the olive oil over medium heat, add the onion and bell pepper, and cook until soft, about 5 minutes. 3. Add the cumin to the onions and bell peppers. Add onion mixture to the rice mixture. 4. Mix thoroughly and season with sea salt, freshly ground pepper, and paprika or cayenne. 5. In a large skillet, heat 2 tablespoons of olive oil over medium heat. 6. Form the rice mixture into 1-inch patties and add them to the skillet. Cook until both sides are browned and crispy. 7. Serve with Greek yogurt or tzatziki on the side.

Per Serving:
calories: 193 | fat: 12g | protein: 3g | carbs: 20g | fiber: 3g | sodium: 6mg

Maple-Roasted Tomatoes

Prep time: 15 minutes | Cook time: 20 minutes | Serves 2

- 10 ounces (283 g) cherry tomatoes, halved
- Kosher salt, to taste
- 2 tablespoons maple syrup
- 1 tablespoon vegetable oil
- 2 sprigs fresh thyme, stems removed
- 1 garlic clove, minced
- Freshly ground black pepper

1. Place the tomatoes in a colander and sprinkle liberally with salt. Let stand for 10 minutes to drain. 2. Transfer the tomatoes cut-side up to a cake pan, then drizzle with the maple syrup, followed by the oil. Sprinkle with the thyme leaves and garlic and season with pepper. Place the pan in the air fryer and roast at 325ºF (163ºC) until the tomatoes are soft, collapsed, and lightly caramelized on top, about 20 minutes. 3. Serve straight from the pan or transfer the tomatoes to a plate and drizzle with the juices from the pan to serve.

Per Serving:
calories: 139 | fat: 7g | protein: 1g | carbs: 20g | fiber: 2g | sodium: 10mg

Garlic Cauliflower with Tahini

Prep time: 10 minutes | Cook time: 20 minutes | Serves 4

Cauliflower:
- 5 cups cauliflower florets (about 1 large head)
- 6 garlic cloves, smashed and cut into thirds
- 3 tablespoons vegetable oil

- ½ teaspoon ground cumin
- ½ teaspoon ground coriander
- ½ teaspoon kosher salt

Sauce:
- 2 tablespoons tahini (sesame paste)
- 2 tablespoons hot water
- 1 tablespoon fresh lemon

- juice
- 1 teaspoon minced garlic
- ½ teaspoon kosher salt

1. For the cauliflower: In a large bowl, combine the cauliflower florets and garlic. Drizzle with the vegetable oil. Sprinkle with the cumin, coriander, and salt. Toss until well coated. 2. Place the cauliflower in the air fryer basket. Set the air fryer to 400°F (204°C) for 20 minutes, turning the cauliflower halfway through the cooking time. 3. Meanwhile, for the sauce: In a small bowl, combine the tahini, water, lemon juice, garlic, and salt. (The sauce will appear curdled at first, but keep stirring until you have a thick, creamy, smooth mixture.) 4. Transfer the cauliflower to a large serving bowl. Pour the sauce over and toss gently to coat. Serve immediately.

Per Serving:
calories: 176 | fat: 15g | protein: 4g | carbs: 10g | fiber: 4g | sodium: 632mg

Chermoula-Roasted Beets

Prep time: 15 minutes | Cook time: 25 minutes | Serves 4

Chermoula:
- 1 cup packed fresh cilantro leaves
- ½ cup packed fresh parsley leaves
- 6 cloves garlic, peeled
- 2 teaspoons smoked paprika
- 2 teaspoons ground cumin

- 1 teaspoon ground coriander
- ½ to 1 teaspoon cayenne pepper
- Pinch crushed saffron (optional)
- ½ cup extra-virgin olive oil
- Kosher salt, to taste

Beets:
- 3 medium beets, trimmed, peeled, and cut into 1-inch chunks
- 2 tablespoons chopped fresh

- cilantro
- 2 tablespoons chopped fresh parsley

1. For the chermoula: In a food processor, combine the cilantro, parsley, garlic, paprika, cumin, coriander, and cayenne. Pulse until coarsely chopped. Add the saffron, if using, and process until combined. With the food processor running, slowly add the olive oil in a steady stream; process until the sauce is uniform. Season to taste with salt. 2. For the beets: In a large bowl, drizzle the beets with ½ cup of the chermoula, or enough to coat. Arrange the beets in the air fryer basket. Set the air fryer to 375°F (191°C) for 25 to minutes, or until the beets are tender. 3. Transfer the beets to a serving platter. Sprinkle with chopped cilantro and parsley and serve.

Per Serving:
calories: 61 | fat: 2g | protein: 2g | carbs: 9g | fiber: 3g | sodium: 59mg

Rosemary New Potatoes

Prep time: 10 minutes | Cook time: 5 to 6 minutes | Serves 4

- 3 large red potatoes (enough to make 3 cups sliced)
- ¼ teaspoon ground rosemary
- ¼ teaspoon ground thyme

- ⅛ teaspoon salt
- ⅛ teaspoon ground black pepper
- 2 teaspoons extra-light olive oil

1. Preheat the air fryer to 330°F (166°C). 2. Place potatoes in large bowl and sprinkle with rosemary, thyme, salt, and pepper. 3. Stir with a spoon to distribute seasonings evenly. 4. Add oil to potatoes and stir again to coat well. 5. Air fry at 330°F (166°C) for 4 minutes. Stir and break apart any that have stuck together. 6. Cook an additional 1 to 2 minutes or until fork-tender.

Per Serving:
calories: 214 | fat: 3g | protein: 5g | carbs: 44g | fiber: 5g | sodium: 127mg

Mushroom-Stuffed Zucchini

Prep time: 15 minutes | Cook time: 46 minutes | Serves 2

- 2 tablespoons olive oil
- 2 cups button mushrooms, finely chopped
- 2 cloves garlic, finely chopped
- 2 tablespoons chicken broth
- 1 tablespoon flat-leaf

- parsley, finely chopped
- 1 tablespoon Italian seasoning
- Sea salt and freshly ground pepper, to taste
- 2 medium zucchini, cut in half lengthwise

1. Preheat oven to 350°F (180°C). 2. Heat a large skillet over medium heat, and add the olive oil. Add the mushrooms and cook until tender, about 4 minutes. Add the garlic and cook for 2 more minutes. 3. Add the chicken broth and cook another 3–4 minutes. 4. Add the parsley and Italian seasoning, and season with sea salt and freshly ground pepper. 5. Stir and remove from heat. 6. Scoop out the insides of the halved zucchini and stuff with mushroom mixture. 7. Place zucchini in a casserole dish, and drizzle a tablespoon of water or broth in the bottom. 8. Cover with foil and bake for 30–40 minutes until zucchini are tender. Serve immediately.

Per Serving:
calories: 189 | fat: 14g | protein: 5g | carbs: 12g | fiber: 3g | sodium: 335mg

Coriander-Cumin Roasted Carrots

Prep time: 10 minutes | Cook time: 20 minutes | Serves 2

- ½ pound (227 g) rainbow carrots (about 4)
- 2 tablespoons fresh orange juice
- 1 tablespoon honey
- ½ teaspoon coriander
- Pinch salt

1. Preheat oven to 400°F(205°C) and set the oven rack to the middle position. 2. Peel the carrots and cut them lengthwise into slices of even thickness. Place them in a large bowl. 3. In a small bowl, mix together the orange juice, honey, coriander, and salt. 4. Pour the orange juice mixture over the carrots and toss well to coat. 5. Spread carrots onto a baking dish in a single layer. 6. Roast for 15 to 20 minutes, or until fork-tender.

Per Serving:
calories: 85 | fat: 0g | protein: 1g | carbs: 21g | fiber: 3g | sodium: 156mg

Potato Vegetable Hash

Prep time: 20 minutes | Cook time: 5 to 7 hours | Serves 4

- 1½ pounds (680 g) red potatoes, diced
- 8 ounces (227 g) green beans, trimmed and cut into ½-inch pieces
- 4 ounces (113 g) mushrooms, chopped
- 1 large tomato, chopped
- 1 large zucchini, diced
- 1 small onion, diced
- 1 red bell pepper, seeded and chopped
- ⅓ cup low-sodium vegetable broth
- 1 teaspoon sea salt
- ½ teaspoon garlic powder
- ½ teaspoon freshly ground black pepper
- ¼ teaspoon red pepper flakes
- ¼ cup shredded cheese of your choice (optional)

1. In a slow cooker, combine the potatoes, green beans, mushrooms, tomato, zucchini, onion, bell pepper, vegetable broth, salt, garlic powder, black pepper, and red pepper flakes. Stir to mix well. 2. Cover the cooker and cook for 5 to 7 hours on Low heat. 3. Garnish with cheese for serving (if using).

Per Serving:
calories: 183 | fat: 1g | protein: 7g | carbs: 41g | fiber: 8g | sodium: 642mg

Chapter 9
Vegetarian Mains

Chapter 9 Vegetarian Mains

Baked Tofu with Sun-Dried Tomatoes and Artichokes

Prep time: 15 minutes | Cook time: 30 minutes | Serves 4

- 1 (16-ounce / 454-g) package extra-firm tofu, drained and patted dry, cut into 1-inch cubes
- 2 tablespoons extra-virgin olive oil, divided
- 2 tablespoons lemon juice, divided
- 1 tablespoon low-sodium soy sauce or gluten-free tamari
- 1 onion, diced
- ½ teaspoon kosher salt
- 2 garlic cloves, minced
- 1 (14-ounce / 397-g) can artichoke hearts, drained
- 8 sun-dried tomato halves packed in oil, drained and chopped
- ¼ teaspoon freshly ground black pepper
- 1 tablespoon white wine vinegar
- Zest of 1 lemon
- ¼ cup fresh parsley, chopped

1. Preheat the oven to 400°F (205°C). Line a baking sheet with foil or parchment paper. 2. In a bowl, combine the tofu, 1 tablespoon of the olive oil, 1 tablespoon of the lemon juice, and the soy sauce. Allow to sit and marinate for 15 to 30 minutes. Arrange the tofu in a single layer on the prepared baking sheet and bake for 20 minutes, turning once, until light golden brown. 3. Heat the remaining 1 tablespoon olive oil in a large skillet or sauté pan over medium heat. Add the onion and salt; sauté until translucent, 5 to 6 minutes. Add the garlic and sauté for 30 seconds. Add the artichoke hearts, sun-dried tomatoes, and black pepper and sauté for 5 minutes. Add the white wine vinegar and the remaining 1 tablespoon lemon juice and deglaze the pan, scraping up any brown bits. Remove the pan from the heat and stir in the lemon zest and parsley. Gently mix in the baked tofu.

Per Serving:
calories: 230 | fat: 14g | protein: 14g | carbs: 13g | fiber: 5g | sodium: 500mg

Crispy Eggplant Rounds

Prep time: 15 minutes | Cook time: 10 minutes | Serves 4

- 1 large eggplant, ends trimmed, cut into ½-inch slices
- ½ teaspoon salt
- 2 ounces (57 g) Parmesan
- 100% cheese crisps, finely ground
- ½ teaspoon paprika
- ¼ teaspoon garlic powder
- 1 large egg

1. Sprinkle eggplant rounds with salt. Place rounds on a kitchen towel for 30 minutes to draw out excess water. Pat rounds dry. 2. In a medium bowl, mix cheese crisps, paprika, and garlic powder. In a separate medium bowl, whisk egg. Dip each eggplant round in egg, then gently press into cheese crisps to coat both sides. 3. Place eggplant rounds into ungreased air fryer basket. Adjust the temperature to 400°F (204°C) and air fry for 10 minutes, turning rounds halfway through cooking. Eggplant will be golden and crispy when done. Serve warm.

Per Serving:
calories: 113 | fat: 5g | protein: 7g | carbs: 10g | fiber: 4g | sodium: 567mg

Roasted Portobello Mushrooms with Kale and Red Onion

Prep time: 15 minutes | Cook time: 30 minutes | Serves 4

- ¼ cup white wine vinegar
- 3 tablespoons extra-virgin olive oil, divided
- ½ teaspoon honey
- ¾ teaspoon kosher salt, divided
- ¼ teaspoon freshly ground black pepper
- 4 large (4 to 5 ounces / 113 to 142 g each) portobello
- mushrooms, stems removed
- 1 red onion, julienned
- 2 garlic cloves, minced
- 1 (8-ounce / 227-g) bunch kale, stemmed and chopped small
- ¼ teaspoon red pepper flakes
- ¼ cup grated Parmesan or Romano cheese

1. Line a baking sheet with parchment paper or foil. In a medium bowl, whisk together the vinegar, 1½ tablespoons of the olive oil, honey, ¼ teaspoon of the salt, and the black pepper. Arrange the mushrooms on the baking sheet and pour the marinade over them. Marinate for 15 to 30 minutes. 2. Meanwhile, preheat the oven to 400°F (205°C). 3. Bake the mushrooms for 20 minutes, turning over halfway through. 4. Heat the remaining 1½ tablespoons olive oil in a large skillet or ovenproof sauté pan over medium-high heat. Add the onion and the remaining ½ teaspoon salt and sauté until golden brown, 5 to 6 minutes. Add the garlic and sauté for 30 seconds. Add the kale and red pepper flakes and sauté until the kale cooks down, about 5 minutes. 5. Remove the mushrooms from the oven and increase the temperature to broil. 6. Carefully pour the liquid from the baking sheet into the pan with the kale mixture; mix well. 7. Turn the mushrooms over so that the stem side is facing up. Spoon some of the kale mixture on top of each mushroom. Sprinkle 1 tablespoon Parmesan cheese on top of each. 8. Broil until golden brown, 3 to 4 minutes.

Per Serving:
calories: 200 | fat: 13g | protein: 8g | carbs: 16g | fiber: 4g | sodium: 365mg

Beet and Carrot Fritters with Yogurt Sauce

Prep time: 15 minutes | Cook time: 15 minutes | Serves 2

For the Yogurt Sauce :
- ⅓ cup plain Greek yogurt
- 1 tablespoon freshly squeezed lemon juice
- Zest of ½ lemon
- ¼ teaspoon garlic powder
- ¼ teaspoon salt

For the Fritters :
- 1 large carrot, peeled
- 1 small potato, peeled
- 1 medium golden or red beet, peeled
- 1 scallion, minced
- 2 tablespoons fresh minced parsley
- ¼ cup brown rice flour or

- unseasoned bread crumbs
- ¼ teaspoon garlic powder
- ¼ teaspoon salt
- 1 large egg, beaten
- ¼ cup feta cheese, crumbled
- 2 tablespoons olive oil (more if needed)

Make the Yogurt Sauce: 1. In a small bowl, mix together the yogurt, lemon juice and zest, garlic powder, and salt. Set aside. Make the Fritters: 1. Shred the carrot, potato, and beet in a food processor with the shredding blade. You can also use a mandoline with a julienne shredding blade or a vegetable peeler. Squeeze out any moisture from the vegetables and place them in a large bowl. 2. Add the scallion, parsley, rice flour, garlic powder, salt, and egg. Stir the mixture well to combine. Add the feta cheese and stir briefly, leaving chunks of feta cheese throughout. 3. Heat a large nonstick sauté pan over medium-high heat and add 1 tablespoon of the olive oil. 4. Make the fritters by scooping about 3 tablespoons of the vegetable mixture into your hands and flattening it into a firm disc about 3 inches in diameter. 5. Place 2 fritters at a time in the pan and let them cook for about two minutes. Check to see if the underside is golden, and then flip and repeat on the other side. Remove from the heat, add the rest of the olive oil to the pan, and repeat with the remaining vegetable mixture. 6. To serve, spoon about 1 tablespoon of the yogurt sauce on top of each fritter.

Per Serving:
calories: 295 | fat: 14g | protein: 6g | carbs: 44g | fiber: 5g | sodium: 482mg

Cheesy Cauliflower Pizza Crust

Prep time: 15 minutes | Cook time: 11 minutes | Serves 2

- 1 (12 ounces / 340 g) steamer bag cauliflower
- ½ cup shredded sharp Cheddar cheese
- 1 large egg
- 2 tablespoons blanched finely ground almond flour

1 teaspoon Italian blend seasoning

1. Cook cauliflower according to package instructions. Remove from bag and place into cheesecloth or paper towel to remove excess water. Place cauliflower into a large bowl. 2. Add cheese, egg, almond flour, and Italian seasoning to the bowl and mix well. 3. Cut a piece of parchment to fit your air fryer basket. Press cauliflower into 6-inch round circle. Place into the air fryer basket. 4. Adjust the temperature to 360ºF (182ºC) and air fry for 11 minutes.

5. After 7 minutes, flip the pizza crust. 6. Add preferred toppings to pizza. Place back into air fryer basket and cook an additional 4 minutes or until fully cooked and golden. Serve immediately.

Per Serving:
calories: 251 | fat: 17g | protein: 15g | carbs: 12g | fiber: 5g | sodium: 375mg

Vegetable Burgers

Prep time: 10 minutes | Cook time: 12 minutes | Serves 4

- 8 ounces (227 g) cremini mushrooms
- 2 large egg yolks
- ½ medium zucchini, trimmed and chopped
- ¼ cup peeled and chopped
- yellow onion
- 1 clove garlic, peeled and finely minced
- ½ teaspoon salt
- ¼ teaspoon ground black pepper

1. Place all ingredients into a food processor and pulse twenty times until finely chopped and combined. 2. Separate mixture into four equal sections and press each into a burger shape. Place burgers into ungreased air fryer basket. Adjust the temperature to 375ºF (191ºC) and air fry for 12 minutes, turning burgers halfway through cooking. Burgers will be browned and firm when done. 3. Place burgers on a large plate and let cool 5 minutes before serving.

Per Serving:
calories: 50 | fat: 3g | protein: 3g | carbs: 4g | fiber: 1g | sodium: 299mg

One-Pan Mushroom Pasta with Mascarpone

Prep time: 10 minutes | Cook time: 20 minutes | Serves 2

- 2 tablespoons olive oil
- 1 large shallot, minced
- 8 ounces (227 g) baby bella (cremini) mushrooms, sliced
- ¼ cup dry sherry
- 1 teaspoon dried thyme
- 2 cups low-sodium
- vegetable stock
- 6 ounces (170 g) dry pappardelle pasta
- 2 tablespoons mascarpone cheese
- Salt
- Freshly ground black pepper

1. Heat olive oil in a large sauté pan over medium-high heat. Add the shallot and mushrooms and sauté for 10 minutes, or until the mushrooms have given up much of their liquid. 2. Add the sherry, thyme, and vegetable stock. Bring the mixture to a boil. 3. Add the pasta, breaking it up as needed so it fits into the pan and is covered by the liquid. Return the mixture to a boil. Cover, and reduce the heat to medium-low. Let the pasta cook for 10 minutes, or until al dente. Stir it occasionally so it doesn't stick. If the sauce gets too dry, add some water or additional chicken stock. 4. When the pasta is tender, stir in the mascarpone cheese and season with salt and pepper. 5. The sauce will thicken up a bit when it's off the heat.

Per Serving:
calories: 517 | fat: 18g | protein: 16g | carbs: 69g | fiber: 3g | sodium: 141mg

Crustless Spinach Cheese Pie

Prep time: 10 minutes | Cook time: 20 minutes | Serves 4

- 6 large eggs
- ¼ cup heavy whipping cream
- 1 cup frozen chopped
- spinach, drained
- 1 cup shredded sharp Cheddar cheese
- ¼ cup diced yellow onion

1. In a medium bowl, whisk eggs and add cream. Add remaining ingredients to bowl. 2. Pour into a round baking dish. Place into the air fryer basket. 3. Adjust the temperature to 320°F (160°C) and bake for 20 minutes. 4. Eggs will be firm and slightly browned when cooked. Serve immediately.

Per Serving:

calories: 263 | fat: 20g | protein: 18g | carbs: 4g | fiber: 1g | sodium: 321mg

Provençal Ratatouille with Herbed Breadcrumbs and Goat Cheese

Prep time: 10 minutes | Cook time: 1 hour 5 minutes | Serves 4

- 6 tablespoons olive oil, divided
- 2 medium onions, diced
- 2 cloves garlic, minced
- 2 medium eggplants, halved lengthwise and cut into ¾-inch thick half rounds
- 3 medium zucchini, halved lengthwise and cut into ¾-inch thick half rounds
- 2 red bell peppers, seeded and cut into 1½-inch pieces
- 1 green bell pepper, seeded and cut into 1½-inch pieces
- 1 (14-ounce / 397-g) can
- diced tomatoes, drained
- 1 teaspoon salt
- ½ teaspoon freshly ground black pepper
- 8 ounces (227 g) fresh breadcrumbs
- 1 tablespoon chopped fresh parsley
- 1 tablespoon chopped fresh basil
- 1 tablespoon chopped fresh chives
- 6 ounces (170 g) soft, fresh goat cheese

1. Preheat the oven to 375°F(190°C). 2. Heat 5 tablespoons of the olive oil in a large skillet over medium heat. Add the onions and garlic and cook, stirring frequently, until the onions are soft and beginning to turn golden, about 8 minutes. Add the eggplant, zucchini, and bell peppers and cook, turning the vegetables occasionally, for another 10 minutes. Stir in the tomatoes, salt, and pepper and let simmer for 15 minutes. 3. While the vegetables are simmering, stir together the breadcrumbs, the remaining tablespoon of olive oil, the parsley, basil, and chives. 4. Transfer the vegetable mixture to a large baking dish, spreading it out into an even layer. Crumble the goat cheese over the top, then sprinkle the breadcrumb mixture evenly over the top. Bake in the preheated oven for about 30 minutes, until the topping is golden brown and crisp. Serve hot.

Per Serving:

calories: 644 | fat: 37g | protein: 21g | carbs: 63g | fiber: 16g | sodium: 861mg

Turkish Red Lentil and Bulgur Kofte

Prep time: 10 minutes | Cook time: 45 minutes | Serves 4

- ⅓ cup olive oil, plus 2 tablespoons, divided, plus more for brushing
- 1 cup red lentils
- ½ cup bulgur
- 1 teaspoon salt
- 1 medium onion, finely
- diced
- 2 tablespoons tomato paste
- 1 teaspoon ground cumin
- ¼ cup finely chopped flat-leaf parsley
- 3 scallions, thinly sliced
- Juice of ½ lemon

1. Preheat the oven to 400°F(205°C). 2. Brush a large, rimmed baking sheet with olive oil. 3. In a medium saucepan, combine the lentils with 2 cups water and bring to a boil. Reduce the heat to low and cook, stirring occasionally, for about 15 minutes, until the lentils are tender and have soaked up most of the liquid. Remove from the heat, stir in the bulgur and salt, cover, and let sit for 15 minutes or so, until the bulgur is tender. 4. Meanwhile, heat ⅓ cup olive oil in a medium skillet over medium-high heat. Add the onion and cook, stirring frequently, until softened, about 5 minutes. Stir in the tomato paste and cook for 2 minutes more. Remove from the heat and stir in the cumin. 5. Add the cooked onion mixture to the lentil-bulgur mixture and stir to combine. Add the parsley, scallions, and lemon juice and stir to mix well. 6. Shape the mixture into walnut-sized balls and place them on the prepared baking sheet. Brush the balls with the remaining 2 tablespoons of olive oil and bake for 15 to 20 minutes, until golden brown. Serve hot.

Per Serving:

calories: 460 | fat: 25g | protein: 16g | carbs: 48g | fiber: 19g | sodium: 604mg

Tortellini in Red Pepper Sauce

Prep time: 15 minutes | Cook time: 10 minutes | Serves 4

- 1 (16-ounce / 454-g) container fresh cheese tortellini (usually green and white pasta)
- 1 (16-ounce / 454-g) jar
- roasted red peppers, drained
- 1 teaspoon garlic powder
- ¼ cup tahini
- 1 tablespoon red pepper oil (optional)

1. Bring a large pot of water to a boil and cook the tortellini according to package directions. 2. In a blender, combine the red peppers with the garlic powder and process until smooth. Once blended, add the tahini until the sauce is thickened. If the sauce gets too thick, add up to 1 tablespoon red pepper oil (if using). 3. Once tortellini are cooked, drain and leave pasta in colander. Add the sauce to the bottom of the empty pot and heat for 2 minutes. Then, add the tortellini back into the pot and cook for 2 more minutes. Serve and enjoy!

Per Serving:

calories: 350 | fat: 11g | protein: 12g | carbs: 46g | fiber: 4g | sodium: 192mg

Cauliflower Steaks with Olive Citrus Sauce

Prep time: 15 minutes | Cook time: 30 minutes | Serves 4

- 1 or 2 large heads cauliflower (at least 2 pounds / 907 g, enough for 4 portions)
- ⅓ cup extra-virgin olive oil
- ¼ teaspoon kosher salt
- ⅛ teaspoon ground black pepper
- Juice of 1 orange
- Zest of 1 orange
- ¼ cup black olives, pitted and chopped
- 1 tablespoon Dijon or grainy mustard
- 1 tablespoon red wine vinegar
- ½ teaspoon ground coriander

1. Preheat the oven to 400ºF (205ºC). Line a baking sheet with parchment paper or foil. 2. Cut off the stem of the cauliflower so it will sit upright. Slice it vertically into four thick slabs. Place the cauliflower on the prepared baking sheet. Drizzle with the olive oil, salt, and black pepper. Bake for about 30 minutes, turning over once, until tender and golden brown. 3. In a medium bowl, combine the orange juice, orange zest, olives, mustard, vinegar, and coriander; mix well. 4. Serve the cauliflower warm or at room temperature with the sauce.

Per Serving:
calories: 265 | fat: 21g | protein: 5g | carbs: 19g | fiber: 4g | sodium: 310mg

Mushroom Ragù with Parmesan Polenta

Prep time: 20 minutes | Cook time: 30 minutes | Serves 2

- ½ ounce (14 g) dried porcini mushrooms (optional but recommended)
- 2 tablespoons olive oil
- 1 pound (454 g) baby bella (cremini) mushrooms, quartered
- 1 large shallot, minced (about ⅓ cup)
- 1 garlic clove, minced
- 1 tablespoon flour
- 2 teaspoons tomato paste
- ½ cup red wine
- 1 cup mushroom stock (or reserved liquid from soaking the porcini mushrooms, if using)
- ½ teaspoon dried thyme
- 1 fresh rosemary sprig
- 1½ cups water
- ½ teaspoon salt
- ⅓ cup instant polenta
- 2 tablespoons grated Parmesan cheese

1. If using the dried porcini mushrooms, soak them in 1 cup of hot water for about 15 minutes to soften them. When they're softened, scoop them out of the water, reserving the soaking liquid. (I strain it through a coffee filter to remove any possible grit.) Mince the porcini mushrooms. 2. Heat the olive oil in a large sauté pan over medium-high heat. Add the mushrooms, shallot, and garlic, and sauté for 10 minutes, or until the vegetables are wilted and starting to caramelize. 3. Add the flour and tomato paste, and cook for another 30 seconds. Add the red wine, mushroom stock or porcini soaking liquid, thyme, and rosemary. Bring the mixture to a boil, stirring constantly until it thickens. Reduce the heat and let it simmer for 10 minutes. 4. While the mushrooms are simmering, bring the water to a boil in a saucepan and add salt. 5. Add the instant polenta and stir quickly while it thickens. Stir in the Parmesan cheese. Taste and add additional salt if needed.

Per Serving:
calories: 451 | fat: 16g | protein: 14g | carbs: 58g | fiber: 5g | sodium: 165mg

Stuffed Pepper Stew

Prep time: 20 minutes | Cook time: 50 minutes | Serves 2

- 2 tablespoons olive oil
- 2 sweet peppers, diced (about 2 cups)
- ½ large onion, minced
- 1 garlic clove, minced
- 1 teaspoon oregano
- 1 tablespoon gluten-free vegetarian Worcestershire
- sauce
- 1 cup low-sodium vegetable stock
- 1 cup low-sodium tomato juice
- ¼ cup brown lentils
- ¼ cup brown rice
- Salt

1. Heat olive oil in a Dutch oven over medium-high heat. Add the sweet peppers and onion and sauté for 10 minutes, or until the peppers are wilted and the onion starts to turn golden. 2. Add the garlic, oregano, and Worcestershire sauce, and cook for another 30 seconds. Add the vegetable stock, tomato juice, lentils, and rice. 3. Bring the mixture to a boil. Cover, and reduce the heat to medium-low. Simmer for 45 minutes, or until the rice is cooked and the lentils are softened. Season with salt.

Per Serving:
calories: 379 | fat: 16g | protein: 11g | carbs: 53g | fiber: 7g | sodium: 392mg

Mediterranean Pan Pizza

Prep time: 5 minutes | Cook time: 8 minutes | Serves 2

- 1 cup shredded Mozzarella cheese
- ¼ medium red bell pepper, seeded and chopped
- ½ cup chopped fresh
- spinach leaves
- 2 tablespoons chopped black olives
- 2 tablespoons crumbled feta cheese

1. Sprinkle Mozzarella into an ungreased round nonstick baking dish in an even layer. Add remaining ingredients on top. 2. Place dish into air fryer basket. Adjust the temperature to 350ºF (177ºC) and bake for 8 minutes, checking halfway through to avoid burning. Top of pizza will be golden brown and the cheese melted when done. 3. Remove dish from fryer and let cool 5 minutes before slicing and serving.

Per Serving:
calories: 108 | fat: 1g | protein: 20g | carbs: 5g | fiber: 3g | sodium: 521mg

Cauliflower Rice-Stuffed Peppers

Prep time: 10 minutes | Cook time: 15 minutes | Serves 4

- 2 cups uncooked cauliflower rice
- ¾ cup drained canned petite diced tomatoes
- 2 tablespoons olive oil
- 1 cup shredded Mozzarella cheese
- ¼ teaspoon salt
- ¼ teaspoon ground black pepper
- 4 medium green bell peppers, tops removed, seeded

1. In a large bowl, mix all ingredients except bell peppers. Scoop mixture evenly into peppers. 2. Place peppers into ungreased air fryer basket. Adjust the temperature to 350ºF (177ºC) and air fry for 15 minutes. Peppers will be tender and cheese will be melted when done. Serve warm.

Per Serving:
calories: 144 | fat: 7g | protein: 11g | carbs: 11g | fiber: 5g | sodium: 380mg

Pistachio Mint Pesto Pasta

Prep time: 10 minutes | Cook time: 10 minutes | Serves 4

- 8 ounces (227 g) whole-wheat pasta
- 1 cup fresh mint
- ½ cup fresh basil
- ⅓ cup unsalted pistachios, shelled
- 1 garlic clove, peeled
- ½ teaspoon kosher salt
- Juice of ½ lime
- ⅓ cup extra-virgin olive oil

1. Cook the pasta according to the package directions. Drain, reserving ½ cup of the pasta water, and set aside. 2. In a food processor, add the mint, basil, pistachios, garlic, salt, and lime juice. Process until the pistachios are coarsely ground. Add the olive oil in a slow, steady stream and process until incorporated. 3. In a large bowl, mix the pasta with the pistachio pesto; toss well to incorporate. If a thinner, more saucy consistency is desired, add some of the reserved pasta water and toss well.

Per Serving:
calories: 420 | fat: 3g | protein: 11g | carbs: 48g | fiber: 2g | sodium: 150mg

Quinoa Lentil "Meatballs" with Quick Tomato Sauce

Prep time: 25 minutes | Cook time: 45 minutes | Serves 4

For the Meatballs:
- Olive oil cooking spray
- 2 large eggs, beaten
- 1 tablespoon no-salt-added tomato paste
- ½ teaspoon kosher salt
- ½ cup grated Parmesan cheese

For the Tomato Sauce:
- 1 tablespoon extra-virgin olive oil
- 1 onion, minced
- ½ teaspoon dried oregano
- ½ teaspoon kosher salt

- ½ onion, roughly chopped
- ¼ cup fresh parsley
- 1 garlic clove, peeled
- 1½ cups cooked lentils
- 1 cup cooked quinoa

- 2 garlic cloves, minced
- 1 (28-ounce / 794-g) can no-salt-added crushed tomatoes
- ½ teaspoon honey
- ¼ cup fresh basil, chopped

Make the Meatballs: 1. Preheat the oven to 400ºF (205ºC). Lightly grease a 12-cup muffin pan with olive oil cooking spray. 2. In a large bowl, whisk together the eggs, tomato paste, and salt until fully combined. Mix in the Parmesan cheese. 3. In a food processor, add the onion, parsley, and garlic. Process until minced. Add to the egg mixture and stir together. Add the lentils to the food processor and process until puréed into a thick paste. Add to the large bowl and mix together. Add the quinoa and mix well. 4. Form balls, slightly larger than a golf ball, with ¼ cup of the quinoa mixture. Place each ball in a muffin pan cup. Note: The mixture will be somewhat soft but should hold together. 5. Bake 25 to 30 minutes, until golden brown. Make the Tomato Sauce: 6. Heat the olive oil in a large saucepan over medium heat. Add the onion, oregano, and salt and sauté until light golden brown, about 5 minutes. Add the garlic and cook for 30 seconds. 7. Stir in the tomatoes and honey. Increase the heat to high and cook, stirring often, until simmering, then decrease the heat to medium-low and cook for 10 minutes. Remove from the heat and stir in the basil. Serve with the meatballs.

Per Serving:
3 meatballs: calories: 360 | fat: 10g | protein: 20g | carbs: 48g | fiber: 14g | sodium: 520mg

Broccoli-Cheese Fritters

Prep time: 5 minutes | Cook time: 20 to 25 minutes | Serves 4

- 1 cup broccoli florets
- 1 cup shredded Mozzarella cheese
- ¾ cup almond flour
- ½ cup flaxseed meal, divided
- 2 teaspoons baking powder
- 1 teaspoon garlic powder
- Salt and freshly ground black pepper, to taste
- 2 eggs, lightly beaten
- ½ cup ranch dressing

1. Preheat the air fryer to 400ºF (204ºC). 2. In a food processor fitted with a metal blade, pulse the broccoli until very finely chopped. 3. Transfer the broccoli to a large bowl and add the Mozzarella, almond flour, ¼ cup of the flaxseed meal, baking powder, and garlic powder. Stir until thoroughly combined. Season to taste with salt and black pepper. Add the eggs and stir again to form a sticky dough. Shape the dough into 1¼-inch fritters. 4. Place the remaining ¼ cup flaxseed meal in a shallow bowl and roll the fritters in the meal to form an even coating. 5. Working in batches if necessary, arrange the fritters in a single layer in the basket of the air fryer and spray generously with olive oil. Pausing halfway through the cooking time to shake the basket, air fry for 20 to 25 minutes until the fritters are golden brown and crispy. Serve with the ranch dressing for dipping.

Per Serving:

calories: 388 | fat: 30g | protein: 19g | carbs: 14g | fiber: 7g | sodium: 526mg

Parmesan Artichokes

Prep time: 10 minutes | Cook time: 10 minutes | Serves 4

- 2 medium artichokes, trimmed and quartered, center removed
- 2 tablespoons coconut oil
- 1 large egg, beaten
- ½ cup grated vegetarian Parmesan cheese
- ¼ cup blanched finely ground almond flour
- ½ teaspoon crushed red pepper flakes

1. In a large bowl, toss artichokes in coconut oil and then dip each piece into the egg. 2. Mix the Parmesan and almond flour in a large bowl. Add artichoke pieces and toss to cover as completely as possible, sprinkle with pepper flakes. Place into the air fryer basket. 3. Adjust the temperature to 400ºF (204ºC) and air fry for 10 minutes. 4. Toss the basket two times during cooking. Serve warm.

Per Serving:

calories: 207 | fat: 13g | protein: 10g | carbs: 15g | fiber: 5g | sodium: 211mg

Chapter
10

Desserts

Chapter 10 Desserts

Blueberry Pomegranate Granita

Prep time: 5 minutes | Cook time: 10 minutes | Serves 2

- 1 cup frozen wild blueberries
- 1 cup pomegranate or
- pomegranate blueberry juice
- ¼ cup sugar
- ¼ cup water

1. Combine the frozen blueberries and pomegranate juice in a saucepan and bring to a boil. Reduce the heat and simmer for 5 minutes, or until the blueberries start to break down. 2. While the juice and berries are cooking, combine the sugar and water in a small microwave-safe bowl. Microwave for 60 seconds, or until it comes to a rolling boil. Stir to make sure all of the sugar is dissolved and set the syrup aside. 3. Combine the blueberry mixture and the sugar syrup in a blender and blend for 1 minute, or until the fruit is completely puréed. 4. Pour the mixture into an 8-by-8-inch baking pan or a similar-sized bowl. The liquid should come about ½ inch up the sides. Let the mixture cool for 30 minutes, and then put it into the freezer. 5. Every 30 minutes for the next 2 hours, scrape the granita with a fork to keep it from freezing solid. 6. Serve it after 2 hours, or store it in a covered container in the freezer.

Per Serving:
calories: 214 | fat: 0g | protein: 1g | carbs: 54g | fiber: 2g | sodium: 15mg

Baklava and Honey

Prep time: 40 minutes | Cook time: 1 hour | Serves 6 to 8

- 2 cups very finely chopped walnuts or pecans
- 1 teaspoon cinnamon
- 1 cup (2 sticks) of unsalted butter, melted
- 1 (16-ounce / 454-g) package phyllo dough, thawed
- 1 (12-ounce / 340-g) jar honey

1. Preheat the oven to 350°F(180°C). 2. In a bowl, combine the chopped nuts and cinnamon. 3. Using a brush, butter the sides and bottom of a 9-by-13-inch inch baking dish. 4. Remove the phyllo dough from the package and cut it to the size of the baking dish using a sharp knife. 5. Place one sheet of phyllo dough on the bottom of the dish, brush with butter, and repeat until you have 8 layers. 6. Sprinkle ⅓ cup of the nut mixture over the phyllo layers. Top with a sheet of phyllo dough, butter that sheet, and repeat until you have 4 sheets of buttered phyllo dough. 7. Sprinkle ⅓ cup of the nut mixture for another layer of nuts. Repeat the layering of nuts and 4 sheets of buttered phyllo until all the nut mixture is gone. The last layer should be 8 buttered sheets of phyllo. 8. Before you bake, cut the baklava into desired shapes; traditionally this is diamonds, triangles, or squares. 9. Bake the baklava for 1 hour or until the top layer is golden brown. 10. While the baklava is baking, heat the honey in a pan just until it is warm and easy to pour. 11. Once the baklava is done baking, immediately pour the honey evenly over the baklava and let it absorb it, about 20 minutes. Serve warm or at room temperature.

Per Serving:
calories: 1235 | fat: 89g | protein: 18g | carbs: 109g | fiber: 7g | sodium: 588mg

Dried Fruit Compote

Prep time: 15 minutes | Cook time: 8 minutes | Serves 6

- 8 ounces (227 g) dried apricots, quartered
- 8 ounces (227 g) dried peaches, quartered
- 1 cup golden raisins
- 1½ cups orange juice
- 1 cinnamon stick
- 4 whole cloves

1. Place all ingredients in the Instant Pot®. Stir to combine. Close lid, set steam release to Sealing, press the Manual button, and set time to 3 minutes. When the timer beeps, let pressure release naturally, about 20 minutes. Press the Cancel button and open lid. 2. Remove and discard cinnamon stick and cloves. Press the Sauté button and simmer for 5–6 minutes. Serve warm or allow to cool, and then cover and refrigerate for up to a week.

Per Serving:
calories: 258 | fat: 0g | protein: 4g | carbs: 63g | fiber: 5g | sodium: 7mg

Greek Yogurt Ricotta Mousse

Prep time: 1 hour 5 minutes | Cook time: 0 minutes | Serves 4

- 9 ounces (255 g) full-fat ricotta cheese
- 4½ ounces (128 g) 2% Greek yogurt
- 3 teaspoons fresh lemon
- juice
- ½ teaspoon pure vanilla extract
- 2 tablespoons granulated sugar

1. Combine all of the ingredients in a food processor. Blend until smooth, about 1 minute. 2. Divide the mousse between 4 serving glasses. Cover and transfer to the refrigerator to chill for 1 hour before serving. Store covered in the refrigerator for up to 4 days.

Per Serving:
calories: 156 | fat: 8g | protein: 10g | carbs: 10g | fiber: 0g | sodium: 65mg

Light and Lemony Olive Oil Cupcakes

Prep time: 10 minutes | Cook time: 24 minutes | Serves 18

- 2 cups all-purpose flour
- 4 teaspoons baking powder
- 1 cup granulated sugar
- 1 cup extra virgin olive oil
- 2 eggs
- 7 ounces (198 g) 2% Greek
Glaze:
- 1 tablespoon lemon juice
- 5 tablespoons powdered sugar

- yogurt
- 1 teaspoon pure vanilla extract
- 4 tablespoons fresh lemon juice
- Zest of 2 lemons

1. Preheat the oven to 350°F (180°C). Line a 12-cup muffin pan with cupcake liners and then line a second pan with 6 liners. Set aside. 2. In a medium bowl, combine the flour and baking powder. Whisk and set aside. 3. In a large bowl, combine the sugar and olive oil, and mix until smooth. Add the eggs, one at a time, and mix well. Add the Greek yogurt, vanilla extract, lemon juice, and lemon zest. Mix until well combined. 4. Add the flour mixture to the batter, ½ cup at a time, while continuously mixing. 5. Spoon the batter into the liners, filling each liner two-thirds full. Bake for 22–25 minutes or until a toothpick inserted into the center of a cupcake comes out clean. 6. While the cupcakes are baking, make the glaze by combining the lemon juice and powdered sugar in a small bowl. Stir until smooth, then set aside. 7. Set the cupcakes aside to cool in the pans for about 5 minutes, then remove the cupcakes from the pans and transfer to a wire rack to cool completely. 8. Drizzle the glaze over the cooled cupcakes. Store in the refrigerator for up to 4 days.

Per Serving:
calories: 225 | fat: 13g | protein: 3g | carbs: 25g | fiber: 1g | sodium: 13mg

Pomegranate-Quinoa Dark Chocolate Bark

Prep time: 10 minutes |Cook time: 10 minutes| Serves: 6

- Nonstick cooking spray
- ½ cup uncooked tricolor or regular quinoa
- ½ teaspoon kosher or sea salt

- 8 ounces (227 g) dark chocolate or 1 cup dark chocolate chips
- ½ cup fresh pomegranate seeds

1. In a medium saucepan coated with nonstick cooking spray over medium heat, toast the uncooked quinoa for 2 to 3 minutes, stirring frequently. Do not let the quinoa burn. Remove the pan from the stove, and mix in the salt. Set aside 2 tablespoons of the toasted quinoa to use for the topping. 2. Break the chocolate into large pieces, and put it in a gallon-size zip-top plastic bag. Using a metal ladle or a meat pounder, pound the chocolate until broken into smaller pieces. (If using chocolate chips, you can skip this step.) Dump the chocolate out of the bag into a medium, microwave-safe bowl and heat for 1 minute on high in the microwave. Stir until the

chocolate is completely melted. Mix the toasted quinoa (except the topping you set aside) into the melted chocolate. 3. Line a large, rimmed baking sheet with parchment paper. Pour the chocolate mixture onto the sheet and spread it evenly until the entire pan is covered. Sprinkle the remaining 2 tablespoons of quinoa and the pomegranate seeds on top. Using a spatula or the back of a spoon, press the quinoa and the pomegranate seeds into the chocolate. 4. Freeze the mixture for 10 to 15 minutes, or until set. Remove the bark from the freezer, and break it into about 2-inch jagged pieces. Store in a sealed container or zip-top plastic bag in the refrigerator until ready to serve.

Per Serving:
calories: 290 | fat: 17g | protein: 5g | carbs: 29g | fiber: 6g | sodium: 202mg

Fresh Figs with Chocolate Sauce

Prep time: 5 minutes | Cook time: 0 minutes | Serves 4

- ¼ cup honey
- 2 tablespoons cocoa powder

- 8 fresh figs

1. Combine the honey and cocoa powder in a small bowl, and mix well to form a syrup. 2. Cut the figs in half and place cut side up. Drizzle with the syrup and serve.
Per Serving:
calories: 112 | fat: 1g | protein: 1g | carbs: 30g | fiber: 3g | sodium: 3mg

Spiced Baked Pears with Mascarpone

Prep time: 10 minutes | Cook time: 20 minutes | Serves 2

- 2 ripe pears, peeled
- 1 tablespoon plus 2 teaspoons honey, divided
- 1 teaspoon vanilla, divided
- ¼ teaspoon ginger

- ¼ teaspoon ground coriander
- ¼ cup minced walnuts
- ¼ cup mascarpone cheese
- Pinch salt

1. Preheat the oven to 350°F(180ºC) and set the rack to the middle position. Grease a small baking dish. 2. Cut the pears in half lengthwise. Using a spoon, scoop out the core from each piece. Place the pears with the cut side up in the baking dish. 3. Combine 1 tablespoon of honey, ½ teaspoon of vanilla, ginger, and coriander in a small bowl. Pour this mixture evenly over the pear halves. 4. Sprinkle walnuts over the pear halves. 5. Bake for 20 minutes, or until the pears are golden and you're able to pierce them easily with a knife. 6. While the pears are baking, mix the mascarpone cheese with the remaining 2 teaspoons honey, ½ teaspoon of vanilla, and a pinch of salt. Stir well to combine. 7. Divide the mascarpone among the warm pear halves and serve.

Per Serving:
calories: 307 | fat: 16g | protein: 4g | carbs: 43g | fiber: 6g | sodium: 89mg

S' mores

Prep time: 5 minutes | Cook time: 30 seconds | Makes 8 s'mores

- Oil, for spraying
- 8 graham cracker squares
- 2 (1½-ounce / 43-g)
- chocolate bars
- 4 large marshmallows

1. Line the air fryer basket with parchment and spray lightly with oil. 2. Place 4 graham cracker squares in the prepared basket. 3. Break the chocolate bars in half and place 1 piece on top of each graham cracker. Top with 1 marshmallow. 4. Air fry at 370°F (188°C) for 30 seconds, or until the marshmallows are puffed and golden brown and slightly melted. 5. Top with the remaining graham cracker squares and serve.

Per Serving:
calories: 154 | fat: 7g | protein: 2g | carbs: 22g | fiber: 2g | sodium: 75mg

Mascarpone and Fig Crostini

Prep time: 10 minutes | Cook time: 10 minutes | Serves 6 to 8

- 1 long French baguette
- 4 tablespoons (½ stick) salted butter, melted
- 1 (8-ounce / 227-g) tub
- mascarpone cheese
- 1 (12-ounce / 340-g) jar fig jam

1. Preheat the oven to 350°F(180°C). 2. Slice the bread into ¼-inch-thick slices. 3. Arrange the sliced bread on a baking sheet and brush each slice with the melted butter. 4. Put the baking sheet in the oven and toast the bread for 5 to 7 minutes, just until golden brown. 5. Let the bread cool slightly. Spread about a teaspoon or so of the mascarpone cheese on each piece of bread. 6. Top with a teaspoon or so of the jam. Serve immediately.

Per Serving:
calories: 445 | fat: 24g | protein: 3g | carbs: 48g | fiber: 5g | sodium: 314mg

Honey-Vanilla Apple Pie with Olive Oil Crust

Prep time: 10 minutes | Cook time: 45 minutes | Serves 8

For the crust:
- ¼ cup olive oil
- 1½ cups whole-wheat flour

For the filling:
- 4 large apples of your choice, peeled, cored, and sliced
- Juice of 1 lemon
- 1 tablespoon pure vanilla

- ½ teaspoon sea salt
- 2 tablespoons ice water

- extract
- 1 tablespoon honey
- ½ teaspoon sea salt
- Olive oil

Make the crust: 1. Put the olive oil, flour, and sea salt in a food processor and process until dough forms. 2. Slowly add the water

and pulse until you have a stiff dough. 3. Form the dough into 2 equal-sized balls, wrap in plastic wrap, and put in the refrigerator while you make the filling. Make the filling: 1. Combine the apples, lemon juice, vanilla, honey, and sea salt in a large bowl. 2. Stir and allow to sit for at least 10 minutes. Preheat oven to 400°F (205°C). 3. Roll 1 crust out on a lightly floured surface. Transfer to a 9-inch pie plate and top with filling. 4. Roll the other ball of dough out and put on top of the pie. Cut a few slices in the top to vent the pie, and lightly brush the top of the pie with olive oil. 5. Bake for 45 minutes, or until top is browned and apples are bubbly. 6. Allow to cool completely before slicing and serving with your favorite frozen yogurt.

Per Serving:
calories: 208 | fat: 8g | protein: 3g | carbs: 34g | fiber: 5g | sodium: 293mg

Grilled Stone Fruit

Prep time: 15 minutes | Cook time: 6 minutes | Serves 2

- 2 peaches, halved and pitted
- 2 plums, halved and pitted
- 3 apricots, halved and pitted
- ½ cup low-fat ricotta cheese
- 2 tablespoons honey

1. Heat grill to medium heat. 2. Oil the grates or spray with cooking spray. 3. Place the fruit cut side down on the grill, and grill for 2–3 minutes per side, until lightly charred and soft. 4. Serve warm with the ricotta and drizzle with honey.

Per Serving:
calories: 263 | fat: 6g | protein: 10g | carbs: 48g | fiber: 4g | sodium: 63mg

Roasted Honey-Cinnamon Apples

Prep time: 15 minutes | Cook time: 20 minutes | Serves 2

- 1 teaspoon extra-virgin olive oil
- 4 firm apples, peeled, cored, and sliced
- ½ teaspoon salt
- 1½ teaspoons ground cinnamon, divided
- 2 tablespoons low-fat milk
- 2 tablespoons honey

1. Preheat the oven to 375°F(190°C). Grease a small casserole dish with the olive oil. 2. In a medium bowl, toss the apple slices with the salt and ½ teaspoon of the cinnamon. Spread the apples in the baking dish and bake for 20 minutes. 3. Meanwhile, in a small saucepan, heat the milk, honey, and remaining 1 teaspoon cinnamon over medium heat, stirring frequently. When it reaches a simmer, remove the pan from the heat and cover to keep warm. 4. Divide the apple slices between 2 dessert plates and pour the sauce over the apples. Serve warm.

Per Serving:
calories: 285 | fat: 3g | protein: 2g | carbs: 70g | fiber: 10g | sodium: 593mg

Date and Honey Almond Milk Ice Cream

Prep time: 10 minutes | Cook time: 5 minutes | Serves 4

- ¾ cup (about 4 ounces/ 113 g) pitted dates
- ¼ cup honey
- ½ cup water
- 2 cups cold unsweetened almond milk
- 2 teaspoons vanilla extract

1. Combine the dates and water in a small saucepan and bring to a boil over high heat. Remove the pan from the heat, cover, and let stand for 15 minutes. 2. In a blender, combine the almond milk, dates, the date soaking water, honey, and the vanilla and process until very smooth. 3. Cover the blender jar and refrigerate the mixture until cold, at least 1 hour. 4. Transfer the mixture to an electric ice cream maker and freeze according to the manufacturer's instructions. 5. Serve immediately or transfer to a freezer-safe storage container and freeze for 4 hours (or longer). Serve frozen.

Per Serving:
calories: 106 | fat: 2g | protein: 1g | carbs: 23g | fiber: 3g | sodium: 92mg

Crispy Apple Phyllo Tart

Prep time: 15 minutes | Cook time: 30 minutes | Serves 4

- 5 teaspoons extra virgin olive oil
- 2 teaspoons fresh lemon juice
- ¼ teaspoon ground cinnamon
- 1½ teaspoons granulated sugar, divided
- 1 large apple (any variety), peeled and cut into ⅛-inch thick slices
- 5 phyllo sheets, defrosted
- 1 teaspoon all-purpose flour
- 1½ teaspoons apricot jam

1. Preheat the oven to 350°F (180°C). Line a baking sheet with parchment paper, and pour the olive oil into a small dish. Set aside. 2. In a separate small bowl, combine the lemon juice, cinnamon, 1 teaspoon of the sugar, and the apple slices. Mix well to ensure the apple slices are coated in the seasonings. Set aside. 3. On a clean working surface, stack the phyllo sheets one on top of the other. Place a large bowl with an approximate diameter of 15 inches on top of the sheets, then draw a sharp knife around the edge of the bowl to cut out a circle through all 5 sheets. Discard the remaining phyllo. 4. Working quickly, place the first sheet on the lined baking sheet and then brush with the olive oil. Repeat the process by placing a second sheet on top of the first sheet, then brushing the second sheet with olive oil. Repeat until all the phyllo sheets are in a single stack. 5. Sprinkle the flour and remaining sugar over the top of the sheets. Arrange the apples in overlapping circles 4 inches from the edge of the phyllo. 6. Fold the edges of the phyllo in and then twist them all around the apple filling to form a crust edge. Brush the edge with the remaining olive oil. Bake for 30 minutes or until the crust is golden and the apples are browned on the edges. 7. While the tart is baking, heat the apricot jam in a small sauce pan over low heat until it's melted. 8. When the tart is done baking, brush the apples with the jam sauce. Slice the tart into 4 equal servings and serve warm. Store at room temperature, covered in plastic wrap, for up to 2 days.

Per Serving:
calories: 165 | fat: 7g | protein: 2g | carbs: 24g | fiber: 2g | sodium: 116mg

Honey Ricotta with Espresso and Chocolate Chips

Prep time: 5 minutes | Cook time: 0 minutes | Serves 2

- 8 ounces (227 g) ricotta cheese
- 2 tablespoons honey
- 2 tablespoons espresso,
- chilled or room temperature
- 1 teaspoon dark chocolate chips or chocolate shavings

1. In a medium bowl, whip together the ricotta cheese and honey until light and smooth, 4 to 5 minutes. 2. Spoon the ricotta cheese-honey mixture evenly into 2 dessert bowls. Drizzle 1 tablespoon espresso into each dish and sprinkle with chocolate chips or shavings.

Per Serving:
calories: 235 | fat: 10g | protein: 13g | carbs: 25g | fiber: 0g | sodium: 115mg

Tortilla Fried Pies

Prep time: 10 minutes | Cook time: 5 minutes per batch | Makes 12 pies

- 12 small flour tortillas (4-inch diameter)
- ½ cup fig preserves
- ¼ cup sliced almonds
- 2 tablespoons shredded, unsweetened coconut
- Oil for misting or cooking spray

1. Wrap refrigerated tortillas in damp paper towels and heat in microwave 30 seconds to warm. 2. Working with one tortilla at a time, place 2 teaspoons fig preserves, 1 teaspoon sliced almonds, and ½ teaspoon coconut in the center of each. 3. Moisten outer edges of tortilla all around. 4. Fold one side of tortilla over filling to make a half-moon shape and press down lightly on center. Using the tines of a fork, press down firmly on edges of tortilla to seal in filling. 5. Mist both sides with oil or cooking spray. 6. Place hand pies in air fryer basket close but not overlapping. It's fine to lean some against the sides and corners of the basket. You may need to cook in 2 batches. 7. Air fry at 390ºF (199ºC) for 5 minutes or until lightly browned. Serve hot. 8. Refrigerate any leftover pies in a closed container. To serve later, toss them back in the air fryer basket and cook for 2 or 3 minutes to reheat.

Per Serving:
1 pie: calories: 137 | fat: 4g | protein: 4g | carbs: 22g | fiber: 2g | sodium: 279mg

Cinnamon-Stewed Dried Plums with Greek Yogurt

Prep time: 5 minutes | Cook time: 3 minutes | Serves 6

- 3 cups dried plums
- 2 cups water
- 2 tablespoons sugar

- 2 cinnamon sticks
- 3 cups low-fat plain Greek yogurt

1. Add dried plums, water, sugar, and cinnamon to the Instant Pot®. Close lid, set steam release to Sealing, press the Manual button, and set time to 3 minutes. 2. When the timer beeps, quick-release the pressure until the float valve drops. Press the Cancel button and open lid. Remove and discard cinnamon sticks. Serve warm over Greek yogurt.

Per Serving:

calories: 301 | fat: 2g | protein: 14g | carbs: 61g | fiber: 4g | sodium: 50mg

Poached Apricots and Pistachios with Greek Yogurt

Prep time: 2 minutes | Cook time: 18 minutes | Serves 4

- ½ cup orange juice
- 2 tablespoons brandy
- 2 tablespoons honey
- ¾ cup water
- 1 cinnamon stick

- 12 dried apricots
- ⅓ cup 2% Greek yogurt
- 2 tablespoons mascarpone cheese
- 2 tablespoons shelled pistachios

1. Place a saucepan over medium heat and add the orange juice, brandy, honey, and water. Stir to combine, then add the cinnamon stick. 2. Once the honey has dissolved, add the apricots. Bring the mixture to a boil, then cover, reduce the heat to low, and simmer for 15 minutes. 3. While the apricots are simmering, combine the Greek yogurt and mascarpone cheese in a small serving bowl. Stir until smooth, then set aside. 4. When the cooking time for the apricots is complete, uncover, add the pistachios, and continue simmering for 3 more minutes. Remove the pan from the heat. 5. To serve, divide the Greek yogurt–mascarpone cheese mixture into 4 serving bowls and top each serving with 3 apricots, a few pistachios, and 1 teaspoon of the syrup. The apricots and syrup can be stored in a jar at room temperature for up to 1 month.

Per Serving:

calories: 146 | fat: 3g | protein: 4g | carbs: 28g | fiber: 4g | sodium: 62mg

Frozen Raspberry Delight

Prep time: 10 minutes | Cook time: 0 minutes | Serves 2

- 3 cups frozen raspberries
- 1 peach, peeled and pitted

- 1 mango, peeled and pitted
- 1 teaspoon honey

1. Add all ingredients to a blender and purée, only adding enough water to keep the mixture moving and your blender from overworking itself. 2. Freeze for 10 minutes to firm up if desired.

Per Serving:

calories: 237 | fat: 2g | protein: 4g | carbs: 57g | fiber: 16g | sodium: 4mg

Chapter
11

Salads

Chapter 11 Salads

Traditional Greek Salad

Prep time: 10 minutes | Cook time: 0 minutes | Serves 4

- 2 large English cucumbers
- 4 Roma tomatoes, quartered
- 1 green bell pepper, cut into 1- to 1½-inch chunks
- ¼ small red onion, thinly sliced
- 4 ounces (113 g) pitted Kalamata olives
- ¼ cup extra-virgin olive oil
- 2 tablespoons freshly
- squeezed lemon juice
- 1 tablespoon red wine vinegar
- 1 tablespoon chopped fresh oregano or 1 teaspoon dried oregano
- ¼ teaspoon freshly ground black pepper
- 4 ounces (113 g) crumbled traditional feta cheese

1. Cut the cucumbers in half lengthwise and then into ½-inch-thick half-moons. Place in a large bowl. 2. Add the quartered tomatoes, bell pepper, red onion, and olives. 3. In a small bowl, whisk together the olive oil, lemon juice, vinegar, oregano, and pepper. Drizzle over the vegetables and toss to coat. 4. Divide between salad plates and top each with 1 ounce (28 g) of feta.

Per Serving:
calories: 256 | fat: 22g | protein: 6g | carbs: 11g | fiber: 3g | sodium: 476mg

Classic Tabouli

Prep time: 30 minutes | Cook time: 0 minutes | Serves 8 to 10

- 1 cup bulgur wheat, grind
- 4 cups Italian parsley, finely chopped
- 2 cups ripe tomato, finely diced
- 1 cup green onion, finely
- chopped
- ½ cup lemon juice
- ½ cup extra-virgin olive oil
- 1½ teaspoons salt
- 1 teaspoon dried mint

1. Before you chop the vegetables, put the bulgur in a small bowl. Rinse with water, drain, and let stand in the bowl while you prepare the other ingredients. 2. Put the parsley, tomatoes, green onion, and bulgur into a large bowl. 3. In a small bowl, whisk together the lemon juice, olive oil, salt, and mint. 4. Pour the dressing over the tomato, onion, and bulgur mixture, tossing everything together. Add additional salt to taste. Serve immediately or store in the fridge for up to 2 days.

Per Serving:
calories: 207 | fat: 14g | protein: 4g | carbs: 20g | fiber: 5g | sodium: 462mg

Sicilian Salad

Prep time: 5 minutes | Cook time: 0 minutes | Serves 2

- 2 tablespoons extra virgin olive oil
- 1 tablespoon red wine vinegar
- 2 medium tomatoes (preferably beefsteak variety), sliced
- ½ medium red onion, thinly sliced
- 2 tablespoons capers, drained
- 6 green olives, halved
- 1 teaspoon dried oregano
- Pinch of fine sea salt

1. Make the dressing by combining the olive oil and vinegar in a small bowl. Use a fork to whisk until the mixture thickens slightly. Set aside. 2. Arrange the sliced tomatoes on a large plate and then scatter the onions, capers, and olives over the tomatoes. 3. Sprinkle the oregano and sea salt over the top, then drizzle the dressing over the salad. Serve promptly. (This salad is best served fresh, but can be stored covered in the refrigerator for up to 1 day.)
Per Serving:
calories: 169 | fat: 15g | protein: 2g | carbs: 8g | fiber: 3g | sodium: 336mg

Greek Potato Salad

Prep time: 15 minutes | Cook time: 15 to 18 minutes | Serves 6

- 1½ pounds (680 g) small red or new potatoes
- ½ cup olive oil
- ⅓ cup red wine vinegar
- 1 teaspoon fresh Greek oregano
- 4 ounces (113 g) feta cheese, crumbled, if desired, or 4 ounces (113 g) grated
- Swiss cheese (for a less salty option)
- 1 green bell pepper, seeded and chopped (1¼ cups)
- 1 small red onion, halved and thinly sliced (generous 1 cup)
- ½ cup Kalamata olives, pitted and halved

1. Put the potatoes in a large saucepan and add water to cover. Bring the water to a boil and cook until tender, 15 to 18 minutes. Drain and set aside until cool enough to handle. 2. Meanwhile, in a large bowl, whisk together the olive oil, vinegar, and oregano. 3. When the potatoes are just cool enough to handle, cut them into 1-inch pieces and add them to the bowl with the dressing. Toss to combine. Add the cheese, bell pepper, onion, and olives and toss gently. Let stand for 30 minutes before serving.

Per Serving:
calories: 315 | fat: 23g | protein: 5g | carbs: 21g | fiber: 3g | sodium: 360mg

Roasted Cauliflower "Steak" Salad

Prep time: 10 minutes | Cook time: 50 minutes | Serves 4

- 2 tablespoons olive oil, divided
- 2 large heads cauliflower (about 3 pounds / 1.4 kg each), trimmed of outer leaves
- 2 teaspoons za'atar
- 1½ teaspoons kosher salt, divided
- 1¼ teaspoons ground black pepper, divided
- 1 teaspoon ground cumin
- 2 large carrots
- 8 ounces (227 g) dandelion greens, tough stems removed
- ½ cup low-fat plain Greek yogurt
- 2 tablespoons tahini
- 2 tablespoons fresh lemon juice
- 1 tablespoon water
- 1 clove garlic, minced

1. Preheat the oven to 450°F(235ºC). Brush a large baking sheet with some of the oil. 2. Place the cauliflower on a cutting board, stem side down. Cut down the middle, through the core and stem, and then cut two 1'-thick "steaks" from the middle. Repeat with the other cauliflower head. Set aside the remaining cauliflower for another use. Brush both sides of the steaks with the remaining oil and set on the baking sheet. 3. Combine the za'atar, 1 teaspoon of the salt, 1 teaspoon of the pepper, and the cumin. Sprinkle on the cauliflower steaks. Bake until the bottom is deeply golden, about 30 minutes. Flip and bake until tender, 10 to 15 minutes. 4. Meanwhile, set the carrots on a cutting board and use a vegetable peeler to peel them into ribbons. Add to a large bowl with the dandelion greens. 5. In a small bowl, combine the yogurt, tahini, lemon juice, water, garlic, the remaining ½ teaspoon salt, and the remaining ¼ teaspoon pepper. 6. Dab 3 tablespoons of the dressing onto the carrot-dandelion mix. With a spoon or your hands, massage the dressing into the mix for 5 minutes. 7. Remove the steaks from the oven and transfer to individual plates. Drizzle each with 2 tablespoons of the dressing and top with 1 cup of the salad.

Per Serving:
calories: 214 | fat: 12g | protein: 9g | carbs: 21g | fiber: 7g | sodium: 849mg

Asparagus Salad

Prep time: 10 minutes | Cook time: 0 minutes | Serves 4

- 1 pound (454 g) asparagus
- Sea salt and freshly ground pepper, to taste
- 4 tablespoons olive oil
- 1 tablespoon balsamic vinegar
- 1 tablespoon lemon zest

1. Either roast the asparagus or, with a vegetable peeler, shave it into thin strips. 2. Season to taste. 3. Toss with the olive oil and vinegar, garnish with a sprinkle of lemon zest, and serve.

Per Serving:
calories: 146 | fat: 14g | protein: 3g | carbs: 5g | fiber: 3g | sodium: 4mg

Riviera Tuna Salad

Prep time: 15 minutes | Cook time: 0 minutes | Serves 4

- ¼ cup olive oil
- ¼ cup balsamic vinegar
- ½ teaspoon minced garlic
- ¼ teaspoon dried oregano
- Sea salt and freshly ground pepper, to taste
- 2 tablespoons capers, drained
- 4–6 cups baby greens
- 1 (6-ounce / 170-g) can solid white albacore tuna, drained
- 1 cup canned garbanzo beans, rinsed and drained
- ¼ cup low-salt olives, pitted and quartered
- 2 Roma tomatoes, chopped

1. To make the vinaigrette, whisk together the olive oil, balsamic vinegar, garlic, oregano, sea salt, and pepper until emulsified. 2. Stir in the capers. Refrigerate for up to 6 hours before serving. 3. Place the baby greens in a salad bowl or on individual plates, and top with the tuna, beans, olives, and tomatoes. 4. Drizzle the vinaigrette over all, and serve immediately.

Per Serving:
calories: 300 | fat: 19g | protein: 16g | carbs: 17g | fiber: 5g | sodium: 438mg

Israeli Salad with Nuts and Seeds

Prep time: 15 minutes | Cook time: 0 minutes | Serves 4

- ¼ cup pine nuts
- ¼ cup shelled pistachios
- ¼ cup coarsely chopped walnuts
- ¼ cup shelled pumpkin seeds
- ¼ cup shelled sunflower seeds
- 2 large English cucumbers, unpeeled and finely chopped
- 1 pint cherry tomatoes, finely chopped
- ½ small red onion, finely chopped
- ½ cup finely chopped fresh flat-leaf Italian parsley
- ¼ cup extra-virgin olive oil
- 2 to 3 tablespoons freshly squeezed lemon juice (from 1 lemon)
- 1 teaspoon salt
- ¼ teaspoon freshly ground black pepper
- 4 cups baby arugula

1. In a large dry skillet, toast the pine nuts, pistachios, walnuts, pumpkin seeds, and sunflower seeds over medium-low heat until golden and fragrant, 5 to 6 minutes, being careful not to burn them. Remove from the heat and set aside. 2. In a large bowl, combine the cucumber, tomatoes, red onion, and parsley. 3. In a small bowl, whisk together olive oil, lemon juice, salt, and pepper. Pour over the chopped vegetables and toss to coat. 4. Add the toasted nuts and seeds and arugula and toss with the salad to blend well. Serve at room temperature or chilled.

Per Serving:
calories: 404 | fat: 36g | protein: 10g | carbs: 16g | fiber: 5g | sodium: 601mg

Tomato and Pepper Salad

Prep time: 10 minutes | Cook time: 0 minutes | Serves 6

- 3 large yellow peppers
- ¼ cup olive oil
- 1 small bunch fresh basil leaves
- 2 cloves garlic, minced
- 4 large tomatoes, seeded and diced
- Sea salt and freshly ground pepper, to taste

1. Preheat broiler to high heat and broil the peppers until blackened on all sides. 2. Remove from heat and place in a paper bag. Seal and allow peppers to cool. 3. Once cooled, peel the skins off the peppers, then seed and chop them. 4. Add half of the peppers to a food processor along with the olive oil, basil, and garlic, and pulse several times to make the dressing. 5. Combine the rest of the peppers with the tomatoes and toss with the dressing. 6. Season the salad with sea salt and freshly ground pepper. Allow salad to come to room temperature before serving.

Per Serving:
calories: 129 | fat: 9g | protein: 2g | carbs: 11g | fiber: 2g | sodium: 8mg

Zucchini and Ricotta Salad

Prep time: 5 minutes | Cook time: 2 minutes | Serves 1

- 2 teaspoons raw pine nuts
- 5 ounces (142 g) whole-milk ricotta cheese
- 1 tablespoon chopped fresh mint
- 1 teaspoon chopped fresh basil
- 1 tablespoon chopped fresh parsley
For the Dressing:
- 1½ tablespoons extra virgin olive oil
- 1 tablespoon fresh lemon juice

- parsley
- Pinch of fine sea salt
- 1 medium zucchini, very thinly sliced horizontally with a mandoline slicer
- Pinch of freshly ground black pepper

- Pinch of fine sea salt
- Pinch of freshly ground black pepper

1. Add the pine nuts to a small pan placed over medium heat. Toast the nuts, turning them frequently, for 2 minutes or until golden. Set aside. 2. In a food processor, combine the ricotta, mint, basil, parsley, and a pinch of sea salt. Process until smooth and then set aside. 3. Make the dressing by combining the olive oil and lemon juice in a small bowl. Use a fork to stir rapidly until the mixture thickens, then add a pinch of sea salt and a pinch of black pepper. Stir again. 4. Place the sliced zucchini in a medium bowl. Add half of the dressing, and toss to coat the zucchini. 5. To serve, place half of the ricotta mixture in the center of a serving plate, then layer the zucchini in a circle, covering the cheese. Add the rest of the cheese in the center and on top of the zucchini, then sprinkle the toasted pine nuts over the top. Drizzle the remaining dressing over the top, and finish with a pinch of black pepper. Store covered in the refrigerator for up to 1 day.

Per Serving:
calories: 504 | fat: 43g | protein: 19g | carbs: 13g | fiber: 3g | sodium: 136mg

Four-Bean Salad

Prep time: 20 minutes | Cook time: 0 minutes | Serves 4

- ½ cup white beans, cooked
- ½ cup black-eyed peas, cooked
- ½ cup fava beans, cooked
- ½ cup lima beans, cooked
- 1 red bell pepper, diced
- 1 small bunch flat-leaf
- parsley, chopped
- 2 tablespoons olive oil
- 1 teaspoon ground cumin
- Juice of 1 lemon
- Sea salt and freshly ground pepper, to taste

1. You can cook the beans a day or two in advance to speed up the preparation of this dish. 2. Combine all ingredients in a large bowl and mix well. Season to taste. 3. Allow to sit for 30 minutes, so the flavors can come together before serving.

Per Serving:
calories: 189 | fat: 7g | protein: 8g | carbs: 24g | fiber: 7g | sodium: 14mg

Melon Caprese Salad

Prep time: 20 minutes |Cook time: 0 minutes| Serves: 6

- 1 cantaloupe, quartered and seeded
- ½ small seedless watermelon
- 1 cup grape tomatoes
- 2 cups fresh mozzarella balls (about 8 ounces / 227 g)
- ⅓ cup fresh basil or mint leaves, torn into small
- pieces
- 2 tablespoons extra-virgin olive oil
- 1 tablespoon balsamic vinegar
- ¼ teaspoon freshly ground black pepper
- ¼ teaspoon kosher or sea salt

1. Using a melon baller or a metal, teaspoon-size measuring spoon, scoop balls out of the cantaloupe. You should get about 2½ to 3 cups from one cantaloupe. (If you prefer, cut the melon into bite-size pieces instead of making balls.) Put them in a large colander over a large serving bowl. 2. Using the same method, ball or cut the watermelon into bite-size pieces; you should get about 2 cups. Put the watermelon balls in the colander with the cantaloupe. 3. Let the fruit drain for 10 minutes. Pour the juice from the bowl into a container to refrigerate and save for drinking or adding to smoothies. Wipe the bowl dry, and put in the cut fruit. 4. Add the tomatoes, mozzarella, basil, oil, vinegar, pepper, and salt to the fruit mixture. Gently mix until everything is incorporated and serve.

Per Serving:
calories: 297 | fat: 12g | protein: 14g | carbs: 39g | fiber: 3g | sodium: 123mg

Easy Greek Salad

Prep time: 10 minutes | Cook time: 0 minutes | Serves 4 to 6

- 1 head iceberg lettuce
- 1 pint (2 cups) cherry tomatoes
- 1 large cucumber
- 1 medium onion
- ½ cup extra-virgin olive oil
- ¼ cup lemon juice
- 1 teaspoon salt
- 1 clove garlic, minced
- 1 cup Kalamata olives, pitted
- 1 (6-ounce / 170-g) package feta cheese, crumbled

1. Cut the lettuce into 1-inch pieces and put them in a large salad bowl. 2. Cut the tomatoes in half and add them to the salad bowl. 3. Slice the cucumber into bite-size pieces and add them to the salad bowl. 4. Thinly slice the onion and add it to the salad bowl. 5. In another small bowl, whisk together the olive oil, lemon juice, salt, and garlic. Pour the dressing over the salad and gently toss to evenly coat. 6. Top the salad with the Kalamata olives and feta cheese and serve.

Per Serving:
calories: 297 | fat: 27g | protein: 6g | carbs: 11g | fiber: 3g | sodium: 661mg

Tossed Green Mediterranean Salad

Prep time: 15 minutes | Cook time: 0 minutes | Serves 4

- 1 medium head romaine lettuce, washed, dried, and chopped into bite-sized pieces
- 2 medium cucumbers, peeled and sliced
- 3 spring onions (white parts only), sliced
- ½ cup finely chopped fresh
- dill
- ⅓ cup extra virgin olive oil
- 2 tablespoons fresh lemon juice
- ¼ teaspoon fine sea salt
- 4 ounces (113 g) crumbled feta
- 7 Kalamata olives, pitted

1. Add the lettuce, cucumber, spring onions, and dill to a large bowl. Toss to combine. 2. In a small bowl, whisk together the olive oil and lemon juice. Pour the dressing over the salad, toss, then sprinkle the sea salt over the top. 3. Sprinkle the feta and olives over the top and then gently toss the salad one more time. Serve promptly. (This recipe is best served fresh.)

Per Serving:
calories: 284 | fat: 25g | protein: 7g | carbs: 10g | fiber: 5g | sodium: 496mg

Italian White Bean Salad with Bell Peppers

Prep time: 15 minutes | Cook time: 0 minutes | Serves 4

- 2 tablespoons extra-virgin olive oil
- 2 tablespoons white wine vinegar
- ½ shallot, minced
- ½ teaspoon kosher salt
- ¼ teaspoon freshly ground black pepper
- 3 cups cooked cannellini
- beans, or 2 (15-ounce / 425-g) cans no-salt-added or low-sodium cannellini beans, drained and rinsed
- 2 celery stalks, diced
- ½ red bell pepper, diced
- ¼ cup fresh parsley, chopped
- ¼ cup fresh mint, chopped

1. In a large bowl, whisk together the olive oil, vinegar, shallot, salt, and black pepper. 2. Add the beans, celery, red bell pepper, parsley, and mint; mix well.

Per Serving:
calories: 300 | fat: 8g | protein: 15g | carbs: 46g | fiber: 11g | sodium: 175mg

Spinach-Arugula Salad with Nectarines and Lemon Dressing

Prep time: 15 minutes | Cook time: 0 minutes | Serves 6

- 1 (7-ounce / 198-g) package baby spinach and arugula blend
- 3 tablespoons fresh lemon juice
- 5 tablespoons olive oil
- ⅛ teaspoon salt
- Pinch (teaspoon) sugar
- Freshly ground black pepper, to taste
- ½ red onion, thinly sliced
- 3 ripe nectarines, pitted and sliced into wedges
- 1 cucumber, peeled, seeded, and sliced
- ½ cup crumbled feta cheese

1. Place the spinach-arugula blend in a large bowl. 2. In a small bowl, whisk together the lemon juice, olive oil, salt, and sugar and season with pepper. Taste and adjust the seasonings. 3. Add the dressing to the greens and toss. Top with the onion, nectarines, cucumber, and feta. 4. Serve immediately.

Per Serving:
1 cup: calories: 178 | fat: 14g | protein: 4g | carbs: 11g | fiber: 2g | sodium: 193mg

Chapter 12

Pizzas, Wraps, and Sandwiches

Chapter 12 Pizzas, Wraps, and Sandwiches

Classic Margherita Pizza

Prep time: 10 minutes | Cook time: 10 minutes | Serves 4

- All-purpose flour, for dusting
- 1 pound (454 g) premade pizza dough
- 1 (15-ounce / 425-g) can crushed San Marzano tomatoes, with their juices
- 2 garlic cloves
- 1 teaspoon Italian seasoning
- Pinch sea salt, plus more as needed
- 1½ teaspoons olive oil, for drizzling
- 10 slices mozzarella cheese
- 12 to 15 fresh basil leaves

1. Preheat the oven to 475°F (245°C). 2. On a floured surface, roll out the dough to a 12-inch round and place it on a lightly floured pizza pan or baking sheet. 3. In a food processor, combine the tomatoes with their juices, garlic, Italian seasoning, and salt and process until smooth. Taste and adjust the seasoning. 4. Drizzle the olive oil over the pizza dough, then spoon the pizza sauce over the dough and spread it out evenly with the back of the spoon, leaving a 1-inch border. Evenly distribute the mozzarella over the pizza. 5. Bake until the crust is cooked through and golden, 8 to 10 minutes. Remove from the oven and let sit for 1 to 2 minutes. Top with the basil right before serving.

Per Serving:
calories: 570 | fat: 21g | protein: 28g | carbs: 66g | fiber: 4g | sodium: 570mg

Sautéed Mushroom, Onion, and Pecorino Romano Panini

Prep time: 10 minutes | Cook time: 20 minutes | Serves 4

- 3 tablespoons olive oil, divided
- 1 small onion, diced
- 10 ounces (283 g) button or cremini mushrooms, sliced
- ½ teaspoon salt
- ¼ teaspoon freshly ground black pepper
- 4 crusty Italian sandwich rolls
- 4 ounces (113 g) freshly grated Pecorino Romano

1. Heat 1 tablespoon of the olive oil in a skillet over medium-high heat. Add the onion and cook, stirring, until it begins to soften, about 3 minutes. Add the mushrooms, season with salt and pepper, and cook, stirring, until they soften and the liquid they release evaporates, about 7 minutes. 2. To make the panini, heat a skillet or grill pan over high heat and brush with 1 tablespoon olive oil. Brush the inside of the rolls with the remaining 1 tablespoon olive oil. Divide the mushroom mixture evenly among the rolls and top each with ¼ of the grated cheese. 3. Place the sandwiches in the hot pan and place another heavy pan, such as a cast-iron skillet, on top to weigh them down. Cook for about 3 to 4 minutes, until crisp and golden on the bottom, and then flip over and repeat on the second side, cooking for an additional 3 to 4 minutes until golden and crisp. Slice each sandwich in half and serve hot.

Per Serving:
calories: 348 | fat: 20g | protein: 14g | carbs: 30g | fiber: 2g | sodium: 506mg

Roasted Vegetable Bocadillo with Romesco Sauce

Prep time: 10 minutes | Cook time: 20 minutes | Serves 4

- 2 small yellow squash, sliced lengthwise
- 2 small zucchini, sliced lengthwise
- 1 medium red onion, thinly sliced
- 4 large button mushrooms, sliced
- 2 tablespoons olive oil
- 1 teaspoon salt, divided
- ½ teaspoon freshly ground black pepper, divided
- 2 roasted red peppers from a jar, drained
- 2 tablespoons blanched almonds
- 1 tablespoon sherry vinegar
- 1 small clove garlic
- 4 crusty multigrain rolls
- 4 ounces (113 g) goat cheese, at room temperature
- 1 tablespoon chopped fresh basil

1. Preheat the oven to 400°F(205°C). 2. In a medium bowl, toss the yellow squash, zucchini, onion, and mushrooms with the olive oil, ½ teaspoon salt, and ¼ teaspoon pepper. Spread on a large baking sheet. Roast the vegetables in the oven for about 20 minutes, until softened. 3. Meanwhile, in a food processor, combine the roasted peppers, almonds, vinegar, garlic, the remaining ½ teaspoon salt, and the remaining ¼ teaspoon pepper and process until smooth. 4. Split the rolls and spread ¼ of the goat cheese on the bottom of each. Place the roasted vegetables on top of the cheese, dividing equally. Top with chopped basil. Spread the top halves of the rolls with the roasted red pepper sauce and serve immediately.

Per Serving:
calories: 379 | fat: 21g | protein: 17g | carbs: 32g | fiber: 4g | sodium: 592mg

Beans and Greens Pizza

Prep time: 11 minutes | Cook time: 14 to 19 minutes | Serves 4

- ¾ cup whole-wheat pastry flour
- ½ teaspoon low-sodium baking powder
- 1 tablespoon olive oil, divided
- 1 cup chopped kale
- 2 cups chopped fresh baby spinach
- 1 cup canned no-salt-added cannellini beans, rinsed and drained
- ½ teaspoon dried thyme
- 1 piece low-sodium string cheese, torn into pieces

1. In a small bowl, mix the pastry flour and baking powder until well combined. 2. Add ¼ cup of water and 2 teaspoons of olive oil. Mix until a dough forms. 3. On a floured surface, press or roll the dough into a 7-inch round. Set aside while you cook the greens. 4. In a baking pan, mix the kale, spinach, and remaining teaspoon of the olive oil. Air fry at 350ºF (177ºC) for 3 to 5 minutes, until the greens are wilted. Drain well. 5. Put the pizza dough into the air fryer basket. Top with the greens, cannellini beans, thyme, and string cheese. Air fry for 11 to 14 minutes, or until the crust is golden brown and the cheese is melted. Cut into quarters to serve.

Per Serving:

calories: 181 | fat: 6g | protein: 8g | carbs: 27g | fiber: 6g | sodium: 103mg

Flatbread Pizza with Roasted Cherry Tomatoes, Artichokes, and Feta

Prep time: 5 minutes | Cook time: 20 minutes | Serves 4

- 1½ pounds (680 g) cherry or grape tomatoes, halved
- 3 tablespoons olive oil, divided
- ½ teaspoon salt
- ½ teaspoon freshly ground black pepper
- 4 Middle Eastern–style flatbread rounds
- 1 can artichoke hearts, rinsed, well drained, and cut into thin wedges
- 8 ounces (227 g) crumbled feta cheese
- ¼ cup chopped fresh Greek oregano

1. Preheat the oven to 500°F(260ºC). 2. In a medium bowl, toss the tomatoes with 1 tablespoon olive oil, the salt, and the pepper. Spread out on a large baking sheet. Roast in the preheated oven until the tomato skins begin to blister and crack, about 10 to 12 minutes. Remove the tomatoes from the oven and reduce the heat to 450°F(235ºC). 3. Place the flatbreads on a large baking sheet (or two baking sheets if necessary) and brush the tops with the remaining 2 tablespoons of olive oil. Top with the artichoke hearts, roasted tomatoes, and cheese, dividing equally. 4. Bake the flatbreads in the oven for about 8 to 10 minutes, until the edges are lightly browned and the cheese is melted. Sprinkle the oregano over the top and serve immediately.

Per Serving:

calories: 436 | fat: 27g | protein: 16g | carbs: 34g | fiber: 6g | sodium: 649mg

Turkish Pizza

Prep time: 20 minutes | Cook time: 10 minutes | Serves 4

- 4 ounces (113 g) ground lamb or 85% lean ground beef
- ¼ cup finely chopped green bell pepper
- ¼ cup chopped fresh parsley
- 1 small plum tomato, seeded and finely chopped
- 2 tablespoons finely chopped yellow onion

For Serving:
- Chopped fresh mint
- Extra-virgin olive oil

- 1 garlic clove, minced
- 2 teaspoons tomato paste
- ¼ teaspoon sweet paprika
- ¼ teaspoon ground cumin
- ⅛ to ¼ teaspoon red pepper flakes
- ⅛ teaspoon ground allspice
- ⅛ teaspoon kosher salt
- ⅛ teaspoon black pepper
- 4 (6-inch) flour tortillas

- Lemon wedges

1. In a medium bowl, gently mix the ground lamb, bell pepper, parsley, chopped tomato, onion, garlic, tomato paste, paprika, cumin, red pepper flakes, allspice, salt, and black pepper until well combined. 2. Divide the meat mixture evenly among the tortillas, spreading it all the way to the edge of each tortilla. 3. Place 1 tortilla in the air fryer basket. Set the air fryer to 400ºF (204ºC) for 10 minutes, or until the meat topping has browned and the edge of the tortilla is golden. Transfer to a plate and repeat to cook the remaining tortillas. 4. Serve the pizzas warm, topped with chopped fresh mint and a drizzle of extra-virgin olive oil and with lemon wedges alongside.

Per Serving:

calories: 172 | fat: 8g | protein: 8g | carbs: 18g | fiber: 2g | sodium: 318mg

Vegetable Pita Sandwiches

Prep time: 15 minutes | Cook time: 9 to 12 minutes | Serves 4

- 1 baby eggplant, peeled and chopped
- 1 red bell pepper, sliced
- ½ cup diced red onion
- ½ cup shredded carrot
- 1 teaspoon olive oil
- ⅓ cup low-fat Greek yogurt
- ½ teaspoon dried tarragon
- 2 low-sodium whole-wheat pita breads, halved crosswise

1. In a baking pan, stir together the eggplant, red bell pepper, red onion, carrot, and olive oil. Put the vegetable mixture into the air fryer basket and roast at 390ºF (199ºC) for 7 to 9 minutes, stirring once, until the vegetables are tender. Drain if necessary. 2. In a small bowl, thoroughly mix the yogurt and tarragon until well combined. 3. Stir the yogurt mixture into the vegetables. Stuff one-fourth of this mixture into each pita pocket. 4. Place the sandwiches in the air fryer and cook for 2 to 3 minutes, or until the bread is toasted. Serve immediately.

Per Serving:

calories: 115 | fat: 2g | protein: 4g | carbs: 22g | fiber: 6g | sodium: 90mg

Grilled Chicken Salad Pita

Prep time: 15 minutes | Cook time: 16 minutes | Serves 1

- 1 boneless, skinless chicken breast
- Sea salt and freshly ground pepper, to taste
- 1 cup baby spinach
- 1 roasted red pepper, sliced
- 1 tomato, chopped
- ½ small red onion, thinly sliced
- ½ small cucumber, chopped
- 1 tablespoon olive oil
- Juice of 1 lemon
- 1 whole-wheat pita pocket
- 2 tablespoons crumbled feta cheese

1. Preheat a gas or charcoal grill to medium-high heat. 2. Season the chicken breast with sea salt and freshly ground pepper, and grill until cooked through, about 7–8 minutes per side. 3. Allow chicken to rest for 5 minutes before slicing into strips. 4. While the chicken is cooking, put all the chopped vegetables into a medium-mixing bowl and season with sea salt and freshly ground pepper. 5. Chop the chicken into cubes and add to salad. Add the olive oil and lemon juice and toss well. 6. Stuff the mixture onto a pita pocket and top with the feta cheese. Serve immediately.

Per Serving:
calories: 653 | fat: 26g | protein: 71g | carbs: 34g | fiber: 6g | sodium: 464mg

Bocadillo with Herbed Tuna and Piquillo Peppers

Prep time: 5 minutes | Cook time: 20 minutes | Serves 4

- 2 tablespoons olive oil, plus more for brushing
- 1 medium onion, finely chopped
- 2 leeks, white and tender green parts only, finely chopped
- 1 teaspoon chopped thyme
- ½ teaspoon dried marjoram
- ½ teaspoon salt
- ¼ teaspoon freshly ground black pepper
- 3 tablespoons sherry vinegar
- 1 carrot, finely diced
- 2 (8-ounce / 227-g) jars Spanish tuna in olive oil
- 4 crusty whole-wheat sandwich rolls, split
- 1 ripe tomato, grated on the large holes of a box grater
- 4 piquillo peppers, cut into thin strips

1. Heat 2 tablespoons olive oil in a medium skillet over medium heat. Add the onion, leeks, thyme, marjoram, salt, and pepper. Stir frequently until the onions are softened, about 10 minutes. Stir in the vinegar and carrot and cook until the liquid has evaporated, 5 minutes. Transfer the mixture to a bowl and let cool to room temperature or refrigerate for 15 minutes or so. 2. In a medium bowl, combine the tuna, along with its oil, with the onion mixture, breaking the tuna chunks up with a fork. 3. Brush the rolls lightly with oil and toast under the broiler until lightly browned, about 2 minutes. Spoon the tomato pulp onto the bottom half of each roll, dividing equally and spreading it with the back of the spoon. Divide the tuna mixture among the rolls and top with the piquillo pepper slices. Serve immediately.

Per Serving:
calories: 416 | fat: 18g | protein: 35g | carbs: 30g | fiber: 5g | sodium: 520mg

Grilled Eggplant and Feta Sandwiches

Prep time: 10 minutes | Cook time: 8 minutes | Serves 2

- 1 medium eggplant, sliced into ½-inch-thick slices
- 2 tablespoons olive oil
- Sea salt and freshly ground pepper, to taste
- 5 to 6 tablespoons hummus
- 4 slices whole-wheat bread, toasted
- 1 cup baby spinach leaves
- 2 ounces (57 g) feta cheese, softened

1. Preheat a gas or charcoal grill to medium-high heat. 2. Salt both sides of the sliced eggplant, and let sit for 20 minutes to draw out the bitter juices. 3. Rinse the eggplant and pat dry with a paper towel. 4. Brush the eggplant slices with olive oil and season with sea salt and freshly ground pepper. 5. Grill the eggplant until lightly charred on both sides but still slightly firm in the middle, about 3–4 minutes a side. 6. Spread the hummus on the bread and top with the spinach leaves, feta, and eggplant. Top with the other slice of bread and serve warm.

Per Serving:
calories: 516 | fat: 27g | protein: 14g | carbs: 59g | fiber: 14g | sodium: 597mg

Herbed Focaccia Panini with Anchovies and Burrata

Prep time: 5 minutes | Cook time: 8 minutes | Serves 4

- 8 ounces (227 g) burrata cheese, chilled and sliced
- 1 pound (454 g) whole-wheat herbed focaccia, cut crosswise into 4 rectangles and split horizontally
- 1 can anchovy fillets packed in oil, drained
- 8 slices tomato, sliced
- 2 cups arugula
- 1 tablespoon olive oil

1. Divide the cheese evenly among the bottom halves of the focaccia rectangles. Top each with 3 or 4 anchovy fillets, 2 slices of tomato, and ½ cup arugula. Place the top halves of the focaccia on top of the sandwiches. 2. To make the panini, heat a skillet or grill pan over high heat and brush with the olive oil. 3. Place the sandwiches in the hot pan and place another heavy pan, such as a cast-iron skillet, on top to weigh them down. Cook for about 3 to 4 minutes, until crisp and golden on the bottom, and then flip over and repeat on the second side, cooking for an additional 3 to 4 minutes until golden and crisp. Slice each sandwich in half and serve hot.

Per Serving:
calories: 596 | fat: 30g | protein: 27g | carbs: 58g | fiber: 5g | sodium: 626mg

Mediterranean-Pita Wraps

Prep time: 5 minutes | Cook time: 14 minutes | Serves 4

- 1 pound (454 g) mackerel fish fillets
- 2 tablespoons olive oil
- 1 tablespoon Mediterranean seasoning mix
- ½ teaspoon chili powder
- Sea salt and freshly ground black pepper, to taste
- 2 ounces (57 g) feta cheese, crumbled
- 4 tortillas

1. Toss the fish fillets with the olive oil; place them in the lightly oiled air fryer basket. 2. Air fry the fish fillets at 400ºF (204ºC) for about 14 minutes, turning them over halfway through the cooking time. 3. Assemble your pitas with the chopped fish and remaining ingredients and serve warm.

Per Serving:

calories: 275 | fat: 13g | protein: 27g | carbs: 13g | fiber: 2g | sodium: 322mg

Jerk Chicken Wraps

Prep time: 30 minutes | Cook time: 15 minutes | Serves 4

- 1 pound (454 g) boneless, skinless chicken tenderloins
- 1 cup jerk marinade
- Olive oil
- 4 large low-carb tortillas
- 1 cup julienned carrots
- 1 cup peeled cucumber ribbons
- 1 cup shredded lettuce
- 1 cup mango or pineapple chunks

1. In a medium bowl, coat the chicken with the jerk marinade, cover, and refrigerate for 1 hour. 2. Spray the air fryer basket lightly with olive oil. 3. Place the chicken in the air fryer basket in a single layer and spray lightly with olive oil. You may need to cook the chicken in batches. Reserve any leftover marinade. 4. Air fry at 375ºF (191ºC) for 8 minutes. Turn the chicken over and brush with some of the remaining marinade. Cook until the chicken reaches an internal temperature of at least 165ºF (74ºC), an additional 5 to 7 minutes. 5. To assemble the wraps, fill each tortilla with ¼ cup carrots, ¼ cup cucumber, ¼ cup lettuce, and ¼ cup mango. Place one quarter of the chicken tenderloins on top and roll up the tortilla. These are great served warm or cold.

Per Serving:

calories: 241 | fat: 4g | protein: 28g | carbs: 23g | fiber: 4g | sodium: 85mg

Mediterranean Tuna Salad Sandwiches

Prep time: 10 minutes | Cook time: 5 minutes | Serves 2

- 1 can white tuna, packed in water or olive oil, drained
- 1 roasted red pepper, diced
- ½ small red onion, diced
- 10 low-salt olives, pitted and finely chopped
- ¼ cup plain Greek yogurt
- 1 tablespoon flat-leaf parsley, chopped
- Juice of 1 lemon
- Sea salt and freshly ground pepper, to taste
- 4 whole-grain pieces of bread

1. In a small bowl, combine all of the ingredients except the bread, and mix well. 2. Season with sea salt and freshly ground pepper to taste. Toast the bread or warm in a pan. 3. Make the sandwich and serve immediately.

Per Serving:

calories: 307 | fat: 7g | protein: 30g | carbs: 31g | fiber: 5g | sodium: 564mg

Chapter

13

Pasta

Chapter 13 Pasta

Toasted Couscous with Feta, Cucumber, and Tomato

Prep time: 15 minutes | Cook time: 10 minutes | Serves 8

- 1 tablespoon plus ¼ cup light olive oil, divided
- 2 cups Israeli couscous
- 3 cups vegetable broth
- 2 large tomatoes, seeded and diced
- 1 large English cucumber, diced
- 1 medium red onion, peeled

- and chopped
- ½ cup crumbled feta cheese
- ¼ cup red wine vinegar
- ½ teaspoon ground black pepper
- ¼ cup chopped flat-leaf parsley
- ¼ cup chopped fresh basil

1. Press the Sauté button on the Instant Pot® and heat 1 tablespoon oil. Add couscous and cook, stirring frequently, until couscous is light golden brown, about 7 minutes. Press the Cancel button. 2. Add broth and stir. Close lid, set steam release to Sealing, press the Manual button, and set time to 2 minutes. When the timer beeps, let pressure release naturally for 5 minutes, then quick-release the remaining pressure until the float valve drops and open lid. 3. Fluff couscous with a fork, then transfer to a medium bowl and set aside to cool to room temperature, about 30 minutes. Add remaining ¼ cup oil, tomatoes, cucumber, onion, feta, vinegar, pepper, parsley, and basil, and stir until combined. Serve at room temperature or refrigerate for at least 2 hours.

Per Serving:
calories: 286 | fat: 11g | protein: 9g | carbs: 38g | fiber: 3g | sodium: 438mg

Penne with Roasted Vegetables

Prep time: 20 minutes | Cook time: 25 to 30 minutes | Serves 6

- 1 large butternut squash, peeled and diced
- 1 large zucchini, diced
- 1 large yellow onion, chopped
- 2 tablespoons extra-virgin olive oil
- ½ teaspoon salt
- ½ teaspoon freshly ground

- black pepper
- 1 teaspoon paprika
- ½ teaspoon garlic powder
- 1 pound (454 g) whole-grain penne
- ½ cup dry white wine or chicken stock
- 2 tablespoons grated Parmesan cheese

1. Preheat the oven to 400°F(205°C). Line a baking sheet with aluminum foil. 2. In a large bowl, toss the vegetables with the olive oil, then spread them out on the baking sheet. Sprinkle the vegetables with the salt, pepper, paprika, and garlic powder and bake just until fork-tender, 25 to 30 minutes. 3. Meanwhile, bring a large stockpot of water to a boil over high heat and cook the penne according to the package instructions until al dente (still slightly firm). Drain but do not rinse. 4. Place ½ cup of the roasted vegetables and the wine or stock in a blender or food processor and blend until smooth. 5. Place the purée in a large skillet and heat over medium-high heat. Add the pasta and cook, stirring, just until heated through. 6. Serve the pasta and sauce topped with the roasted vegetables. Sprinkle with Parmesan cheese.

Per Serving:
calories: 456 | fat: 7g | protein: 9g | carbs: 92g | fiber: 14g | sodium: 241mg

No-Drain Pasta alla Norma

Prep time: 5 minutes |Cook time: 25 minutes| Serves: 6

- 1 medium globe eggplant (about 1 pound / 454 g), cut into ¾-inch cubes
- 1 tablespoon extra-virgin olive oil
- 1 cup chopped onion (about ½ medium onion)
- 8 ounces (227 g) uncooked thin spaghetti
- 1 (15-ounce / 425-g) container part-skim ricotta

- cheese
- 3 Roma tomatoes, chopped (about 2 cups)
- 2 garlic cloves, minced (about 1 teaspoon)
- ¼ teaspoon kosher or sea salt
- ½ cup loosely packed fresh basil leaves
- Grated Parmesan cheese, for serving (optional)

1. Lay three paper towels on a large plate, and pile the cubed eggplant on top. (Don't cover the eggplant.) Microwave the eggplant on high for 5 minutes to dry and partially cook it. 2. In a large stockpot over medium-high heat, heat the oil. Add the eggplant and the onion and cook for 5 minutes, stirring occasionally. 3. Add the spaghetti, ricotta, tomatoes, garlic, and salt. Cover with water by a ½ inch (about 4 cups of water). Cook uncovered for 12 to 15 minutes, or until the pasta is just al dente (tender with a bite), stirring occasionally to prevent the pasta from sticking together or sticking to the bottom of the pot. 4. Remove the pot from the heat and let the pasta stand for 3 more minutes to absorb more liquid while you tear the basil into pieces. Sprinkle the basil over the pasta and gently stir. Serve with Parmesan cheese, if desired.

Per Serving:
calories: 299 | fat: 9g | protein: 15g | carbs: 41g | fiber: 5g | sodium: 174mg

Mixed Vegetable Couscous

Prep time: 20 minutes | Cook time: 10 minutes | Serves 8

- 1 tablespoon light olive oil
- 1 medium zucchini, trimmed and chopped
- 1 medium yellow squash, chopped
- 1 large red bell pepper, seeded and chopped
- 1 large orange bell pepper, seeded and chopped
- 2 tablespoons chopped fresh

- oregano
- 2 cups Israeli couscous
- 3 cups vegetable broth
- ½ cup crumbled feta cheese
- ¼ cup red wine vinegar
- ¼ cup extra-virgin olive oil
- ½ teaspoon ground black pepper
- ¼ cup chopped fresh basil

1. Press the Sauté button on the Instant Pot® and heat light olive oil. Add zucchini, squash, bell peppers, and oregano, and sauté 8 minutes. Press the Cancel button. Transfer to a serving bowl and set aside to cool. 2. Add couscous and broth to the Instant Pot® and stir well. Close lid, set steam release to Sealing, press the Manual button, and set time to 2 minutes. When the timer beeps, let pressure release naturally for 5 minutes, then quick-release the remaining pressure and open lid. 3. Fluff with a fork and stir in cooked vegetables, cheese, vinegar, extra-virgin olive oil, black pepper, and basil. Serve warm.

Per Serving:
calories: 355 | fat: 9g | protein: 14g | carbs: 61g | fiber: 7g | sodium: 588mg

Fettuccine with Tomatoes and Pesto

Prep time: 15 minutes | Cook time: 10 minutes | Serves 4

- 1 pound (454 g) whole-grain fettuccine
- 4 Roma tomatoes, diced
- 2 teaspoons tomato paste
- 1 cup vegetable broth
- 2 garlic cloves, minced
- 1 tablespoon chopped fresh oregano

- ½ teaspoon salt
- 1 packed cup fresh basil leaves
- ¼ cup extra-virgin olive oil
- ¼ cup grated Parmesan cheese
- ¼ cup pine nuts

1. Bring a large stockpot of water to a boil over high heat, and cook the fettuccine according to the package instructions until al dente (still slightly firm). Drain but do not rinse. 2. Meanwhile, in a large, heavy skillet, combine the tomatoes, tomato paste, broth, garlic, oregano, and salt and stir well. Cook over medium heat for 10 minutes. 3. In a blender or food processor, combine the basil, olive oil, Parmesan cheese, and pine nuts and blend until smooth. 4. Stir the pesto into the tomato mixture. Add the pasta and cook, stirring frequently, just until the pasta is well coated and heated through. 5. Serve immediately.

Per Serving:
calories: 636 | fat: 22g | protein: 11g | carbs: 96g | fiber: 3g | sodium: 741mg

Couscous with Crab and Lemon

Prep time: 10 minutes | Cook time: 7 minutes | Serves 4

- 1 cup couscous
- 1 clove garlic, peeled and minced
- 2 cups water
- 3 tablespoons extra-virgin olive oil, divided
- ¼ cup minced fresh flat-leaf parsley
- 1 tablespoon minced fresh

- dill
- 8 ounces (227 g) jumbo lump crabmeat
- 3 tablespoons lemon juice
- ½ teaspoon ground black pepper
- ¼ cup grated Parmesan cheese

1. Place couscous, garlic, water, and 1 tablespoon oil in the Instant Pot® and stir well. Close lid, set steam release to Sealing, press the Manual button, and set time to 7 minutes. When the timer beeps, let pressure release naturally for 10 minutes, then quick-release the remaining pressure and open lid. 2. Fluff couscous with a fork. Add parsley, dill, crabmeat, lemon juice, pepper, and remaining 2 tablespoons oil, and stir until combined. Top with cheese and serve immediately.

Per Serving:
calories: 360 | fat: 15g | protein: 22g | carbs: 34g | fiber: 2g | sodium: 388mg

Couscous with Tomatoes and Olives

Prep time: 5 minutes | Cook time: 3 minutes | Serves 4

- 1 tablespoon tomato paste
- 2 cups vegetable broth
- 1 cup couscous
- 1 cup halved cherry tomatoes
- ½ cup halved mixed olives
- ¼ cup minced fresh flat-leaf parsley
- 2 tablespoons minced fresh

- oregano
- 2 tablespoons minced fresh chives
- 1 tablespoon extra-virgin olive oil
- 1 tablespoon red wine vinegar
- ½ teaspoon ground black pepper

1. Pour tomato paste and broth into the Instant Pot® and stir until completely dissolved. Stir in couscous. Close lid, set steam release to Sealing, press the Manual button, and set time to 3 minutes. When the timer beeps, let pressure release naturally for 10 minutes, then quick-release the remaining pressure and open lid. 2. Fluff couscous with a fork. Add tomatoes, olives, parsley, oregano, chives, oil, vinegar, and pepper, and stir until combined. Serve warm or at room temperature.

Per Serving:
calories: 232 | fat: 5g | protein: 7g | carbs: 37g | fiber: 2g | sodium: 513mg

Spicy Broccoli Pasta Salad

Prep time: 10 minutes | Cook time: 10 minutes | Serves 2

- 8 ounces (227 g) whole-wheat pasta
- 2 cups broccoli florets
- 1 cup carrots, peeled and shredded
- ¼ cup plain Greek yogurt

- Juice of 1 lemon
- 1 teaspoon red pepper flakes
- Sea salt and freshly ground pepper, to taste

1. Cook the pasta according to the package directions for al dente and drain well. 2. When the pasta is cool, combine it with the veggies, yogurt, lemon juice, and red pepper flakes in a large bowl, and stir thoroughly to combine. 3. Taste for seasoning, and add sea salt and freshly ground pepper as needed. 4. This dish can be served at room temperature or chilled.

Per Serving:

calories: 473 | fat: 2g | protein: 22g | carbs: 101g | fiber: 13g | sodium: 101mg

Walnut Spaghetti

Prep time: 10 minutes | Cook time: 20 minutes | Serves 6

- 1 pound (454 g) whole-wheat spaghetti
- ½ cup olive oil
- 4 cloves garlic, minced
- ¾ cup walnuts, toasted and finely chopped

- 2 tablespoons low-fat ricotta cheese
- ½ cup freshly grated, lowfat Parmesan cheese
- ¼ cup flat-leaf parsley, chopped
- Sea salt and freshly ground pepper, to taste

1. Prepare the spaghetti in boiling water according to package directions for al dente, reserving 1 cup of the pasta water. 2. Heat the olive oil in a large skillet on medium-low heat. Add the garlic and sauté for 1–2 minutes. 3. Ladle ½ cup of the pasta water into the skillet, and continue to simmer for 5–10 minutes. 4. Add the chopped walnuts and ricotta cheese. 5. Toss the walnut sauce with the spaghetti in a large serving bowl. Top with the Parmesan cheese and parsley. Season and serve.

Per Serving:

calories: 551 | fat: 31g | protein: 16g | carbs: 60g | fiber: 7g | sodium: 141mg

Penne with Broccoli and Anchovies

Prep time: 10 minutes | Cook time: 10 minutes | Serves 4

- ¼ cup olive oil
- 1 pound (454 g) whole-wheat pasta
- ½ pound (227 g) broccoli or broccoli rabe cut into 1-inch florets
- 3 to 4 anchovy fillets, packed in olive oil

- 2 cloves garlic, sliced
- Pinch red pepper flakes
- ¼ cup freshly grated, lowfat Parmesan
- Sea salt and freshly ground pepper, to taste

1. Heat the olive oil in a deep skillet on medium heat. 2. In the meantime, prepare the pasta al dente, according to the package directions. 3. Fry the broccoli, anchovies, and garlic in the oil until the broccoli is almost tender and the garlic is slightly browned, about 5 minutes or so. 4. Rinse and drain the pasta, and add it to the broccoli mixture. Stir to coat the pasta with the garlic oil. Transfer to a serving dish, toss with red pepper flakes and Parmesan, and season.

Per Serving:

calories: 568 | fat: 17g | protein: 21g | carbs: 89g | fiber: 11g | sodium: 203mg

Chapter

14

Staples, Sauces, Dips, and Dressings

Chapter 14 Staples, Sauces, Dips, and Dressings

Creamy Grapefruit-Tarragon Dressing

Prep time: 5 minutes | Cook time: 0 minutes | Serves 4to 6

- ½ cup avocado oil mayonnaise
- 2 tablespoons Dijon mustard
- 1 teaspoon dried tarragon or 1 tablespoon chopped fresh tarragon
- Zest and juice of ½
- grapefruit (about 2 tablespoons juice)
- ½ teaspoon salt
- ¼ teaspoon freshly ground black pepper
- 1 to 2 tablespoons water (optional)

1. In a large mason jar or glass measuring cup, combine the mayonnaise, Dijon, tarragon, grapefruit zest and juice, salt, and pepper and whisk well with a fork until smooth and creamy. If a thinner dressing is preferred, thin out with water.

Per Serving:

calories: 49 | fat: 4g | protein: 0g | carbs: 4g | fiber: 0g | sodium: 272mg

Melitzanosalata (Greek Eggplant Dip)

Prep time: 10 minutes | Cook time: 3 minutes | Serves 8

- 1 cup water
- 1 large eggplant, peeled and chopped
- 1 clove garlic, peeled
- ½ teaspoon salt
- 1 tablespoon red wine vinegar
- ½ cup extra-virgin olive oil
- 2 tablespoons minced fresh parsley

1. Add water to the Instant Pot®, add the rack to the pot, and place the steamer basket on the rack. 2. Place eggplant in steamer basket. Close lid, set steam release to Sealing, press the Manual button, and set time to 3 minutes. When the timer beeps, quick-release the pressure until the float valve drops. Press the Cancel button and open lid. 3. Transfer eggplant to a food processor and add garlic, salt, and vinegar. Pulse until smooth, about 20 pulses. 4. Slowly add oil to the eggplant mixture while the food processor runs continuously until oil is completely incorporated. Stir in parsley. Serve at room temperature.

Per Serving:

calories: 134 | fat: 14g | protein: 1g | carbs: 3g | fiber: 2g | sodium: 149mg

Classic Basil Pesto

Prep time: 5 minutes | Cook time: 13 minutes | Makes about 1½ cups

- 6 garlic cloves, unpeeled
- ½ cup pine nuts
- 4 cups fresh basil leaves
- ¼ cup fresh parsley leaves
- 1 cup extra-virgin olive oil
- 1 ounce (28 g) Parmesan cheese, grated fine (½ cup)

1. Toast garlic in 8-inch skillet over medium heat, shaking skillet occasionally, until softened and spotty brown, about 8 minutes. When garlic is cool enough to handle, remove and discard skins and chop coarsely. Meanwhile, toast pine nuts in now-empty skillet over medium heat, stirring often, until golden and fragrant, 4 to 5 minutes. 2. Place basil and parsley in 1-gallon zipper-lock bag. Pound bag with flat side of meat pounder or with rolling pin until all leaves are bruised. 3. Process garlic, pine nuts, and herbs in food processor until finely chopped, about 1 minute, scraping down sides of bowl as needed. With processor running, slowly add oil until incorporated. Transfer pesto to bowl, stir in Parmesan, and season with salt and pepper to taste. (Pesto can be refrigerated for up to 3 days or frozen for up to 3 months. To prevent browning, press plastic wrap flush to surface or top with thin layer of olive oil. Bring to room temperature before using.)

Per Serving:

¼ cup: calories: 423 | fat: 45g | protein: 4g | carbs: 4g | fiber: 1g | sodium: 89mg

Spicy Cucumber Dressing

Prep time: 5 minutes | Cook time: 0 minutes | Serves 2

- 1½ cups plain, unsweetened, full-fat Greek yogurt
- 1 cucumber, seeded and peeled
- ½ lemon, juiced and zested
- 1 tablespoon dried, minced garlic
- ½ tablespoon dried dill
- 2 teaspoons dried oregano
- Salt

1. In a food processor, combine the yogurt, cucumber, lemon juice, garlic, dill, oregano, and a pinch of salt and process until smooth. Adjust the seasonings as needed and transfer to a serving bowl.

Per Serving:

calories: 209 | fat: 10g | protein: 18g | carbs: 14g | fiber: 2g | sodium: 69mg

Chermoula

Prep time: 10 minutes | Cook time: 0 minutes | Makes about 1½ cups

- 2¼ cups fresh cilantro leaves
- 8 garlic cloves, minced
- 1½ teaspoons ground cumin
- 1½ teaspoons paprika
- ½ teaspoon cayenne pepper
- ½ teaspoon table salt
- 6 tablespoons lemon juice (2 lemons)
- ¾ cup extra-virgin olive oil

1. Pulse cilantro, garlic, cumin, paprika, cayenne, and salt in food processor until cilantro is coarsely chopped, about 10 pulses. Add lemon juice and pulse briefly to combine. Transfer mixture to medium bowl and slowly whisk in oil until incorporated and mixture is emulsified. Cover and let sit at room temperature for at least 30 minutes to allow flavors to meld. (Sauce can be refrigerated for up to 2 days; bring to room temperature before serving.)

Per Serving:
¼ cup: calories: 253 | fat: 27g | protein: 1g | carbs: 3g | fiber: 1g | sodium: 199mg

Herbed Butter

Prep time: 10 minutes | Cook time: 0 minutes | Makes ½ cup

- ½ cup (1 stick) butter, at room temperature
- 1 garlic clove, finely minced
- 2 teaspoons finely chopped fresh rosemary
- 1 teaspoon finely chopped fresh oregano
- ½ teaspoon salt

1. In a food processor, combine the butter, garlic, rosemary, oregano, and salt and pulse until the mixture is well combined, smooth, and creamy, scraping down the sides as necessary. Alternatively, you can whip the ingredients together with an electric mixer. 2. Using a spatula, scrape the butter mixture into a small bowl or glass container and cover. Store in the refrigerator for up to 1 month.

Per Serving:
⅛ cup: calories: 206 | fat: 23g | protein: 0g | carbs: 206g | fiber: 0g | sodium: 294mg

Arugula and Walnut Pesto

Prep time: 5 minutes | Cook time: 0 minutes | Serves 8 to 10

- 6 cups packed arugula
- 1 cup chopped walnuts
- ½ cup shredded Parmesan cheese
- 2 garlic cloves, peeled
- ½ teaspoon salt
- 1 cup extra-virgin olive oil

1. In a food processor, combine the arugula, walnuts, cheese, and garlic and process until very finely chopped. Add the salt. With the processor running, stream in the olive oil until well blended. 2. If the mixture seems too thick, add warm water, 1 tablespoon at a time, until smooth and creamy. Store in a sealed container in the refrigerator.

Per Serving:
calories: 292 | fat: 31g | protein: 4g | carbs: 3g | fiber: 1g | sodium: 210mg

Apple Cider Dressing

Prep time: 5 minutes | Cook time: 0 minutes | Serves 2

- 2 tablespoons apple cider vinegar
- ⅓ lemon, juiced
- ⅓ lemon, zested
- Salt and freshly ground black pepper, to taste

1. In a jar, combine the vinegar, lemon juice, and zest. Season with salt and pepper, cover, and shake well.

Per Serving:
calories: 7 | fat: 0g | protein: 0g | carbs: 1g | fiber: 0g | sodium: 1mg

Olive Tapenade

Prep time: 10 minutes | Cook time: 0 minutes | Makes about 1 cup

- ¾ cup pitted brine-cured green or black olives, chopped fine
- 1 small shallot, minced
- 2 tablespoons extra-virgin olive oil
- 1 tablespoon capers, rinsed and minced
- 1½ teaspoons red wine vinegar
- 1 teaspoon minced fresh oregano

1. Combine all ingredients in bowl. (Tapenade can be refrigerated for up to 1 week.)

Per Serving:
¼ cup: calories: 92 | fat: 9g | protein: 0g | carbs: 2g | fiber: 1g | sodium: 236mg

Parsley-Mint Sauce

Prep time: 5 minutes | Cook time: 0 minutes | Serves 6

- ½ cup fresh flat-leaf parsley
- 1 cup fresh mint leaves
- 2 garlic cloves, minced
- 2 scallions (green onions), chopped
- 2 tablespoons pomegranate molasses
- ¼ cup olive oil
- 1 tablespoon fresh lemon juice

1. Combine all the ingredients in a blender and blend until smooth. Transfer to an airtight container and refrigerate until ready to use. Can be refrigerated for 1 day.

Per Serving:
calories: 90 | fat: 9g | protein: 1g | carbs: 2g | fiber: 0g | sodium: 5mg

Basic Brown-Onion Masala

Prep time: 20 minutes | Cook time: 6½ hours | Makes 4 cups

- 2 tablespoons rapeseed oil
- 6 onions, finely diced
- 8 garlic cloves, finely chopped
- 1¾ pounds (794 g) canned plum tomatoes
- 3-inch piece fresh ginger, grated
- 1 teaspoon salt
- 1½ teaspoons turmeric
- Handful fresh coriander stalks, finely chopped
- 3 fresh green chiles, finely chopped
- 1 teaspoon chili powder
- 1 teaspoon ground cumin seeds
- 1 cup hot water
- 2 teaspoons garam masala

1. Preheat the slow cooker on high (or to the sauté setting, if you have it). Then add the oil and let it heat. Add the onions and cook for a few minutes until they start to brown. Make sure you brown the onions well so you get a deep, flavorsome base. 2. Add the garlic and continue to cook on high for about 10 minutes. 3. Add the tomatoes, ginger, salt, turmeric, coriander stalks, chopped chiles, chili powder, cumin seeds, and water. 4. Cover the slow cooker and cook on low for 6 hours. 5. Remove the lid and stir. Let the masala cook for another 30 minutes uncovered to reduce a little. 6. Add the garam masala after the masala has cooked. 7. Use right away, or freeze it in small tubs or freezer bags. Just defrost what you need, when you need it.

Per Serving:
calories: 286 | fat: 8g | protein: 7g | carbs: 52g | fiber: 8g | sodium: 656mg

Roasted Harissa

Prep time: 5 minutes | Cook time: 15 minutes | Makes ¾ cup

- 1 red bell pepper
- 2 small fresh red chiles, or more to taste
- 4 garlic cloves, unpeeled
- ½ teaspoon ground coriander
- ½ teaspoon ground cumin
- ½ teaspoon ground caraway
- 1 tablespoon fresh lemon juice
- ½ teaspoon salt

1. Preheat the broiler to high. 2. Put the bell pepper, chiles, and garlic on a baking sheet and broil for 6 to 8 minutes. Turn the vegetables over and broil for 5 to 6 minutes more, until the pepper and chiles are softened and blackened. Remove from the broiler and set aside until cool enough to handle. Remove and discard the stems, skin, and seeds from the pepper and chiles. Remove and discard the papery skin from the garlic. 3. Put the flesh of the pepper and chiles with the garlic cloves in a blender or food processor. Add the coriander, cumin, caraway, lemon juice, and salt and blend until smooth. 4. This may be stored refrigerated for up to 3 days. Store in an airtight container, and cover the sauce with a ¼-inch layer of oil.

Per Serving:
calories: 28 | fat: 0g | protein: 1g | carbs: 6g | fiber: 1g | sodium: 393mg

Vinaigrette

Prep time: 5 minutes | Cook time: 0 minutes | Serves 4

- 2 tablespoons balsamic vinegar
- 2 large garlic cloves, minced
- 1 teaspoon dried rosemary, crushed
- ¼ teaspoon freshly ground black pepper
- ¼ cup olive oil

1. In a small bowl, whisk together the vinegar, garlic, rosemary, and pepper. While whisking, slowly stream in the olive oil and whisk until emulsified. Store in an airtight container in the refrigerator for up to 3 days.

Per Serving:
1 cup: calories: 129 | fat: 1g | protein: 3g | carbs: 0g | fiber: 0g | sodium: 2mg

Pepper Sauce

Prep time: 10 minutes | Cook time: 20 minutes | Makes 4 cups

- 2 red hot fresh chiles, seeded
- 2 dried chiles
- ½ small yellow onion, roughly chopped
- 2 garlic cloves, peeled
- 2 cups water
- 2 cups white vinegar

1. In a medium saucepan, combine the fresh and dried chiles, onion, garlic, and water. Bring to a simmer and cook for 20 minutes, or until tender. Transfer to a food processor or blender. 2. Add the vinegar and blend until smooth.

Per Serving:
1 cup: calories: 41 | fat: 0g | protein: 1g | carbs: 5g | fiber: 1g | sodium: 11mg

Appendix 1: Measurement Conversion Chart

VOLUME EQUIVALENTS(DRY)

US STANDARD	METRIC (APPROXIMATE)
1/8 teaspoon	0.5 mL
1/4 teaspoon	1 mL
1/2 teaspoon	2 mL
3/4 teaspoon	4 mL
1 teaspoon	5 mL
1 tablespoon	15 mL
1/4 cup	59 mL
1/2 cup	118 mL
3/4 cup	177 mL
1 cup	235 mL
2 cups	475 mL
3 cups	700 mL
4 cups	1 L

WEIGHT EQUIVALENTS

US STANDARD	METRIC (APPROXIMATE)
1 ounce	28 g
2 ounces	57 g
5 ounces	142 g
10 ounces	284 g
15 ounces	425 g
16 ounces (1 pound)	455 g
1.5 pounds	680 g
2 pounds	907 g

VOLUME EQUIVALENTS(LIQUID)

US STANDARD	US STANDARD (OUNCES)	METRIC (APPROXIMATE)
2 tablespoons	1 fl.oz.	30 mL
1/4 cup	2 fl.oz.	60 mL
1/2 cup	4 fl.oz.	120 mL
1 cup	8 fl.oz.	240 mL
1 1/2 cup	12 fl.oz.	355 mL
2 cups or 1 pint	16 fl.oz.	475 mL
4 cups or 1 quart	32 fl.oz.	1 L
1 gallon	128 fl.oz.	4 L

TEMPERATURES EQUIVALENTS

FAHRENHEIT(F)	CELSIUS(C) (APPROXIMATE)
225 °F	107 °C
250 °F	120 °C
275 °F	135 °C
300 °F	150 °C
325 °F	160 °C
350 °F	180 °C
375 °F	190 °C
400 °F	205 °C
425 °F	220 °C
450 °F	235 °C
475 °F	245 °C
500 °F	260 °C

Appendix 2: The Dirty Dozen and Clean Fifteen

The Environmental Working Group (EWG) is a nonprofit, nonpartisan organization dedicated to protecting human health and the environment Its mission is to empower people to live healthier lives in a healthier environment. This organization publishes an annual list of the twelve kinds of produce, in sequence, that have the highest amount of pesticide residue-the Dirty Dozen-as well as a list of the fifteen kinds ofproduce that have the least amount of pesticide residue-the Clean Fifteen.

THE DIRTY DOZEN	THE CLEAN FIFTEEN
• The 2016 Dirty Dozen includes the following produce. These are considered among the year's most important produce to buy organic:	• The least critical to buy organically are the Clean Fifteen list. The following are on the 2016 list:

THE DIRTY DOZEN

Strawberries	Spinach
Apples	Tomatoes
Nectarines	Bell peppers
Peaches	Cherry tomatoes
Celery	Cucumbers
Grapes	Kale/collard greens
Cherries	Hot peppers

The Dirty Dozen list contains two additional itemskale/collard greens and hot peppers-because they tend to contain trace levels of highly hazardous pesticides.

THE CLEAN FIFTEEN

Avocados	Papayas
Corn	Kiw
Pineapples	Eggplant
Cabbage	Honeydew
Sweet peas	Grapefruit
Onions	Cantaloupe
Asparagus	Cauliflower
Mangos	

Some of the sweet corn sold in the United States are made from genetically engineered (GE) seedstock. Buy organic varieties of these crops to avoid GE produce.

Appendix 3: Recipes Index

Made in the USA
Columbia, SC
16 November 2024

46713806R00059